3RD EDITION

THE POLITICS OF CONGRESS

DAVID J. VOGLER
Wheaton College

ALLYN AND BACON, INC.
Boston • London • Sydney • Toronto

*To all the Voglers and Marshalls,
and to Alice, who is both*

Library of Congress Cataloging in Publication Data

Vogler, David J
 The politics of Congress.

 Bibliography: p.
 Includes index.
 1. United States. Congress. I. Title.
JK1061.V63 1980   328.73   79-25085
ISBN 0-205-06975-4

Printed in the United States of America

Cover photo courtesy of *U.S. News & World Report*
Credits—Pages 1, 2, 76, 77, 79, quotes from Richard F. Fenno,
Jr., *Home Style: House Members in Their Districts.* Copyright
© 1978 by Little, Brown and Company (Inc.). Reprinted by permission. Pages 131, 132, quotes from Harrison W. Fox, Jr., and
Susan Webb-Hammond, *Congressional Staffs: The Invisible Force
in American Lawmaking* (The Free Press, 1977). Excerpts from
pages 5 and 143 and a table on page 171 reprinted with permission of Macmillan Publishing Co., Inc. Copyright © 1977 by
The Free Press, a Division of Macmillan Publishing Co. Pages
163, 171, 172, 174–177, 179, 307, quotes; page 173, table from
Richard F. Fenno, Jr., *Congressmen in Committees.* Copyright ©
1973 by Little, Brown and Company (Inc.). Reprinted by permission. Pages 71, 227, 233, 265, 267, quotes from Donald R.
Matthews, *U.S. Senators and Their World.* Copyright © 1960 by
The University of North Carolina Press. Reprinted by permission of the publisher.

CONTENTS

PREFACE

A POLITICAL LEADER observing another Congress in 1814 commented that "Congress doesn't run—it waltzes." To students of Congress the pace of change seems a fast waltz indeed. Changes in the membership and structure of Congress since publication of the second edition of this book have required extensive revisions and additions. Almost half of the third edition is new material designed to cover both changes in the institution of Congress and recent political science research on the subject. The basic framework of analysis, however, remains the same. The many reforms and changes of the last decade have, in fact, reinforced the value of viewing Congress in terms of the opposing goals of representation and lawmaking.

In addition to the many policy and political examples drawn from recent sessions of Congress, the third edition contains new or expanded material on about thirty structural and institutional changes that took place in Congress in the late 1970s. These topics include: the continuing unpopularity of Congress as an institution, coupled with a high rate of reelection of incumbent legislators; the new emphasis on congressional oversight of the federal bureaucracy; the growing number of legislators who see themselves as ombudsmen rather than as lawmakers; the emergence of the post-cloture filibuster and changes in the Senate filibuster rule enacted in 1979; the extensive studies conducted by the House Commission on Administrative Review; current proposals to limit terms of service for both representatives and senators; the effects of reapportionment in the 1970s; the changing age structure of Congress; the role of issues in congressional campaigns; the importance of party identification in congressional elections; party loyalty among legislators; the increasing power of the party caucus and party leaders in the House; the growth of congressional staffs; the growing importance of district offices; the proliferation of subcommittees; the Senate committee reorganization of 1977; changes in the hierarchy of committee preferences; an evaluation of the first five years of the congressional budget process; House leaders' increasing use of the suspension-of-the-rules procedure in recent sessions; the development of the House Rules Committee into an arm of the House leadership; Senate unanimous consent agreements; the declining importance of seniority in both chambers; lobby reform proposals; the role of regional and other special caucuses in the House; politics in an age of scarcity; the growth of single-issue politics and interest groups; the role of political action committees in campaign funding; congressional controls over executive impoundment of funds; increased use of the legislative veto; and the impact of the War Powers Act of 1973 and other legislation on the congressional role in the making of foreign policy.

In writing all three editions of *The Politics of Congress,* I have been guided by two central questions: How do we evaluate Congress? and, So what? By providing some different perspectives for judging congressional performance and by relating these to reform proposals, I have sought to show that a person's judgment of Congress and his or her support of or opposition to specific reform proposals depend on a broad evaluation of the entire political system and not just on short-term legislative goals such as efficiency or standing up to the president. Judgment of Congress requires some information about the way things are, and I have sought to provide this without imposing my own interpretations of the way things ought to be. Unless these facts about Congress are viewed within a framework of alternative ways in which the system might operate, they do little toward expanding our critical understanding of the politics of Congress. That is why the first chapter is more concerned with alternative views of the way things ought to be than with the way things are.

Even if one understands the legislative process, one might ask, So what? Politics, after all, determines who gets what, and detailed explanations about congressional rules or the structure of the subcommittee system might seem irrelevant to people concerned about their children's education, the energy crisis, inflation, taxes, and medical costs. Political scientists have come to realize the architectonic role of policies in American politics. I have sought to provide some answers to the question of "So what?" by showing how the politics of Congress are related to the policies that emerge from that body.

Each election brings more women into political office. The use of masculine pronouns at times in this book is not meant to imply that all of our representatives are men or that they should be. The pronouns are used merely to avoid confusion and the awkwardness of expressions such as "she or he" in sentences that may already have several pronouns.

Many people helped me with this book. The first two editions contained an extensive listing of those who helped with each edition, and I thank them all again. Professor Burdett Loomis of the University of Kansas and Walter Oleszek of the Congressional Research Service suggested changes and new topics for the third edition, and I have incorporated almost all of their suggestions into the present text. Professors Henry Kenski of the University of Arizona and Philip Brenner of the University of Maryland, Baltimore County, have been most generous with their suggestions and ideas for changes in the book over the years. Burt Hoffman, special assistant of the House majority whip, shared with me his insights on the changes occurring in Congress in recent years. The American Political Science Association (APSA) Congressional Fellows Program provided me with an opportunity to experience firsthand the hectic world of a congressional office. The director of the APSA Program, Thomas E. Mann, organized the year in Washington in a way that greatly enhanced my understanding of Congress, and he continues to add to that knowledge through his research on congressional elections. My former boss and present congressman, Gerry Studds, has taught me what an effective representative can do, and he and his staff have been most helpful in making my many trips to Washington productive ones. I would also like to thank Alice Bogert; Al Levitt; Barbara, Irl, Carol, and Susan Marshall; and Alice Vogler for their patience in putting up with a compulsive writer during the revision of the text; and Diane Lawlor, Alice Peterson, Beth Rushford, Nancy Shepardson, and Abbe Levine for their assistance in production of the book.

1

JUDGING CONGRESS

"I HAVE BEEN A MEMBER OF THE HOUSE for twenty years. During the whole of that time, we have been attacked, denounced, despised, hunted, harried, blamed, looked down upon, excoriated, and flayed." That was the complaint of a Speaker of the House about fifty years ago. The Speaker did go on to say that this vilification of Congress was nothing new. Congress was unpopular when John Quincy Adams was a congressman. It was unpopular when Abraham Lincoln was a congressman. "From the beginning of the Republic it has been the duty of every voter to look down upon us and the duty of every humorist to make jokes at us." [1] If the Speaker were able to come back and visit some congressional districts during the 1970s and 1980s, he would be further chagrined to find that many legislators had joined the humorists. Here is how one representative described to his constituents a Marine Corps dinner that he had attended earlier: "We drank a whole bunch of toasts. When we toasted the air force, the band played 'Wild Blue Yonder.' Then we toasted the navy, and the band played 'Anchors Aweigh.' We toasted the marines, and the band played the Marine Hymn. And the infantry. As it came my turn to make a toast, I turned to the person next to me and said, 'What do you think the band will play for a congressman?' And he said, 'Here Comes Santa Claus.'" To the question, "Isn't there any sanity up there on the Hill?" another representative responded: "Not much. No, let me phrase that positively. There is some sanity on the Hill." When a group of business-men asked him, "How are things in Congress?" the representative replied: "Things in Congress are about usual—no, they are better than usual because we are in recess." [2] Congress as a topic seems to rank right up there with spouses and the postal service as a certain source of laughs for the after-dinner speaker, especially when the speaker is a member of Congress.

The U.S. Congress is an institution that is subject to continual evaluation and judgment by all citizens. Sometimes that judgment takes the form of a willingness to laugh at jokes about Congress. It is also reflected in individual decisions to participate in demon-strations and lobbying efforts on Capitol Hill and in individual reactions to such demonstrations and lobbying activities. Writing letters and personally engaging in dialogue with members of Con-gress are also ways for constituents to express judgments not only about the job that their own senators and representatives are doing but also about the institution of Congress as a whole. Every two years all United States citizens over the age of eighteen have the opportunity to judge Congress formally through voting. About 160 million people are eligible to vote, but in the last two decades a majority of those eligible have not voted in congressional elec-tions. Some would say that nonvoting is also an indication of in-dividuals judging Congress as an institution.

Articulated opinions of Congress as an institution, both positive and negative, provide a good starting point for any consideration of our national legislative body. They show that there is a wide variety of opinions not only about how well Congress does its job but also about what exactly that job is or should be. Consider some of the following evaluations of the legislative process and its pro-duct.

In one of the many clashes between state political leaders and congressional leaders about renewal of the revenue sharing program in 1980, a governor from New England asserted that the nation-wide tax revolt and uproar over government spending were caused by "the inability of Congress, with its more than 300 committees and subcommittees, to control hundreds of billions of dollars in narrow, categorical grant programs, each supported by a special interest group and Federal bureaucracies." [3] At about the same time, speaking of the vote of twenty-eight of the required thirty-four state legislatures that had, by early 1979, passed resolutions calling for a constitutional convention to propose a balanced budget amendment to the Constitution, the executive director of the National Taxpayers Union said: "It's a vote of no confidence in Congress. It says Congress is screwing up." [4]

The close of the Ninety-fifth Congress in the fall of 1978—a Congress of which the president said he was "very proud" and to which the Senate majority leader gave a grade of "A"—brought forward this general assessment by another observer of the congressional process:

> People who say that Congress doesn't know what it's doing are wrong. Amid a bleak spectacle of rushing to adjournment last weekend by wildly passing or killing dozens of complicated bills in a matter of hours or minutes, with many members voting blindly, it chose to close shop at the best possible of moments: on a weekend when the public was mightily distracted by the World Series and football games.[5]

Part of the blame for this congressional irresponsibility was put on the large number of members of Congress who have been voluntarily retiring in recent years: over 10 percent of the total membership in the Ninety-fifth Congress (1977–1978) voluntarily retired.[6] The above observer also noted, "Congress is becoming a place of transients. Sound political philosophies, whether liberal or conservative, can't be shaped, advanced or refined in a group eroded by rapid turnovers." [7]

One senator who was resigning after one term in office was asked if he had any regrets about leaving Congress. With the cameras rolling in the radio-television gallery of the Senate, he replied: "I can't wait to get out of this chicken——outfit." [8] A number of state officeholders expressed a similar view of Congress when asked why they had decided against running for the House or Senate. "I've been there, I know what happens," said the attorney general of North Carolina, who had ten years of staff experience on Capitol Hill. "When I go up to Washington now I see all those people scurrying about making all this noise about this piece of legislation or that piece, which will probably never see the light of day." New York's Suffolk County executive, in saying why he would not be a candidate for the House, commented: "I can make a decision, order it implemented and in six months see if it has worked or not. But in Congress, it is like elephants making love.

It takes two years before you can see whether what you've done has had any results." [9]

Political scientists who study Congress also offer some summary judgments about the institution. One scholar recently evaluated the national legislature's responsibility, responsiveness, and accountability and had this to say:

> Congress simply is not equipped to be responsible on a regular basis; its organization and procedures are not designed to allow efficient and rapid formulation of policy. Congress has even delegated much of its policy-making power to the President, especially in international relations, and only the war in Indochina and the Watergate affair have provided much incentive for it to flex its muscles and try to recapture its atrophied authority.
>
> The legislature's performance is better in responsiveness. The same structural shortcomings that inhibit responsibility encourage representativeness. Many groups—but not all, and particularly not those interests lacking in money and skill—can find the time and the locus in the legislature to present their views prior to enactment of policy.
>
> Finally, Congress is held accountable in the sense that dissatisfied citizens can retire its members; in practice, these citizens lack the knowledge and/or the electoral opportunity to exercise meaningful popular control over public policy.
>
> Whatever the evaluative criteria employed, critics of all persuasions find Congress wanting. Each set, from its own particular vantage points, has specified reform proposals intended to make the legislature a "better" institution.[10]

Writing at about the same time, another political scientist addressed the generally accepted notion that the modern Congress has lost much of its influence and power to the executive branch. He concluded that these reports about the decline of the power of the legislature are greatly exaggerated: "We have sought to examine the 'decline' of Congress in terms of a decline in power (initiation), efficiency, public esteem, public interest, and manners or standards of behavior. We have found that only in terms of public interest (as indicated by a decline in newspaper coverage) can we discern any evidence for a congressional decline." [11] Another assessment is provided by the author of a recent book on Congress:

> When majorities want change, Congress can act with speed and effectiveness, but when minorities seek swift solutions to national

problems, it may act slowly or not at all. It is sensitive to majorities, penetrable by persistent minorities, and much less sensitive to newly organized minority interests.

It represents constituencies and a public that has been less attentive to national affairs. This means that in times requiring highmindedness and a national view, it may be transfixed by the parochial and the particular. Yet it has power to criticize and check the executive (who also may be transfixed by the parochial and the particular).

Indeed Congress is probably the most powerful national assembly that can be found in political life.[12]

All of these observations suggest that those professionals who study or participate in the national legislative process have various opinions on Congress. Public opinion polls and election results suggest that the general public also generates some seemingly contradictory notions about Congress and how well it does its job.

Figure 1–1 provides a broad picture of public opinion of Congress as it is reflected (1) in national surveys that ask whether people generally approve or disapprove of the way Congress is handling its job and (2) in results of elections, in which voters have the opportunity to reelect their incumbent representative and senators.[13] Public opinion polls consistently show that the public does not think very highly of the institution of Congress. Approval ratings of Congress declined from 59 percent in 1964 to 28 percent in 1978. The election data, however, give us a picture which is different from that provided by survey data. Of House members seeking reelection, more than 90 percent were returned to office by voters during the last decade. Incumbent senators have not fared as well as House members, especially in recent years, but the percentage of incumbent senators returned to office has still been far above the percentage of the population having a favorable view of how well Congress as an institution is doing its job. What, then, can we say about the public's judgment of Congress? Most of us do not think highly of the institution, but we act as though we do. At every election we vote back in the same cast of characters who have given us the supposedly bad performance of the past two years.

Professor Glenn R. Parker has analyzed the fluctuations in congressional popularity for the period 1939–1974. In his article, "Some Themes in Congressional Unpopularity," Professor Parker concludes that negative public ratings of Congress seem to be most closely connected to declining economic conditions, the absence of

FIGURE 1–1 Public Opinion of Congress as Reflected in Public Evaluation of Congressional Performance and Reelection of Incumbents

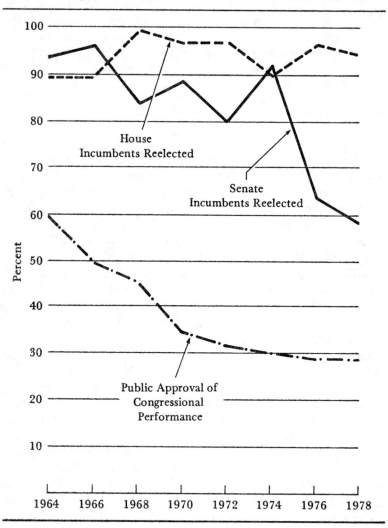

international crises, and the election of "active-positive" presidents.[14] Another congressional scholar has demonstrated that the high points of positive public opinion of Congress during the 1960s and early 1970s coincided with the high points of congressional productivity in passage of bills requested by the president.[15] Public judgments about how well Congress is doing its job appear to be based on some evaluation of the congressional role of making public policy by passage of legislation.

There is another dimension of public opinion of Congress that helps to explain the seemingly contradictory pattern of negatively evaluating congressional performance yet voting to return incumbents to office. Some of the more recent public opinion polls have asked people to evaluate not only the way that Congress has been handling its job but also the way the representatives from their own districts have been handling their jobs. A Gallup poll taken in March 1977 showed that 36 percent of the public approved of the job Congress was doing while 55 percent approved of the job being done by their own representative.[16] Similarly, a *New York Times* poll in April 1978 showed that 31 percent approved of Congress while 62 percent approved of their own representative.[17] A national poll conducted in 1977 for the U.S. House Commission on Administrative Review uncovered the same pattern: about twice as many people gave a positive rating to the job their own representative was doing as compared with those who gave a positive rating to the job Congress as a whole was doing.[18]

What is most significant about this latter poll is the fact that people seem to be using different standards by which to judge Congress as an institution and their own representative. The reasons given for both negative and positive evaluations of the institution of Congress focused on the legislative function, whereas the standards by which people judged the performance of individual members of Congress focused on the representative function. To see how well the institution of Congress is doing, we look at its legislative track record; to see how well an individual member is doing, we look at his or her performance in advancing the interests of the district. We can see this difference when we look at some of the specific reasons given in this national poll for respondents' evaluations of Congress and their representatives. Both positive and negative evaluations of the institution of Congress focused on the legislative function: "they are doing their work, passed a lot of bills"; "passed many good bills that were later vetoed"; "they passed increases in Social Security, helped the economy"; "can't see that anything has changed, no signs of improvement, they have not done anything"; "haven't done anything about inflation, prices, the economy"; "haven't done all they could, lots of problems they did not deal with, e.g., energy, crime, etc." The reasons given for both positive and negative evaluations of the performance of individual members, on the other hand, had more to do with representation of district interests than with legislation: "represents his district well, works hard for the district"; "his contact, listens to you, is available, cares about his constituents and what they think"; "keeps you well informed, sends newsletters, bulletins"; "haven't heard about him"; "all he did was vote the party line, played party politics"; "doesn't keep in touch, doesn't keep us informed." [19]

The findings of this national poll help us to understand the dichotomous nature of public opinion about Congress that is reflected in Figure 1–1. Generally, negative ratings of Congress as an institution seem to be tied to evaluations of legislative performance. Positive evaluations of individual members and the high reelection rate of incumbents seem to be tied to evaluations of representational performance. While the American people seem to think very little of Congress as a whole, they seem to feel their own particular representatives and senators are doing a good enough job to deserve reelection.

Whenever professional observers, participants, and the general public judge Congress and individual members of Congress, they are responding to some basic notions about what Congress and its individual members should be doing. It is clear that most voters may hold, at the same time, diametrically opposed opinions with regard to how well Congress as a whole is doing and how well their own representatives are doing. In the next chapter we will consider some of the different measures used to evaluate representation provided by individual members of Congress. First, however, we want to look at some of the broader standards people use when evaluating Congress as an institution.

Disparate views of Congress are not confined to voting patterns. Presidents and presidential candidates are quick to use Congress as a scapegoat when citizens are disgruntled. Editorial cartoonists of every ideological stripe know that the public will recognize their symbol of the typical congressman—the bloated figure with the watch chain stretched across his potbelly. The country is filled with people who cannot quite remember the name of their own representatives or senators but who do know that one of them helped their nephew come home from naval duty overseas to attend his father's funeral. They know that some members of Congress are reputed to be closely tied in with figures in organized crime, and many still hold to the broader belief that the only good politician is a dead one (a dead politician becomes a statesman).

There is clearly some difference in the amount of information about Congress that is possessed by journalists, political scientists, former legislators, and the majority of the American public who neither vote nor pay close attention to congressional politics. More important than the amount of each person's information, however, are his or her political values. As quotes earlier in this chapter indicate, people who have the same amount of information about Congress do not necessarily make the same judgments of congressional performance or share political values for determining the quality of that performance. And the same political values may be held by members of both the politically informed and the politically uninformed groups in society. If you could get a group of professional Congress-watchers in a pub with a group of football, hockey, or baseball fans who were not interested in politics and have them discuss congressional politics, it is likely that factions and coalitions would form not on the basis of information about the legislative process but rather on the basis of some shared values about what the real job of Congress should be. Regimental-tie types and bowling-jacket types would line up together against other such disparate coalitions. Knowing a lot about congressional behavior does not lead to an evaluative consensus about how well Congress is doing its job or even what that job really is.

A short introductory book on Congress is expected to cover the more important facts about congressional behavior. In the following pages I will present some of the findings of political scientists who have studied Congress. But a clear understanding of any such empirical information must be built upon a realization of the different frameworks within which such facts may be interpreted. The purpose of any political science course is to develop a critical faculty for interpreting and evaluating information, not simply memorizing facts. Laying out some intricate scheme of how members of Congress are chosen to serve on particular committees might help give teachers a basis for exam questions and students a focus of study for such exams, but it does little to bring either party closer to an answer to the underlying question, "So what?" That question can only be answered by first looking at the divergent views of what Congress is really supposed to be doing in the American political system and then evaluating the information about actual congressional behavior within these normative frameworks. "What is" takes on life only when we compare it with different notions of "what should be." Throughout this book I will include discussions of reform proposals, whether successful or not, because of their tendency to bring to the surface the gut issues of congressional politics. Recurring issues and actions of congressional reform provide one ground for bringing underlying values and empirical information face to face.

In this chapter I outline some of the different ideas people have about what Congress is supposed to do. By presenting various notions about what Congress is and should be, I hope to provide not only a framework for evaluating the various reforms and proposed changes in the system but also a means for interpreting the facts about how the present system operates.

THE FUNCTIONS OF CONGRESS

Everyone will agree that there are certain functions that Congress should perform for the political system as a whole. Voters have expectations about what their representatives and senators should be doing for them. Politicians, political scientists, and the general public all have standards for evaluating the performance of Congress. Reformers seek to change certain parts of the system to make it better able to perform some functions. We all agree that Congress should be the representative branch and that a member of Congress should perform many activities as representative for his or her district. We will soon have a closer look at the different ways in which people think of representation and how their beliefs affect their expectations and evaluation of Congress and its members. But first, I think it would be helpful to consider the many functions that Congress is expected to perform.

A general list of such expectations includes representation through the articulation of constituency interests; lawmaking, or representation of constituency interests and/or national interest by reaching decisions; administrative oversight; public education by gathering and disseminating information; and constituent service, or casework.[20] All of these specific functions may be considered part of the process of representation, and there is considerable overlap among the different functions. A congressman's helping a constituent solve a minor problem with a federal agency might lead to the congressman's obtaining information useful in drafting legislation and passing a law or to his beginning public hearings concerning that agency. It is worth considering these functions at specific levels because the relative importance each person attaches to different activities will lead to quite different conceptions of the proper legislative role.

Representation through Interest Articulation

The common notion of Congress is that of a forum where the interests and demands of all groups in society are expressed. A member of Congress is expected to act as a spokesperson for the ethnic, economic, religious, political, and professional groups within his or her geographic district. The idea of Congress as a slow-moving, deliberative body is closely associated with representation in this sense. Political scientists often say that Congress maintains the stability of the political system by acting as a safety valve that partially disarms potentially disruptive groups by permitting expression of grievances and demands. Similarly, the agonizingly slow movement toward decision on matters such as civil rights is regarded by some observers as important because the consensus produced by such deliberation means that the decision, when it comes, will be regarded as legitimate by almost all groups in society.

Many of the points made in current debates over the role of Congress are directly related to expectations stemming from this conception of representation. If a presidential victory (such as that of Lyndon Johnson in 1964, Richard Nixon in 1972, and Jimmy Carter in 1976) is interpreted as a mandate for implementing presidential policies concerning Indochina, dismantling the welfare state, or cutting the defense budget, how can the citizen who disagrees with such policies have his or her views expressed? If blacks constitute 20 percent of a particular congressional district, should a congressional representative devote all of his or her efforts to implementing the white majority position on a civil rights measure or should the representative also articulate the demands of his or her black constituents? If certain interest groups in a district support the losing candidate, must they suffer lack of representation for two years?

All of these questions point out the duty of members of Congress not only to implement majority decisions through their voting behavior but also to express the interests of electoral minorities when participating in debate, casework, and other activities. Associated with this conception of representation are the ideas of decentralization, access of a vast number of groups to the government, and predominance of local interests over some national interest expressed through presidential elections and national parties, and, generally, the idea that Congress should be an avenue for providing inputs into the political system that are independent of those that come through the executive branch.

Lawmaking

The term representation is used in another sense when we talk about the need for Congress to be responsive to policy mandates expressed in the last election. To be representative in this sense requires that Congress at some point call a halt to the articulation of interests and debate—that it arrive at a policy decision. When the Senate considers a tax bill, for example, a lot of time is given to the representation of groups, individuals, and industries seeking tax benefits. Most senators feel that they should articulate the demands made by the significant groups in their states. If depletion allowances for Florida's phosphate industry are proposed by that state's senators, no final action on the bill should be taken until Louisiana's senators are able to suggest depletion allowances for industries in their state. But at some point the Senate must call a halt to this sort of interest representation. It also has a responsibility to decide on a final bill; it must end its deliberations and vote. If it does not, then it is failing to represent all the voters who supported one or the other party's candidates in the last election because of that party's pledge on tax policy.

There are a number of questions associated with representation by lawmaking. When should a congressman vote against constituency interests in favor of the national interest? If a majority of his constituents takes a position that the legislator regards as harmful to them, should he vote in line with the expressed will of his constituents or in favor of his perception of their real interests? How much time should the congressman devote to acquiring expertise in areas so that he can cast a well-informed, rational vote? How much time should he spend talking with constituent groups so that he can vote the way they want him to? All of these considerations clearly relate to representation, but there is an important difference between the two ways in which the term is used.

Representation through interest articulation includes the representation of a broad array of minority interests. The congressman is expected to introduce into legislative deliberations not just the positions of the electoral majority in his district but also the positions of significant minorities. In other words, he should bring the policy debate from his constituency into the legislative process. But when it comes to actual voting, normal expectations of representation seem quite different. A congressman's vote is expected to be in accordance with some electoral majority relevant to him. This may be his district's majority, an electoral decision in the past presidential election, or what he regards as a policy mandate given his political party. A congressman from a district that is 20 percent black might feel that he should represent his black constituents in policy debates over school busing but that he should represent the white majority's position in voting on the matter.

We have touched on a number of complex questions about the nature of representation that will be discussed more fully later. For now it should be enough to mention that the following characteristics associated with representation as interest ariculation are not associated with representation as lawmaking: a decentralized legislative system with many access points, which makes it hard for Congress to arrive at policy decisions within a limited period of time; congressional emphasis on local matters, which makes it difficult to achieve consensus on policies designed to deal with a national or international problem; and a need to cut off debate and deliberation at some point to transform party or presidential mandates into policies (a limiting of minorities' expression in order to enact the majority's decision).

Administrative Oversight

If Congress is to perform its lawmaking function effectively, it must see that the laws it has passed are administered so as to produce the results intended. Congress seeks to do this through the process of administrative oversight. Committee hearings provide a means for representatives and senators to hear the testimony of those who administer the law and to review the bureaucracy's implementation of its policies. Effectively used, administrative oversight can be a powerful tool for maintaining the integrity of legislation already passed; for gathering information that can serve as the basis for future legislation; and for reducing the amount of discretion, and thus political power, granted to the executive bureaucracy.

Questions of representation also enter into evaluations of congressional performance in overseeing the bureaucracy. It has been suggested that the decentralized structure of Congress allows representatives and senators to perform representation through articulation by giving vent to the myriad individual dissatisfactions with bureaucratic operations. This sort of challenge to official testimony in hearings is an important avenue of access to the system for groups outside the administration.

Some people argue that most of the oversight through hearings is relatively worthless because it does not really change the way bureaucracy behaves and because it is cursory and ill informed. Others contend that Congress has abdicated much of its lawmaking power by increasing the discretionary power of bureaucracy. If Congress lets administrators decide the meaning of a bill's phrase, how then can it later criticize the administrators for not following the dictates of the legislation?

In recent years administrative oversight has moved from being one of those dusty topics considered only by congressional scholars to being an activity with great political importance. Common to many successful congressional campaigns in 1976 and 1978 was an antibureaucratic theme that promised greater congressional control over what many perceived as a federal bureaucracy that was out of control. "If I were to describe the difference between the 1974 freshmen and the 1976 freshmen," said one representative, "I'd say the '74 class probably ran against Congress more than anything except Watergate and the '76 class probably ran more against bureaucracy and the tentacles of the federal government." [21] Representatives and senators elected by running against the bureaucracy can keep their campaign promises by supporting government reorganization, deregulation of private sectors of the economy, and an enhanced congressional role of administrative oversight. After the 1978 election the chairman of the House Republican Conference said that the first priority of the Ninety-sixth Congress (1979–1980) should be to make itself an "oversight Congress" by declaring a one-year moratorium on new spending programs, enacting "sunset" legislation (which would automatically terminate funding for federal programs unless they were specifically renewed by Congress every ten years), and requiring that every congressional committee establish an oversight subcommittee.[22]

A number of additional reforms aimed at improving the oversight capabilities of Congress have been proposed in recent years.

These include reorganization of the congressional committee structure in order to clarify committee jurisdictions and responsibilities in overseeing government agencies, strengthening the role of the Government Operations Committees of the Senate and the House of Representatives in coordinating the oversight activities of standing committees, moving to two-year periods of authorization for government programs to give Congress time for a thorough review of an agency's programs before authorizing funds, and setting aside certain time periods in the legislative calendar during which congressional activity would focus exclusively on oversight. The Senate's overwhelming (87–1) passage of a "sunset" bill in 1978 suggests that of all these reform proposals some form of "sunset" legislation is likely to be the first major step toward Congress's improving its oversight capabilities.

How well Congress will ever be able to perform the oversight function, even with these reforms, is a matter of great debate.[23] Still, it is clear that most people accept such oversight as a legitimate function of Congress and an integral part of representative government.

Education

The importance of Congress's responsibility of raising issues and providing forums for educating the public on political matters has long been recognized. Woodrow Wilson, writing in 1885, emphasized this function: "Quite as important as legislation is vigilant oversight of administration; and even more important than legislation is the instruction and guidance in political affairs which the people might receive from a body which kept all national concerns suffused in a broad daylight of discussion." [24]

Much of Congress's gathering and dissemination of information is a by-product of its other functions. Public hearings can be convenient forums for articulation of interests, gathering of information useful to lawmaking, and performance of administrative oversight. But sometimes a legislator or group of legislators will seek to raise issues and disseminate information even when this activity is not directly related to these other functions. Some recent examples are the hearings on the assassinations of John Kennedy and Martin Luther King conducted by the House Select Committee on Assassinations in 1977 and 1978 and the four months of hearings on the future of the North Atlantic Treaty Organization (NATO) conducted by a special subcommittee of the House Armed Services Committee in 1978. Both chambers have select committees that are charged with studying and investigating a particular area rather than reporting legislation. In the Ninety-sixth Congress the Senate Select Small Business Committee, the Senate Special Aging Committee, the House Select Aging Committee, and the House Select Narcotics Abuse and Control Committee all had the primary function of investigation and education; none of these committees had the power to report legislation.

There are many reasons for engaging in such activities. A representative or senator might hope that publicizing the extent of problems in one area will generate constituent demands that will lead to new legislation. While writing off the likelihood of new programs, a legislator might feel that the general education of the public is one of the goals of any political system. Or, a representative or senator might feel that such educational activities are important for developing public tolerance of minorities and a sense of community and for maintaining civil liberties.

Constituent Service

An important function of the individual member of Congress in the American system is acting as a go-between for the private citizen and the large, impersonal federal government. The legislator and his or her staff spend much of their time doing casework—intervention on behalf of a constituent faced with a problem stemming from government activity (or inactivity). Individual representation means that a member of Congress is expected not only to articulate constituency interests in debate and vote in accordance with the electoral majority but also to be available to constituents who have a problem.

Former Representative Luther Patrick captured the essence of this constituent service function in suggesting that:

> A Congressman has become an expanded messenger boy, an employment agency, getter-out of the Navy, Army, and Marines, a wardheeler, a wound healer, trouble shooter, law explainer, bill finder, issue translator, resolution interpreter, controversy-oil-pourer, glad hand extender, business promoter, veterans affairs adjuster, ex-servicemen's champion, watchdog for the underdog, sympathizer for the upperdog, kisser of babies, recoverer of lost baggage, soberer of delegates, adjuster for traffic violations and voters straying into the

toils of the law, binderup of broken hearts, financial wet nurse, a good samaritan, contributor of good causes, cornerstone layer, public building and bridge dedicator and ship christener.[25]

A number of members of Congress and scholars of the institution have expressed concern over the increasing amount of time that legislators spend on what is called their ombudsman role (i.e., helping constituents to deal with the federal bureaucracy). Professor Morris P. Fiorina, in his book *Congress: Keystone of the Washington Establishment,* suggests that most members of Congress benefit a great deal from the existence of an extensive and confusing bureaucracy and complex government programs, which continually require constituents to seek the assistance of their representatives in dealing with the government.[26] While most members of Congress would agree with Fiorina's assessment that the high rate of reelection of incumbents is directly related to their emphasis on constituent service, many are also aware of the problems this emphasis on casework creates for Congress as an institution. This concern about "the manner in which Congress has changed from legislators to ombudsmen" was articulated by one representative at a hearing of the House Commission on Administrative Review in 1977:

> Rightly or wrongly, we have become the link between the frustrated citizen and the very involved Federal Government in the citizens' lives. Because the Federal Government is so often hard for them to deal with, they end up writing letters, getting letters back from computers, after a while throwing up their hands, and the last stop is the congressional office. So we become the ombudsmen.
>
> I am not sure that it is a proper role for us to play, but we are in it. We do not have much choice. We continually use more and more of our staff time to handle citizen's complaints, constituents' problems.
>
> I do not know how you get out of this, since it becomes apparent to most people that if you want to be reelected it is more important how you handle your constituents in their relationships and problems with the Government than it is how you vote. I think it is one of the reasons that at the same time that Congress is going down, down, down in the overall opinion of the American public, the rate of incumbents being reelected is going up, up, up. I think that has nothing to do with how we vote, but I think it has a lot to do with the fact that we have a staff which spends an incredible amount of its time handling constituent problems.[27]

A survey of 153 House members and their staffs by the House Commission on Administrative Review in 1977 reflected this same awareness of the electoral importance of the constituency service function and the feeling that it is a role that is forced upon House members rather than one that is freely chosen. When House members were asked which roles the House of Representatives *should* play, 82 percent mentioned the legislative role and 27 percent mentioned the ombudsman role. When they were asked which roles the public *expected* them to play, 87 percent mentioned the legislative role and 79 percent mentioned the ombudsman role.[28]

CONFLICTING FUNCTIONS

So far we have had a brief look at some generally agreed upon ideas regarding what functions Congress should be performing in the political system and how a member of Congress should be spending his or her time. But what individual people expect of Congress is bound to vary with their different conceptions of political goals and with their relative economic and political position within society. Any list of universally accepted functions of Congress is bound to gloss over important conflicts about what the proper legislative role is. Let's consider the congressional functions discussed so far and determine some areas of potential conflict.

In Table 1-1, I have summarized the different conceptions of representation. I have arranged them within a framework suggesting the inherent conflict between maximizing representation through interest articulation and maximizing representation through enactment of electoral mandates. I have used the term *representation* for the former and *lawmaking* for the latter. While I do not want to suggest that these categories are mutually exclusive, I do think that they lead to quite different conceptions of the legislative process and thus to goals that conflict. Increasing the potential for achieving one goal decreases the chances of satisfying the other.

It should be emphasized that this list is not presented with the idea of suggesting two completely distinct and logically incompatible schools of thought as to congressional functions. A particular reformer might feel that Congress should strengthen its lawmaking ability so as to become a source of policy that is independent of the president and national party leadership. The difference between this person and the one who wants efficient legislative ratification of

TABLE 1–1 Differing Views on the Primary Function of Congress

Representation	Lawmaking
1. Congress is a forum for articulating group interests.	1. Congress is a decision-maker that translates popular mandates into law.
2. Emphasis is put on representation of minorities.	2. Emphasis is put on majority rule.
3. Decentralized legislative structure is favored.	3. Centralized legislative system under party presidential leadership is favored.
4. Legislative coalitions are formed after elections—likely to be shifting pattern of dissimilar groups brought together through logrolling.	4. Legislative coalitions are formed at elections. Members of Congress are expected to follow party and presidential mandates reflected in elections.
5. *Public interest* is defined as the sum of the many constituency interests.	5. *Public interest* is defined in national terms as being more than just the sum of constituency interests.
6. Constituency casework is considered an important part of an individual legislator's role.	6. Casework is relegated largely to staff so as to free the legislator for important work.
7. Administrative oversight is regarded as a process for advancing ideas and information and for representing interests of constituent groups.	7. Administrative oversight is regarded as a process of insuring that mandates of earlier legislation are being carried out.
8. Chief criterion for evaluating legislative performance is the number of groups and interests considered in the legislative process.	8. Chief criterion for evaluating legislative performance is the efficiency with which electoral mandates are translated into policies.

presidential programs lies more in defining representation in terms of legislative constituencies and national interests than in defining it in terms of lawmaking and representation. Yet I do think that many of the differences in evaluating Congress and the debates over reform reflect an underlying conflict between representation and lawmaking. This conflict can be seen both in the choices an individual member of Congress must make and in the debate at the institutional level.

At the level of an individual representative's or senator's decision-making, this conflict is reflected in the demand that he or she devote considerable time to the study and reflection needed for responsible lawmaking and at the same time be ready to respond to the unending flow of small favors sought by constituents. "I thought I was going to be Daniel Webster," remarked one congressman, "but I found that most of my work consisted of personal work for constituents." Said another: "The least appealing aspect of my job is the service we have to perform for constituents. . . . Too much of our time and energy is diverted in that direction with the result that the opportunity for creative thinking in a legislative way is greatly lessened." [29]

The conflict between representational and lawmaking functions is seen in the choice a representative must make between pursuing a "House career" and articulating the interests of his constituency. To climb the committee and seniority ladder until reaching a pinnacle, such as the Ways and Means Committee, a representative must specialize in one policy area and devote full time to lawmaking functions. Those who articulate a broad array of constituent interests over many policy areas often find that they must give up hope of advancement through the House decision-making hierarchy and seek a Senate seat instead.

The conflict between representation and lawmaking is even more pronounced at the institutional level, both in general evaluations of Congress and in proposals for reform. If a Congress maximizes the lawmaking function of efficiently passing legislation, some will denounce it as a "rubber stamp" or "me too" Congress. If it maximizes representation and delays legislation so that all interests can have a say, it runs the risk of being tagged a "do nothing" Congress. Specific reform proposals also highlight the inherent conflict between representation and lawmaking. Debate over reform will generally produce one side arguing for measures to increase the efficiency with which Congress may perform its lawmaking function, and the other contending that inefficiency is the price the legislature must pay if it is to maximize its representational potential.

Two changes in the Senate filibuster rule, one in 1975 and the other in 1979, illustrate this conflict between representation and lawmaking. The rules change in 1975 reduced the number of senators needed to invoke cloture, a vote to limit debate and end a filibuster. The rules change in 1979 established an absolute one hundred-hour limit on debate time after a cloture vote and was aimed at ending the practice of post-cloture filibustering that had developed after the 1975 rules change. Prior to the 1975 reform, the support of two-thirds of those present and voting (sixty-seven if all one hundred senators were present) was needed to invoke cloture and cut off a filibuster. The cloture reform, which was proposed and seriously considered in 1971 but not passed until 1975, changed the number of senators needed to invoke cloture to three-fifths (sixty senators) of the total membership.

The debate over this rules change raised the most fundamental issues involving the representational and lawmaking functions of Congress. Those senators who emphasized the representational function of the Senate opposed any attempts to reduce the number of senators needed to invoke cloture. Senator William Fulbright suggested that the debate over changing the cloture rule raised the larger question of whether the Senate would "remain an element in the American constitutional process." Stressing the importance of representation over lawmaking, he went on to say: "Some issues, such as civil rights and war-making power, arise in our kind of governmental community that need delay and consideration so that a compromise can be worked out. A simple majority—and that's what it would be if this rule is changed—should not have the right to impose a decision on a significant minority." [30] Supporters of the old cloture system felt that it represented the most important contribution of the United States Senate to the political process, for it allowed full expression of the widest possible array of views.

Senators in favor of the rules change were clearly emphasizing the lawmaking responsibilities of Congress. "Eventually, the right of the Senate to vote will win out over the right of the Senate to debate," declared one such senator early in the debate over the rules change.[31] After the successful passage of the reform of Rule 22 (the Senate rule governing cloture) in 1975, another senator predicted that the reform "will make the Senate more efficient, more democratic and more effective. With the reform of Rule 22 the Senate will be able to deal with the pressing problems of America in 1975." [32]

The following year, however, a conservative southern senator, James Allen of Alabama, introduced the concept of the post-cloture filibuster in opposing an antitrust enforcement bill. After the Senate had voted cloture, Allen introduced scores of amendments to the bill, continually demanded time-consuming quorum calls and roll-call votes, and carried on what amounted to a filibuster. He was able to do this because the time spent on debating amendments and taking roll-call votes and quorum calls did not count against the one-hour time limit on debate imposed on each senator by the cloture vote. In 1977, two liberal senators used the same post-cloture filibuster tactics to tie up debate on a natural gas pricing bill for nine days after the Senate had voted cloture. Widespread use of the post-cloture filibuster in the Ninety-fifth Congress (1977–1978) led Senate majority leader Robert Byrd to complain that the problem "is not so much in getting cloture. The problem is what happens after cloture is invoked." [33] At Byrd's strong urging, the Senate adopted a resolution in February, 1979, that provided an absolute one hundred–hour limit on the time allowed for debate, roll-call votes, and quorum calls and that limited the number of amendments that any senator could propose to a bill after cloture.

Like the 1975 rules change, the 1979 Senate rules change highlighted the conflict between those emphasizing the lawmaking function and those emphasizing representation. "We have to expedite the legislative process," argued Senator Byrd, "we don't live in the leisurely world of 75 years ago." [34] Opponents of the change charged that Senate majority leader Byrd was "more interested in the passage of legislation than in the content of legislation" and said that the leadership "should not be permitted to operate the Senate like an automated data processor spewing forth law with machine-like precision." [35]

On the House side there have been even greater changes in voting procedures. There the debate over reform revealed the same conflicting positions seen in the Senate's debate over changing the cloture rule. The Legislative Reorganization Act of 1970 planted the seeds of reform in two provisions. Now that both are in effect, watching a close roll-call vote in the House is similar to watching the closing minutes of a nip and tuck basketball game. The first provision makes it easier to get recorded teller votes; the second provides for an electronic voting system. In the following paragraphs I will briefly outline the changes made since the 1970 Act, which clearly indicate the demands of efficient lawmaking and accountable representation.

Most of the business on the House floor since the first Congress in 1790 has been conducted under a procedure known as the Committee of the Whole House. That procedure is intended to maximize the lawmaking function of Congress. Instead of needing a majority (218 members) of the total membership to conduct business, the Committee of the Whole needs a quorum of only 100 members. Before the 1970 changes, there were only three ways of taking votes in the Committee of the Whole, and all votes were nonrecorded (that is, no record was made of how each member voted on the measure). The three procedures for voting were (1) a voice vote, in which members yelled out ayes or nays; (2) a division vote, in which members stood to be counted; and (3) a teller vote, in which members filed past tellers (clerks) who counted those favoring and those opposing a measure. Roll-call votes were not permitted under the Committee of the Whole procedure; they were subject to the larger quorum limitation of 218 members, a majority of the entire House membership. By acting on measures by voice, division, or teller votes, the Committee of the Whole is able to dispose of legislative measures rapidly and efficiently. A teller vote, the longest of the Committee of the Whole procedures, would take about ten minutes to complete as compared with the thirty minutes necessary for each roll-call vote under the system before the electronic voting changes.

Because they allowed quick decision-making, the fast voting procedures under the Committee of the Whole were seen as an efficient way for the House to meet its lawmaking responsibilities. But because the nonrecorded voting prevented accountability, many people regarded it as an obstacle to the House's effective fulfillment of its representational functions. Two basic patterns of behavior led to objections from those seeking accountability in House voting. First, only a fraction of the total House membership reported to the floor for the nonrecorded voting. Therefore, major policy issues were, in effect, being decided by only a small number of representatives. The record showed only a voice vote, division vote, or teller vote passage, allowing no way for interested constituents to see how or if their representatives voted. Second, the Committee of the Whole voting procedures permitted members of the House to practice fence-straddling, best-of-both-worlds type of voting behavior. On roll-call votes, when their position on a measure would be known to interested constituents, representatives could vote one way. Then they could gut the bill they had supported in roll call by anonymously voting for measures that undercut it in any of the nonrecorded voting procedures.

The conflicting demands of lawmaking and representation are

clearly evident in this discussion of House voting procedures. To be an effective lawmaker, the House must clearly have a way to facilitate voting and reduce the amount of time spent on passing or not passing bills. The various methods of voting under the Committee of the Whole procedure contributed to this goal. But to meet the demands of representation there had to be some way for constituents to know how their representative voted on a measure. If the House used a series of time-consuming roll-call votes, it would cripple itself as a major policy- and decision-maker. The Legislative Reorganization Act of 1970 contained a two-step solution to this dilemma: (1) a procedure for making recorded teller votes easier to come by and (2) an electronic voting system, which greatly reduced the time spent on roll-call voting.

The Legislative Reorganization Act provided that one-fifth of a quorum of the Committee of the Whole (twenty members) could call for a recorded teller vote. (In 1979, the number of members required to call for a recorded teller vote was changed to twenty-five.) Members would still march down the aisles and hand their cards to tellers, but now the cards would contain the representatives' names as well as how they voted. The effect was one that, in essence, brought roll-call voting into the previously anonymous pattern of voting under the Committee of the Whole procedure. No longer could major amendments to bills be tacked on in the Committee of the Whole by a small group of representatives whose votes would not be known.

The impact of the recorded teller vote was dramatic. A survey during the first year of operation showed that voting participation increased by more than 90 percent over that of the previous year.[36]

Substantive as well as participatory changes were brought about by this reform. One occurred soon after the new system took effect. After procrastinating for many years, the House finally defeated funds for a supersonic transport plane (the SST) in the first recorded vote on the issue. Under the new system committee chairmen could not be assured of controlling the amending process on the floor, and liberal representatives could no longer hide their votes on popular conservative amendments such as antibusing measures. The recorded teller vote reform, by itself, clearly improved the representational nature of congressional voting. But the time required for such roll calls worked against the Committee of the Whole's purpose of quickly and efficiently dispatching business before the House.

The second provision of the Legislative Reorganization Act of

1970 corrected that problem. It states that "the names of members voting or present may be recorded through the use of electronic equipment." The electronic voting system went into effect in January, 1973. On the floor of the House there are forty-four voting stations. When an electronic recorded vote is in progress, each member on the floor approaches one of these stations and pushes in a coded identification card, voting aye, nay, or present by pushing the appropriate button. At each end of the chamber a clock ticks down the remaining seconds of the fifteen minutes allowed for each vote, while a display panel above the Speaker's chair shows a running compilation of how each member voted. Individual consoles are provided for both the majority leader and the minority leader so that they may attempt to change members' votes during the fifteen-minute time limit.

The electronic voting system saves time and increases the number of roll-call votes taken on the floor of the House. A House committee survey of the use of this system concluded that during the remainder of the 1973 session the electronic system was used for a total of 1,453 rolls calls, which represented a savings of approximately 500 hours of legislative time that would otherwise have been needed to answer roll calls under the old manual system.[37]

The provisions of the 1970 Act would seem to be advancing the representational and the lawmaking functions of Congress equally. But in reality the victory goes to representation over lawmaking. The great increase in roll-call votes made possible by the new system has led to a situation in which representatives are continually being called out of committee and subcommittee meetings (where the real fashioning of legislation takes place) to take part in roll-call votes on the floor. The dramatic changes produced by the Legislative Reorganization Act of 1970 have served to highlight the underlying conflict between maximizing representation and maximizing lawmaking. Reforms that make it easier to call for recorded votes and that reduce the amount of time needed for such votes inevitably lead to an increase in floor votes that, under the old system, would have been resolved in committee. Perhaps most important, the floor votes are constantly calling members out of hearings or committee markup sessions to perform their representational commitments on the floor. There is an obvious overlap between the two spheres of action (committees and the House floor) and the two functions (representation and lawmaking), but the tension between them remains.

The Washington journalist Louis Kohlmeier, Jr., points out

that "Congress is the least efficient, and most democratic, of the three branches." [38] Senator Dennis DeConcini of Arizona, in Senate hearings conducted in 1978 on a proposal to limit the terms of members of Congress, expressed a similar perception of the conflict between efficiency and democracy: "What is sought here, then, is greater responsiveness and greater representativeness. By shortening terms I feel that legislative accountability will be enhanced and the forces which nurture it will be strengthened. This may be another way of saying that I have come to prefer democracy over efficiency." [39] The measure of democracy in these cases is the representativeness of Congress as compared with the executive and judicial branches. Implicit in such an evaluation is the idea that efficiency and representativeness, while not mutually exclusive, pull in different directions. To maximize efficiency, Congress would have to sacrifice some procedures that assure fuller representation. The basic conflict between the lawmaking and the representation functions is perhaps best seen by looking at two evaluations of Congress that start from opposing points of view.

The lawmaking function was stressed in a study conducted by the Cambridge, Massachusetts, management consulting firm of Arthur D. Little.

> Congressional decision-making is the heart of all Congressional action and effectiveness. Congress does contribute to the process of government not only by its formal decisions; merely its investigation and discussion of public issues assist public understanding, help develop consensus, and thereby facilitate Congressional decisions. But important as they are, neither investigation nor public discussion can justify Congress in the public eye if it does not decide, for when as a body it makes no decisions, it fails to perform its great constitutional function of setting national policy.[40]

The Arthur D. Little people came up with a number of reform proposals. These were designed to improve the efficiency of Congress by reducing the existing points of delay (or points of representation) produced by such procedures as those requiring a full hearing in the Senate and the House committee before acting on legislation.

If we emphasize the legislative function of representation, the reforms proposed to streamline the "creaking machinery of the U.S. Congress"—as the Arthur D. Little consultants called it—would do more harm than good. While the present system may be inefficient, it does provide for fuller representation of all interests than would be achieved in a more streamlined legislative system. A quite different view of what Congress is, and should be, is offered by a leading student of the Senate, Ralph K. Huitt, who starts from a value premise emphasizing the representational function of the legislature:

> Congress has the strength of the free enterprise system; it multiplies the decision makers, the points of access to influence and power, and the creative moving agents. It is hard to believe that a small group of leaders could do better. What would be gained in orderliness might well be lost in vitality and in sensitiveness to the pressures for change.
>
> Moreover, Congress resembles the social system it serves; it reflects the diversity of the country. There is much to be said for a system in which almost every interest can find some spokesman, in which every cause can strike a blow, however feeble, in its own behalf.[41]

The relative emphasis one gives to the lawmaking and representation functions of Congress structures how one evaluates the legislature and determines the nature of one's proposed reforms. In the rest of this chapter we will look at various models of Congress used to evaluate the legislature and at reform proposals related to these models. One should always keep in mind the inherent conflict between representation and lawmaking. For as Theodore Lowi reminds us, "a *perfectly representative* government would be virtually incapable of making a decision!" [42] Alexander Hamilton spoke for five hours one day at the Constitutional Convention of 1787 in order to "give my sentiments of the best form of government—not as a thing attainable by us, but as a model which we ought to approach as near as possible." [43] More recently, the political scientist Ralph K. Huitt noted that "there is no 'model' of a proper legislature to which men of good intentions can repair." [44]

Both men use the term *model* to refer to a set of interrelated assumptions and statements about the proper role of the legislature in the American political system. In constructing a model of Congress, the political theorist creates a simplified view of reality by choosing to emphasize certain legislative functions. Evaluations of Congress and reform proposals arise when people compare the existing system with the idealized legislative model.

Four models of Congress will be outlined in this chapter. While both representation and lawmaking are deemed appropriate legislative functions in all four models, in each model one of these function is valued over the other. As a result, each model comes to different conclusions about the proper role of Congress and about the type of reforms needed to improve that institution. Two of the models focus on the lawmaking function of Congress; the others emphasize the representational function.

Models Emphasizing the Lawmaking Function

The Hamiltonian, or Strong President, Model.[45] "A feeble Executive," wrote Hamilton, "implies a feeble execution of the government. A feeble execution is but another phrase for a bad execution; and a government ill executed, whatever it may be in theory, must be, in practice, a bad government." [46] So it was that Hamilton and the early Federalists developed a model of executive-legislative relations that emphasized the need for a president who would dominate the national government. The Congress would have a modifying and ratifying role, but the real initiation and implementation of policy was to lie with the executive branch. Leonard White has described the Federalist concept of government as one in which "decisions on programs thought out by national leaders might be subject to the vote of popular assemblies, but the latter . . . had neither the capacity, nor the unity, to work out the plans themselves." [47]

The Hamiltonian model was developed as the result of a desire to enact a comprehensive Federalist program coupled with a distrust of the people. Over a century later, Woodrow Wilson outlined a conception of executive-legislative relations similar to Hamilton's. "Leadership in government," said Wilson, "naturally belongs to its executive officers, who are daily in contact with practical conditions and exigencies and whose reputations alike for good judgement and for fidelity are at stake much more than are those of the members of the legislative body." [48] Wilson's justification for a strong presidency was that it more accurately reflected the wishes of the people. The president should initiate and implement policy because "the nation as a whole has chosen him, and is conscious that it has no other political spokesman. His is the only national voice in affairs." [49]

In the closing decades of the twentieth century, many political scientists have adopted the strong presidency view of Hamilton and Wilson. Even after Vietnam and Watergate seemed to demonstrate the dangers of excessive presidential power, many presidential scholars returned to a Hamiltonian conception of the president's proper role in the American political system. In the 1976 edition of *Presidential Power*, Richard Neustadt repeats his earlier assertion that "Our Constitution, our traditions, and our politics provide no better source for the initiatives a President can take." [50] "Presidents must lead Congress," says Richard Pious in his 1979 book, *The American Presidency:*

> Congress will accept strong presidential leadership because it simply is not very good at developing or passing comprehensive programs when left to its own devices.
>
> The president is best situated to propose comprehensive programs, articulate a conception of the national interest, and educate the public to the dimensions of national problems. A president who is weak as a leader does not, by his failure to lead Congress, create conditions for legislative policymaking: there is no "see-saw" effect. When the president cannot lead Congress the result is scattered innovation, incremental rather than comprehensive programming, or deadlock between the branches.[51]

The Hamiltonian model may be summarized as one that advocates a strong, vigorous president acting within a somewhat unbalanced system of checks and balances. The Congress is not ignored, but its chief function becomes one of modifying and providing legitimacy for programs and policies emanating from the executive branch. The lawmaking function is deemed the most important legislative function by advocates of the Hamiltonian model. In order to create a Congress capable of acting with dispatch on programs submitted by the president, proponents of the Hamiltonian model suggest reforms that would centralize leadership in the legislature and make it more responsive to the executive's programs.

One suggested reform is that Congress be required to act on all executive proposals within a specified time period. By having a deadline for legislative action, Congress would be forced to change its work patterns in order to deal more rapidly and efficiently with presidential proposals. This, of course, would require giving up the present system of slow deliberation that maximizes representation.

Reforms that would reduce the individual legislator's work load and allow him or her to concentrate on passing legislation also fit into the Hamiltonian framework. Legislation giving broad mandates and long-term authorization to executive agencies would greatly reduce the time a legislator had to devote annually to re-viewing programs established the previous year. He would have more time to devote to performing his or her lawmaking function. Another reform proposal designed to achieve the same end is to create a congressional bureaucracy to handle legislators' constituent casework.

All of these proposals share the basic assumption that is the defining characteristic of the Hamilton model: the preferred po-litical system is one in which the lawmaking function of Congress is maximized. All of these reforms would make Congress less able to carry out its representational function by reducing the points of access of interests to the legislature and by speeding up the de-liberative process. Some representation would be sacrificed in order to improve legislative efficiency.

The Jeffersonian, or Party Government, Model. The Hamiltonian model emerged at a time when most political leaders in the country felt that political parties, or factions, were evil institutions that could imperil the existence of the new government. However, oppo-sition to the Federalist economic programs and pro-British foreign policy soon led to the organization of state parties to combat those policies through elections. Unlike most of the other early American political thinkers, Thomas Jefferson regarded parties as an integral part of politics. "In every free and deliberating society," he said, "there must, from the nature of man, be opposite parties, and vio-lent dissensions and discords; and one of these, for the most part must prevail over the other for a longer or a shorter time." [52]

After winning the election of 1800, Jefferson instituted an ex-tensive system of party organization in the legislature. By joining the executive and legislative branches, the party became a vehicle for translating the will of the majority into policy. The president and his advisors would propose policy, and Republican legislators, working through party caucuses, would transmute the proposals into law. Republican legislators who acted independently of the party were called "wayward freaks" by the president and were sometimes the targets of electoral purges.[53] An extensive intelli-gence system and selective dispersal of patronage were important instruments in the implementation of the Jeffersonian system of party government.

As we have already seen, Woodrow Wilson thought the Ameri-can system worked best when the executive was dominant. Like

Jefferson, he regarded the political party as the most likely vehicle for achieving that dominance. Openly admiring the British parliamentary system, Wilson saw the political party as a vital link between the executive and legislative branches. By bringing together the two branches, which were separated in the constitutional system, the political party could produce an effective government, responsive to the majority. Emphasizing the role of the party in uniting the two branches of government, Wilson laid down the political maxim that:

> When the several Chief organs of government are separated by organic law and offset against each other in jealous seclusion, no common legal authority set over them, no necessary community of interest subsisting amongst them, no common origin or purpose dominating them, they must of necessity, if united at all, be united by pressure from without; and they must be united if government is to proceed. They cannot remain checked and balanced against one another; they must act and act together. They must, therefore, of their own will or of mere necessity obey an outside master.[54]

Elected as a minority president in 1912, Wilson set about to build a strong national Democratic party by providing patronage rewards to party legislators in return for policy support. Twice during his presidency Wilson considered resigning from office and seeking reelection in a party referendum similar to that in British practice.

In 1950, members of the American Political Science Association's Committee on Political Parties analyzed the existing party system and proposed a set of reforms that were similar to those of the Jeffersonian model. The political scientists shared Jefferson and Wilson's view of political parties as an essential link between public mandates voiced in elections and policies emanating from Congress. The populist "responsible two-party system" favored by the committee was one in which: (1) both presidential and congressional candidates would campaign on a platform of consistent party policy proposals; (2) there would be a significant difference between the two parties' policies; (3) voters would make their choice between parties on the basis of these consistent platforms; and (4) once elected, both the president and his or her congressional colleagues from the same party would seek to implement the party platform by passing laws.[55] The continuing deterioration of political parties in the 1970s has led a number of political analysts to restate this call for a more responsible two-party system.[56]

Reforms suggested by advocates of party government are aimed not just at Congress and the president, but at the entire political system. Changes would be effected not only in legislative organization but also in grass-roots party organizations. Voters would be able to perceive the policy differences between parties and act in terms of those differences. Central to all of these changes is the notion of providing party leaders with sanctions to employ against "wayward freak" legislators who do not support party programs. Rather than gaining the party label simply by winning a primary, a congressional candidate would have to demonstrate clearly his support of the national party's program. Another sanction which advocates of the party government model would like to see in the hands of party leaders is the power to control the dispersal of campaign funds. In the debate in 1979 surrounding the proposal for public funding of congressional campaigns, party government advocates emphasized the importance of having the state and local party organizations disperse these campaign funds rather than having them go directly to the individual candidates. Supporters of this model want a change from the present system in which party organizations in the state or district are irrelevant to most congressional campaigns and in which the times when a majority of Democrats in both the House and the Senate oppose a majority of Republicans are far fewer than the number of massive defections from the party position. In 1978, for example, a majority of House Democrats opposed a majority of House Republicans on only 33 percent of all roll-call votes, and a majority of Senate Democrats opposed a majority of Senate Republicans on only 45 percent of all roll-call votes.[57] Most of the roll-call votes in both chambers do not reflect the level of party unity sought by supporters of the Jeffersonian model.

Specific reforms advocated by party government spokespersons are similar to those put forward by Hamiltonians. Both seek to centralize leadership in order to maximize the lawmaking functions of Congress. Some of the reforms proposed by those who want a party government include (1) nationalizing the party organizations by requiring that congressional candidates bearing the party label be approved by the national party headquarters and that national party leaders have a voice in selecting the party's legislative leaders; (2) using party caucus votes to bind all members to support the party position on important issues; (3) creating strong party policy

committees in Congress to make committee assignments on the basis of demonstrated party loyalty and to handle matters of legislative scheduling; and (4) expanding committee staff assistance so that both minority and majority members have the resources for developing meaningful party positions on committee matters.[58]
While the low incidence of party unity voting mentioned above shows that Congress is a long way from achieving the goals sought with these reforms by party government advocates, House Democrats in the 1970s did begin to exercise powers along the lines suggested in proposals 2 and 3 above. A newly active House Democratic Caucus exercises a great deal more control over the selection process for committee chairpersons and members and increasingly advances a party position on substantive issues.[59]

The Jeffersonian model is like the Hamiltonian model in that it seeks to overcome the dangers of inaction implicit in the Madisonian system of checks and balances. Both models advocate a central role for presidential leadership. The differences between the models lie in the nature of that leadership and its resources. In the Hamiltonian model, the president relies on his or her personal sources of power. Legislative majorities must be put together with each new issue. In the Jeffersonian model, the president has a continuing base of support on all issues in his or her party's legislative coalition. Because these legislators have been elected on the basis of support for the party program, the president can expect their support without having to employ tactics to build a majority coalition on each issue. The party government model also gives the legislators a more central role in the formulation of party policy. Because they have been elected on the same party platform as the president, legislators can be expected to initiate programs designed to implement that policy. They do not need to wait for executive initiatives. And they can count on support from the White House for programs in line with the platform.

Decision-Making Emphasis of Both Models

The strong president and party government models both deal with the question of representation. The *public interest* is defined in terms of electoral mandates. The people are *represented* when legislators pass laws that reflect the mandates. Advocates of both models contend that increasing the ability of Congress to perform its lawmaking function allows Congress to be representative because it can then enact the programs desired by a majority.

The definition of representation in both models is one emphasizing the importance of electoral mandates and the ability of elected officials to transform those mandates into policies through a process of virtual representation. This definition is subject to criticism. For example, a voter who disagrees with the Democratic party's position on foreign policy and civil rights may nevertheless vote for a Democratic candidate because of his or her position on economic matters. If the successful Democratic candidate interprets his or her winning as a mandate for all Democratic programs, then the process of representing that voter's opinions becomes distorted. Making Congress better able to transform electoral mandates into policy quickly greatly reduces the legislator's chances of representing that constituent's dissenting opinions on civil rights and foreign policy.

In a system that stresses the party label and virtual representation, *representation* has a different meaning than it has in a system emphasizing geographic representation. Simply put, the question is this: Is a Democratic congressman from Alabama being more representative by voting consistently with his party, or is he being more representative by speaking for the economic and social interests of his district in Alabama even when they run counter to the Democratic party's programs?

By defining representation solely in terms of electoral mandates and the legislator's transforming that mandate into policy, advocates of the Hamiltonian and Jeffersonian models tend to favor any reforms that would increase the ability of Congress to perform its lawmaking function. But making Congress more efficient in this way results in fewer points of access for electoral minorities to state their case and a shorter time period in which all interests are given a hearing in the deliberative process. If representation is thought of primarily as interest articulation rather than as policy-making in accordance with an electoral majority, then the reforms suggested by these two models can be regarded as sacrificing the representational function of Congress to the lawmaking function.

Models Emphasizing the Representation Function

The Madisonian System. Although both Hamilton and Madison envisioned a government structured in a form of checks and balances, there is a distinct difference of emphasis between the two modes of thought. While Hamilton sought a government capable of vigorous action, Madison feared that such action might endanger individual liberties. Rather than fearing an undemocratic minority, Madison felt that the real threat to a republic would come from a majority faction able to execute policies detrimental to minority groups by gaining control of the government. He proposed to prevent such majority control "by so contriving the interior structure of the government as that its several constituent parts may, by their mutual relations, be the means of keeping each other in their proper places." [60] Seeking to establish a state where "the private interest of every individual may be a sentinel over the public rights," Madison proposed an executive branch and a legislative branch with equal powers but with means for each to check the actions of the others. Instead of being separate institutions with separate powers, the president and Congress were to be separate institutions sharing powers. The presidential veto and the Senate's role in making foreign policy and approving presidential appointments, as well as shared control of the military and congressional control of the purse strings, were checks on precipitous government action in response to majority demands. "I am part of the legislative process," President Eisenhower often remarked, for the Madisonian system had made it so.[61]

The Madisonian model of Congress is essentially negative. Rather than focusing on joint executive-legislative actions, it emphasizes a system of mutual distrust. As one scholar has noted: "In the system that Madison envisages, the danger is action and the safeguard is stalemate, or, as he would have it, balance. Factious interests are to be 'broken,' 'controlled,' and 'balanced' against each other to produce 'stability.' " [62]

Twentieth-century variations of the Madisonian model are generally called the *constitutional*, or *literary*, models of Congress because they find their support in a strict reading of the Constitution.[63] They generally advocate greatly increasing congressional strength vis-à-vis the executive to restore a balance that most feel has been seriously upset. Emphasis is generally placed, not on streamlining Congress so that it might more readily respond to presidential initiatives, but on strengthening the congressional role of blocking legislation and checking the executive. In *Obstacle Course on Capitol Hill*, Robert Bendiner discusses this role:

> A United States Congressman has two principal functions: to make laws and to keep laws from being made. The first of these he and his colleagues perform only with sweat, patience, and a remarkable

skill in the handling of creaking machinery; but the second they perform daily, with ease and infinite variety. Indeed, if that government is best that governs least, then Congress is one of the most perfect instruments of government ever devised.[64]

Senator Harry Byrd of Virginia expressed the same idea in the debate over the filibuster rule change in 1979: "It is in the very nature of the Senate as an institution that some legislation during the year not be enacted. The system is intended to operate in that fashion because, in a free society, there is a fundamental presumption against new law and new restrictions on our citizens."[65]

Some of the strongest advocates of the Madisonian model are members of Congress themselves. A study by Davidson, Kovenock, and O'Leary found that 55 percent of the members of Congress they interviewed agreed with the statement, "Congress and the executive should be equal partners in the making of public policy."[66] As part of the American political culture, the system of checks and balances also receives support from the public. In a series of national polls over the last three decades, people have been asked whether they thought that the president or Congress should have the major responsibility in the making of foreign, economic, and racial policy. A large majority (about 60 percent) have continually said that they should have equal responsibility. "Unsophisticated as the public may be in knowledge of constitutional provisions for the separation of powers," notes one close student of these polls, "they have systematically given implied consent to the principle of checks and balances."[67]

Support for the Madisonian model is often tied to conservatism in American politics, but this depends, to a great extent, on who is president. Before the election of Richard Nixon in 1968, conservatives tended to favor a Madisonian model of Congress. This was certainly true during the Kennedy and Johnson administrations, when those who opposed the Democratic programs sought to have those programs blocked by Congress.

With the election of Richard Nixon, however, these same conservatives looked to the executive branch for leadership. The presidency rather than the Congress become the ally of those who sought a reduction in funds for domestic programs. At the same time, many of those who had earlier advocated a strong presidency became ardent Madisonians, seeking to make Congress an effective force for blocking presidential programs and for appropriating more money for education, poverty, and medical programs than that requested in the president's budget. Congress's passing of the War Powers Resolution of 1973 and the Congressional Budget and Impoundment Control Act of 1974 is an example of the type of Madisonian checks on presidential power that Congress sought to institutionalize during the Nixon administration. Liberal opponents of both the Vietnam War and presidential impoundments of funds for social programs were among the staunchest advocates of the Madisonian model. The election of a Democratic president (Carter) in 1976, however, produced a return to the earlier pattern of conservative support for the Madisonian system. Although Congress did not disassemble the many institutional checks on presidential power created during the Nixon years and although many liberals continually sought to increase and expand the government programs advanced by President Jimmy Carter, the pattern in the late 1970s resembled that of the pre-Nixon era in which the strongest supporters of the Madisonian model were conservatives who viewed Congress as a check on too much government action.

The Madisonian model may be called conservative if we define it in broad terms rather than give it its American political connotations. The system of checks and balances is conservative in that it minimizes government activity and is greatly weighted toward maintenance of the status quo. Madison's system is founded on the premise that government action constitutes the greatest threat to individual liberties. To protect these liberties it is necessary to devise a government that can perform its lawmaking function only with great difficulty. Given a choice between representation and lawmaking, supporters of the Madisonian model will always choose the former.

This emphasis on representation rather than lawmaking generally takes two forms when it is used to evaluate the present system and when it is applied to reform proposals. On the one hand, followers of Madison want to increase legislative representation in the decision-making process. Senate doves in the late 1960s and early 1970s were not advocating that the Senate make foreign policy decisions, but rather that the president include the representation of Senate opinions in policy-making. On the other hand, the Madisonians' fear of secret and overly hasty executive policy-making extends to legislative decision-making, so that Madisonians generally uphold the same decentralized structure that makes it difficult for Congress to play an active representational role in executive decision-making.

"Congressional acts, like the common law, ought to move carefully from precedent to precedent" is the way one congressman puts it.[68] To insure that legislation is not passed without a thorough airing of all interests, adherents of this model generally support reform proposals that would maintain and extend a congressional system giving minorities greater access and control over the legislative process. While supporters of a checks and balances model sometimes oppose reform proposals that would change the existing system, and at other times favor such reforms, they always support procedures that seek to maximize the representational function. Madisonians thus opposed changes in the filibuster rule that diluted minority representation, although they supported the 1970 change providing for recorded teller votes.

Madisonians supported many reforms in the Legislative Reorganization Act of 1970 because they increased the legislature's representational capabilities. Included were (1) the requirement that committees make public all roll-call votes taken in committee meetings; (2) a provision giving committee members three days within which they may file minority views to a committee report on a bill; (3) a rule that divides debate on a conference report between majority and minority positions; (4) a stipulation that committee meetings and hearings be open to the public unless the committee votes to close them; (5) a provision that open committee hearings be broadcast over radio or television as long as a majority of the committee agrees; and (6) a requirement that committees announce hearings at least one week in advance unless there is an obvious reason for starting hearings at once.

Other reforms favored by adherents of the Madisonian model show the same concern for representation. Expanding congressional sources of information independent of the executive by increasing the size of the staffs of the legislators and the committees is such a proposal. Madisonians oppose any efforts to increase the individual legislator's lawmaking function by turning over his or her constituent casework to a central legislative bureau. Instead of streamlining the legislative process by cutting down on the time spent on administrative oversight, Madisonians suggest expanding that function by providing only limited grants of authority to executive agencies and giving Congress an active oversight role through hearings and investigations, review of appointments, and tight budgetary controls.

The Pluralist System. We find many of the values associated with the Madisonian system in contemporary pluralist descriptions of Congress. Without getting too deeply involved in the debate over the merits of pluralism, we should at least review the representative aspects of the pluralist model and its similarity to Madison's.[69]

In *The End of Liberalism,* Theodore Lowi has outlined the basic assumptions of the pluralist model as articulated in its ideological form, *interest-group liberalism.* These are (1) that organized interests are homogeneous and easy to define and that any "duly elected" spokesperson for an interest accurately reflects the opinions of the members of that group; (2) that organized interests represent almost all sectors of our lives so that there is always an organized group to check effectively the demands made by another organized group; and (3) that government's role is to provide access to organized groups and to ratify the agreement and adjustments reached by competing group leaders.[70]

It is clear that the first two assumptions deal directly with the question of representation. The validity of the pluralist model as an empirical description of reality and as a normative model for evaluating other political systems and institutions hinges on the correctness of its assumptions that group leaders accurately represent membership opinions and that organized interest groups provide a truly representative picture of the total society. Studies of political, corporate, and labor leadership and policy-making in such diverse areas as taxes and agriculture cast doubt on both assumptions.[71] These matters will be dealt with at greater length in Chapters 2 and 6. It is enough now to note the representational base on which the pluralist model rests and to observe that assumptions or hypotheses about the nature of this representation are often treated as observed facts rather than hypotheses.

The pluralists' emphasis on group interaction as the basic process of politics is closely tied to the way they define *the public interest.* In the Hamiltonian and Jeffersonian models the public interest is defined in terms of policy goals favored by an electoral majority. For Madisonians, the public interest is achieved by protecting individual liberties from incursions by the state. Pluralists, on the other hand, tend to deny that there is some substantive definition of the public interest apart from that which emerges by balancing group interests; they define the public interest solely in terms of this group process.[72] Contrasting notions of the public interest and the role of government were presented by Edmund Burke in 1774 and David Truman in 1951:

> *Burke:* "Parliament is not a congress of ambassadors from different and hostile interests, which interests each must maintain, as an agent and advocate against other agents and advocates; but Parliament is a deliberative assembly of one nation, with one interest, that of the whole—where not local purposes, not local prejudices, ought to guide, but the general good, resulting from the general reason of the whole." [73]

> *Truman:* "Assertion of an inclusive 'national' or 'public interest' is an effective device. . . . In themselves these claims are a part of the data of politics. However, they do not describe any actual or possible political situation within a complex modern nation. In developing a group interpretation of politics, therefore, we do not need to account for a totally inclusive interest, because one does not exist." [74]

Whereas Burke was articulating a normative model of politics, an attempt to achieve the good society, political scientists such as Truman have generally presented the pluralist model as an empirical one, a description of "the way things are." By eliminating such considerations as the public good or the public interest, group theorists sought to skirt problems of definition associated with models that try to avoid "tyranny" or achieve "democracy." They attempted to provide a model that would permit objective study of the American political system—study not tainted by their own political predilections.

At the beginning of this chapter, it was suggested that the framework one employs for observing reality greatly affects the picture of reality one obtains. "It is the theory," Einstein once said, "which decides what we can observe." [75] By viewing American politics within the framework of an empirical pluralist model, political scientists found a system that seemed to maximize representational values. Most pluralists would agree with Ralph Huitt's favorable view of a Congress that has "the strength of the free enterprise system" because it seems to provide for the representation of all societal interests. In considering the findings of studies that employed a pluralist framework, we should look for ways in which the theoretical framework may have affected the results. Since most congressional research is carried on within a pluralist framework emphasizing interest articulation and policy-making through long-term bargaining, we often find political scientists defending aspects of the legislative process that many others consider silly.

One of the criticisms leveled at pluralists is that they avoid basic value conflicts and judge political questions on the basis of how many people favor which position rather than weighing the merits of opposing arguments.[76] Whenever people judge Congress and offer reform proposals, there exists the same danger of overlooking fundamental conflicts and attempting to provide a wide variety of reforms that actually move in different directions. We want our representatives and senators to assist us in our encounters with the bureaucracy, and we want the institution of Congress to pass laws. Reforms that make it easier for representatives and senators to perform the first function make it harder for the institution to perform the second. This fundamental conflict between representation and lawmaking needs to be kept in mind if we are to evaluate accurately both congressional behavior and proposed reforms. Members of Congress themselves sometimes commit the pluralist fallacy of ignoring basic value conflicts in attempting to provide something for everyone. Fifteen years ago the Joint Committee on the Organization of Congress introduced its final report with the observation that "the members of the joint committee agree that Congress should be maintained as a study and deliberative body, that the machinery of Congress must be modernized in order to provide for efficient handling of the nation's affairs, and that the rule by majority must be preserved with adequate protection for the rights of the minority."[77] A general statement such as this one seems to ignore the fact that reforms aimed at maintaining Congress as "a study and deliberative body" are likely to make it more difficult for the institution to handle efficiently the nation's affairs. Reforms that facilitate representation, in other words, are likely to hinder efficient lawmaking.

A more recent overall review and assessment of the workings of the House of Representatives accurately identifies this conflict between representation and lawmaking as the major institutional constraint affecting congressional reform. In its final report, the House Commission on Administrative Review discusses those characteristics of the House that identify it as a representative institution: a decision-making process with consensus-building at numerous decision points, constituent service work, and the general accessibility of members and staff aides. "At the same time," the Commission's report says:

> A counter-pressure arises from legislative or policy responsibility, which emphasizes decisionmaking and policy output. Changes in House and caucus rules and procedures in recent years reflect this dichotomy: some reforms (the Speaker's responsibility to nominate Democratic members of the Rules Committee, the role of the Steering and Policy Committee, changes in the numbers required for various floor procedures) have been designed to effect more efficient decisionmaking; others (recorded teller votes, various committee procedures) have enhanced the representative function.
>
> The representative nature of the institution, which emphasizes consensus-building and a deliberative decisionmaking process, argues against an overriding emphasis on efficiency. An important function of the House is to represent citizen concerns, and to achieve policy outputs which can be accepted by all. An emphasis on efficient decisionmaking resulting in rapid passage of numerous statutes, for example, may in fact not allow time for needed consensus-building. Similarly, some duplication of office operations, although perhaps not as efficient as a central service, may be more effective as a means of carrying out representative and even legislative and oversight responsibilities.
>
> Recognizing the existence of these institutional constraints gives the Commission less leeway in proposing solutions to the problems noted.[78]

This conflict between the representative and lawmaking functions emerges in the Senate as well as in the House. Debate over changes in the filibuster rule, as we have seen, centers on the desire of some to make the Senate a more efficient lawmaker and the desire of others to maximize the Senate role of full representation.

Both chambers of the national legislature are expected to fill both the representative and the lawmaking roles. Differences over the value of particular legislative practices or proposed reforms are often, in fact, differences over the relative importance of the lawmaking and representative functions of Congress. Whether or not one thinks that Congress *should* adopt a particular reform will often depend on what one thinks of the broader values of representation and efficient lawmaking, and these values, in turn, are related to even broader considerations about the proper role of government in American society.

The purpose of this chapter has been to acquaint you with the fact that there are many different answers to the question of what Congress is supposed to be doing in the American political system. A familiarity with the different value frameworks used to judge Congress provides a firmer ground for both evaluating and understanding the politics of Congress. The following five chapters attempt to present a picture of what goes on in Congress. Chapter 2 deals with the question of representation, Chapter 3 with the political party as an instrument for transforming electoral mandates into policies, Chapter 4 with the committee system in the House and Senate, Chapter 5 with rules and norms, and Chapter 6 with the impact of interest groups and executive lobbying on legislative policies.

NOTES

1. Representative Nicholas Longworth, quoted in U.S. Congress, House, *Congressional, Media, and People Who Work the Hill Panels, Hearings Before the Commission on Administrative Review*, Ninety-fourth Congress, second session, November 30, and December 1, 1976, p. 70.

2. Richard Fenno, *Home Style: House Members in Their Districts* (Little, Brown, 1978), pp. 165 and 166.

3. John Herbers, "Tax Revolt is Squeezing the States," *New York Times*, February 25, 1979, p. E5.

4. *Congressional Quarterly Weekly Report*, February 17, 1979, p. 277.

5. Colman McCarthy, "At Season's End, No Joy in Washington," *Boston Globe*, October 21, 1978, p. 23.

6. In 1978, the total number of voluntary resignations (House and Senate) for the Ninety-fifth Congress was fifty-nine. In 1976, there were fifty-five; in 1974, fifty-one. Figures for earlier years include: 1950, twenty-nine; 1956, twenty-five; 1960, thirty; 1966, twenty-four; and 1970, thirty-two. For more on this phenomenon, see Steven V. Roberts, "Many Members of House Retiring as Pressures Outweigh Rewards," *New York Times*, March 27, 1978, p. A1; Marguerite Michaels, "Why Congressmen Want Out," *Parade Magazine*, November 5, 1978, p. 11; "Retirements: A Mix of Ambition and Fatigue," *Congressional Quarterly Weekly Report*, April 24, 1976; and Stephen E. Frantzich, "Opting Out: Retirement from the House of Representatives, 1966–1974," *American Politics Quarterly*, vol. 6, no. 3 (July, 1978), pp. 251–273.

7. Colman McCarthy, p. 23.

8. Quoted in Mary Russell and Robert G. Kaiser, "The Marathon: Non-

stop 34 Hours of Waltzing, Stumbling, Struggling," *Washington Post,* October 16, 1978, p. A6.

9. "The Non-Candidates: Why Didn't They Run?" *Congressional Quarterly Weekly Report,* April 15, 1978, p. 892.

10. Leroy N. Rieselbach, *Congressional Reform in the Seventies* (General Learning Press, 1977), pp. 32–33. Reprinted by permission of the Silver Burdett Company.

11. Alan P. Balutis, "Congress: Reports of Its Demise Have Been Greatly Exaggerated," *Congressional Record,* February 9, 1977, pp. H1037–H1043.

12. Barbara Hinckley, *Stability and Change in Congress* (Harper & Row, 1978, 2nd ed.), pp. 207–208.

13. The public opinion data in Figure 1–1 are from Gallup and Harris polls as reported in *The Gallup Opinion Index* (Scholarly Resources) and the *Harris Survey Yearbook of Public Opinion* (Louis Harris and Associates) for the years indicated between 1964 and 1978.

14. Glenn R. Parker, "Some Themes in Congressional Unpopularity," *American Journal of Political Science,* vol. 21, no. 1 (February, 1977), pp. 93–109. See also Glenn R. Parker, "A Note on the Impact and Saliency of Congress," *American Politics Quarterly,* vol. 4, no. 4 (October, 1976), pp. 413–421.

15. Randall B. Ripley, *Congress: Process and Policy* (W. W. Norton, 1978, second edition), pp. 388ff.

16. *Gallup Opinion Index,* report no. 144 (July, 1977).

17. "Approval of Carter Drops to 46% in Poll," *New York Times,* April 14, 1978, p. 10.

18. The results of the national poll conducted by Louis Harris and Associates for the U.S. House Commission on Administrative Review are reported in Thomas E. Cavanagh, "The Two Arenas of Congress: Electoral and Institutional Incentives for Performance," a paper prepared for delivery at the 1978 annual meeting of the American Political Science Association, New York, N.Y., August 31 to September 3, 1978, p. 25.

19. Ibid., appendix, tables 5 and 6.

20. A representative sample of discussions of the various functions of Congress may be found in Roger Davidson, David Kovenock, and Michael O'Leary, *Congress in Crisis: Politics and Congressional Reform* (Wadsworth, 1969), pp. 34ff; Malcolm Jewell and Samuel Patterson, *The Legislative Process in the United States* (Random House, 1977, third edition), pp. 5ff; William Keefe and Morris Ogul, *The American Legislative Process* (Prentice-Hall, 1977, fourth edition), pp. 14ff; and Randall Ripley, *Congress: Process and Policy,* pp. 30ff.

21. Mary Russell, "New House Democrats Called More Restrained," *Washington Post*, December 2, 1976, p. A4.

22. Representative John B. Anderson, "House Reform Agenda for the 96th Congress," *Congressional Record*, October 11, 1978, reprinted in House Republican Conference press release, October 23, 1978.

23. For a thorough discussion see Morris Ogul, *Congress Oversees the Bureaucracy* (University of Pittsburgh Press, 1976).

24. Woodrow Wilson, *Congressional Government* (World Publishing Company, 1967), p. 195.

25. Luther Patrick, "What Is a Congressman?" *Congressional Record*, May 13, 1963, p. H2978. Quoted in Joseph S. Clark, *Congress: The Sapless Branch* (Harper & Row, 1964), p. 62.

26. Morris P. Fiorina, *Congress: Keystone of the Washington Establishment* (Yale University Press, 1977).

27. Representative Joel Pritchard, statement in U.S. Congress, House, *Administrative Reorganization and Legislative Management, Hearings Before the Commission on Administrative Review*, Ninety-fifth Congress, first session, June 2, 1977, p. 62.

28. Thomas E. Cavanagh, "The Two Arenas of Congress: Electoral and Institutional Incentives for Performance," appendix, tables 1 and 3.

29. Quoted in Charles Clapp, *The Congressman: His Work as He Sees It* (Brookings Institution, 1963), pp. 57, 61, and 62.

30. *Congressional Quarterly Weekly Report*, February 19, 1971, p. 416.

31. Ibid.

32. *Congressional Quarterly Weekly Report*, March 15, 1975, p. 545.

33. Quoted in Jack Germond and Jules Witcover, "Minority Hamstrings U.S. Senate," *Boston Globe*, February 9, 1978, p. 18.

34. Quoted in David Broder, "Byrd vs. Byrd Over Senate Rules," *Boston Globe*, February 4, 1979, p. A7.

35. Senator Harrison Schmitt, quoted in Ann Cooper, "The Senate and the Filibuster: War of Nerves—and Hardball," *Congressional Quarterly Weekly Report*, September 2, 1978, p. 2309; and Senator Harry Byrd, quoted in David Broder, "Byrd vs. Byrd Over Senate Rules," p. A7.

36. Norman J. Ornstein, ed., *Congress in Change* (Praeger, 1975), p. 192. Further discussion and analysis of the recorded teller vote change may be found in Norman J. Ornstein and David W. Rohde, "The Strategy of Reform: Recorded Teller Voting in the House of Representatives," a paper presented at the 1974 annual meeting of the Midwest Political Science Association, Chicago, April, 1974.

37. Committee on House Administration, *The Electronic Voting System*

for the United States House of Representatives, (U.S. Government Printing Office, January 31, 1975), p. 1.

38. Louis M. Kohlmeier, Jr., *The Regulators* (Harper & Row, 1969), p. 291.

39. U.S. Congress, Senate, *Congressional Tenure, Hearings Before the Subcommittee on the Constitution of the Committee on the Judiciary,* Ninety-fifth Congress, second session, March 14, 1978, p. 6.

40. Philip Donham and Robert Fahey, *Congress Needs Help* (Random House, 1966), p. 148.

41. Ralph K. Huitt, "Congressional Organization in the Field of Money and Credit," in Commission on Money and Credit, *Fiscal Debt and Management Policies* (Prentice-Hall, 1963), p. 494.

42. Theodore Lowi, *Legislative Politics, U.S.A.* (Little, Brown, 1962), p. x.

43. James MacGregor Burns, *Presidential Government* (Avon Books, 1965), p. 24.

44. Ralph K. Huitt, "What Can We Do About Congress?" *Milwaukee Journal,* December 13, 1964, Part 5, p. 1. Quoted in Davidson et al., *Congress in Crisis,* p. 16.

45. The term for this and the Madisonian and Jeffersonian models are taken from James MacGregor Burns's discussion in *Presidential Government,* pp. 43–47.

46. Alexander Hamilton, *The Federalist Papers,* Federalist paper number 70, (Modern Library edition, n.d.), p. 455.

47. Leonard White, *The Federalists* (Macmillan, 1948), p. 510.

48. Woodrow Wilson, *Constitutional Government in the United States* (first published 1908; Columbia University Press edition, 1964), p. 72.

49. Ibid.

50. Richard E. Neustadt, *Presidential Power: The Politics of Leadership with Reflections on Johnson and Nixon* (John Wiley and Sons, 1976), p. 74.

51. Richard M. Pious, *The American Presidency* (Basic Books, 1979), p. 177.

52. Saul K. Padover, *Jefferson* (Mentor Books, 1955), p. 107.

53. Quoted in Louis Koenig, *The Chief Executive* (Harcourt, Brace & World, 1964), p. 102. James Young's incisive study of legislative-executive interaction under Jefferson suggests that the President's legislative coalitions were more a result of personal interaction and skillful lobbying by Jefferson than they were a result of party control. See James Young, *The Washington Community: 1800–1828* (Harcourt, Brace & World, 1966).

54. Woodrow Wilson, *Constitutional Government in the United States,* p. 211.

55. American Political Science Association Committee on Political Parties, *Toward a More Responsible Two Party System* (Holt, Rinehart & Winston, 1950).

56. See, for example, Everett Carl Ladd, Jr., *Where Have All the Voters Gone?* (W. W. Norton, 1978) and Ruth K. Scott and Ronald J. Hrebenar, *Parties in Crisis* (John Wiley and Sons, 1979).

57. Bob Livernash, "Party Unity Down in House, Up in Senate," *Congressional Quarterly Weekly Report*, December 16, 1978, pp. 3447-3449.

58. Davidson et al., *Congress in Crisis*, p. 34, outline these reforms. Other discussions of party government reform proposals can be found in Richard Bolling, *House Out of Order* (E. P. Dutton, 1966); James MacGregor Burns, *The Deadlock of Democracy* (Prentice-Hall, 1963); Joseph Clark, *Congressional Reform* (Thomas Y. Crowell, 1965); and the American Political Science Association Committee on Political Parties, *Toward a More Responsible Two Party System*.

59. Lawrence Dodd, "Emergence of Party Government in the House of Representatives," *DEA News Supplement* American Political Science Association (Summer, 1976).

60. Federalist paper number 51, *The Federalist Papers*, p. 336.

61. Richard E. Neustadt, *Presidential Power: The Politics of Leadership with Reflections on Johnson and Nixon*, p. 101.

62. Hannah Fenichel Pitkin, *The Concept of Representation* (University of California Press, 1967), p. 195.

63. See, for instance, John Saloma, *Congress and the New Politics* (Little, Brown, 1969), pp. 44-45; and Davidson et al., *Congress in Crisis*, pp. 17-25.

64. Robert Bendiner, *Obstacle Course on Capitol Hill* (McGraw-Hill, 1964), p. 15.

65. Quoted in David Broder, "Byrd vs. Byrd Over Senate Rules," *Boston Globe*, February 4, 1979, p. A7.

66. Davidson et al., *Congress in Crisis*, p. 69.

67. Hazel Erskine, "The Polls: Presidential Power," *Public Opinion Quarterly*, 37 (Fall, 1973), p. 491. The quotation and the poll data are reported in Robert E. DiClerico, *The American President* (Prentice-Hall, 1979), pp. 153-154.

68. Edwin M. Yoder, Jr., "Washington Report: Eckhardt of Texas," *Harpers*, June, 1970, p. 36.

69. For a good discussion and analysis of pluralism and its critics, see Jerrold E. Schneider, *Ideological Coalitions in Congress* (Greenwood Press, 1979), pp. 20-41.

70. Theodore Lowi, *The End of Liberalism* (W. W. Norton, 1969).

71. See, for example, Theodore Lowi's *The End of Liberalism* and *The*

Politics of Disorder; Murray Edelman, *The Symbolic Uses of Politics* (University of Illinois Press, 1964); Philip Green and Sanford Levinson, eds., *Power and Community* (Vintage, 1970); Grant McConnell, *Private Power and American Democracy* (Vintage, 1966); and E. E. Schattschneider, *The Semi-Sovereign People* (Holt, Rinehart & Winston, 1961). For agriculture and tax policies see the notes to Chapter 6.

72. For a good discussion of the conservative effects of this "balancing definition" of the public interest in administrative law, see Charles Reich, "The New Property," *Yale Law Journal,* vol. 73, no. 5 (April, 1964), pp. 733–787; and Reich, "The Law of the Planned Society," *Yale Law Journal,* vol. 75, no. 8 (July, 1966), pp. 1227–1270.

73. Edmund Burke, "Speech to the Electors of Bristol," *Writings and Speeches of Edmund Burke* (Little, Brown, 1901), pp. 93–98; reprinted in Neal Riemer, *The Representative* (D. C. Heath, 1967), p. 11.

74. David Truman, *The Governmental Process* (Alfred A. Knopf, 1962), p. 51.

75. Norwood Hanson, *Patterns of Discovery* (Cambridge University Press, 1958).

76. Charles Reich, "The New Property."

77. "Organization of Congress," *Final Report of the Joint Committee on the Organization of Congress* (U.S. Government Printing Office, 1966), pp. 1–2.

78. U.S. Congress, House, *Final Report of the Commission on Administrative Review,* Ninety-fifth Congress, first session, December 31, 1977, vol. 1, pp. 677–678.

REPRESENTATION

"WHEN MY FATHER FIRST WENT TO CONGRESS," the Senate Republican leader Howard Baker remembered, "he came up here with full expectations of returning to Tennessee regularly, keeping his family down there, keeping his interest in a range of things. He stayed in his law firm, he continued to have interests in a number of businesses." Senator Baker suggested that the modern Congress might benefit from the old way of doing things. He proposed that Congress should consider meeting in Washington for only six or seven months a year instead of its current almost year-round schedule, that it stop dealing with tiny legislative details, and that members of Congress should spend the rest of the time at home practicing law, teaching, farming, or carrying on their private businesses. "That would enable members to find out what their constituency thinks and reimmerse themselves in the mainstream of the country's life," he said.[1] As Figure 2–1 indicates, one would have to go way back to the first half of this century to find a congressional schedule that might fit the pattern sought by Senator Baker. The length of congressional sessions increased dramatically during and after World War II, making the job of being a representative or senator very much a full-time endeavor. The average length of time that Congress was in session between the Ninety-second and Ninety-fifth Congresses (1971–1978) was 627 out of the available 730 days for each two-year period covered in a congressional term.

While the length of congressional sessions shown in Figure 2–1

FIGURE 2–1 Average Length of Congressional Sessions in Days by Decade, 1791–1978

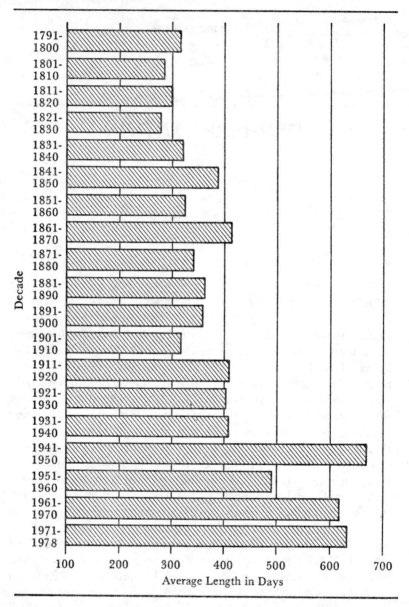

Source: The data for 1971–1978 are from *Congressional Directory 1977* (U.S. Government Printing Office), p. 400 and *Congressional Quarterly Weekly Report* (October 21, 1978), p. 2999. All other data are adapted from Randall B. Ripley, *Congress: Process and Policy* (Norton, 1978, second edition), p. 60.

does not leave much time for mingling with the home folks or carrying on a career in the state or district as suggested by Senator Baker, the congressional schedule does provide about two months a year when Congress is not in session and members of Congress do not have to be in Washington. Prior to 1977 these periods when Congress was not in session were known as recesses or, to critics of Congress, vacations. Sensitive to criticism about how representatives and senators were spending their time during these periods, leaders in the House changed the name from recesses to "district work periods" and leaders in the Senate changed it to "nonlegislative days" when they announced the legislative work schedule for 1977.[2]

Most members of Congress spend most of these nonlegislative days back home in the state or district. The two months of nonlegislative days are spread throughout the year. They consist primarily of weekends and are used by members of Congress for meeting with constituents in a wide variety of settings: luncheons; district office hours; town meetings; awards ceremonies; interview sessions with the media; tours of industrial, business, or government program sites and projects; and the like. A study conducted in 1973 found that House members averaged thirty-five trips home during the year.[3] When these trips occur around election time, they appear to many people more as campaigning for reelection than as serving as a member of Congress. Senators and representatives, however, are quick to point out the essential tie between such trips and their service as a representative of the people living in their state or district. Says one representative:

> My going home can be characterized, if you wish, as strictly trying to get myself reelected, but its impact on me is to force me to face up to people who have problems. It forces me to talk to someone who is unemployed. Nobody we talk to around here on a daily basis is unemployed. No matter how well motivated you are, one of the biggest problems in Congress or anywhere is that you can so isolate yourself from the people you are serving that you forget.[4]

The trips home and the attendant listening to constituents are regarded by members of Congress as an important part of their job. Specifically, it has more to do with their job as representative than it does with their job as lawmaker. While the ideas presented to them during these meetings with constituents might serve to generate legislation upon the member's return to Washington, the major justification for trips home and meeting with constituents is to permit

Congress to serve as a representational institution in American politics.

In chapter 1, I mentioned that one of the best ways to identify various notions about the functions of Congress is to look at specific reform proposals. This is true whether one is looking at Congress from the perspective of an insider or as an outside observer. A leading inside proponent of general congressional reforms verbalized an appreciation of the underlying conflicts:

> One of the things that has preoccupied me over quite a few years in my evaluation of the problems of reform and reorganization has been the reconciliation of seemingly incompatible goals. One is that you want greater efficiency for reasons that are pretty obvious. However, on the other hand, you never want to lose sight of the importance of the representative nature of the institution. That raises a lot of curious conflicts.[5]

To get some beginning insight into the representational function of Congress, it is worth looking at a specific reform proposal that raises some of those "curious conflicts" between the functions of representation and lawmaking. The reform proposal, introduced in the opening months of the Ninety-sixth Congress (1979–1980) and the subject of Senate committee hearings in the previous Congress, is one that would limit the number of terms that members of Congress can serve. The proposal appears in the form of a joint resolution calling for a constitutional amendment that would limit senators to two full terms (twelve years) and members of the House to six full terms (twelve years).

In July, 1977, a nonpartisan, nonprofit organization known as the Foundation for the Study of Presidential and Congressional Terms was formed for the purpose of study and public debate on three constitutional amendments that would: (1) limit the number of years that a senator and representative could remain in office; (2) extend the term of office for House members from two to three or four years; and (3) limit the president to a single, six-year term in office. In the Ninety-fifth Congress (1977–1978), more than fifteen resolutions calling for a constitutional amendment to limit terms of senators and representatives were introduced. A subcommittee of the Senate Judiciary Committee held hearings on the subject in the spring of 1978, but the House Judiciary Committee failed to take any action on the matter in the Ninety-fifth Congress.

Since the two-year House term and six-year Senate term were

established in the Constitution in 1789, close to seventy resolutions have been introduced in Congress calling for a constitutional amendment to limit the terms of service for representatives and senators. None of the resolutions got very far. The Senate hearings in the spring of 1978 represented the first serious consideration of the term limitation proposal in over thirty years. One reason for the failure of earlier efforts to limit congressional terms was the opposition of incumbent senators and representatives, especially senior ones. A poll taken by the Foundation for the Study of Presidential and Congressional Terms elicited a response from 148 members of the House and the Senate. By a margin of more than two-to-one, incumbent senators and representatives rejected any form of term limitation.[6] Public support for a term limitation, on the other hand, was growing. A Gallup Poll taken in 1977 showed that 60 percent of the public favored a twelve-year limit on congressional terms; this was an increase from the 49 percent who favored such a measure in 1964.[7]

The chief target of supporters of a congressional term limitation is the professional politician or career legislator, who is the antithesis of the citizen legislator eulogized by Senator Baker at the beginning of this chapter. In the last century, a high electoral turnover of from 40 to 50 percent at each election filled each session of Congress with new members and provided a kind of automatic representation of viewpoints by members from many different occupations. In the twentieth century, however, the high number of members seeking reelection and the high rate of return of incumbent candidates have produced a Congress in which the turnover is low. Figures 2–2 and 2–3 demonstrate the stability in membership in both the House and the Senate for the last four decades. The low percentage of new members in both the House and the Senate for these years reflects the fact, pointed out by an advocate of congressional term limitation, that "in all elections since, World War II, approximately 93% of the Members of Congress have sought to be returned to Congress, and of that number about 93% have won their bids." [8]

While those who see no need for a limit on terms do not deny these data on the high success rate of incumbents seeking reelection, they do point out that the high rate of retirement of members in recent years (discussed in Chapter 1) and even the low rate of electoral turnover—when looked at over a number of elections rather than in one year—do produce a Congress with plenty of new blood

FIGURE 2–2   Percentage of New Senators by Congress, 1940–1978

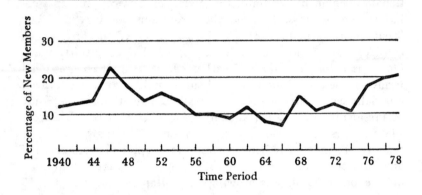

Source: Adapted from data contained in *Congressional Quarterly Weekly Report*, December 30, 1978, p. 3499.

FIGURE 2–3   Percentage of New Representatives by Congress, 1940–1978

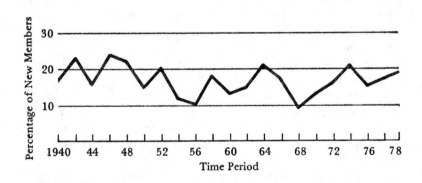

Source: Adapted from data contained in Nelson W. Polsby, "Institutionalization in the U.S. House of Representatives," *American Political Science Review* 62 (1968), p. 146, and updated from data in *Congressional Quarterly Weekly Reports.*

in it. When the Ninety-sixth Congress convened in January, 1979, for instance, more than half of the Senate membership had joined that chamber since 1970; in the House, more than 60 percent of the members had served two terms or less.[9]

Debate over a term limitation for members of Congress gets to the heart of the meaning of representation and provides, once again, an insight into the conflicting goals of representation and lawmaking. The gist of the argument advanced by supporters of the term limitation proposal is that a twelve-year limit on service would make Congress a more truly representative body, while opponents of the measure generally argue that such a change would undercut the ability of Congress to function as a responsible lawmaking institution. The conflict between these goals can be seen by looking at a summary of the arguments advanced by supporters of the term limitation proposal and of the arguments put forward by those who oppose such a change.

Proponents of the twelve-year limit on congressional service make the following arguments:[10]

> Limited terms of service would ensure infusion of new blood from the mainstream of our communities into the American political system. New Members of Congress would bring to their jobs a fresh outlook and approach to the nation's problems. A greater number of people with diverse backgrounds would be drawn from the private sector. We would certainly be offering greater opportunity to a variety of people who wish to serve their country.

> Limited terms would counteract the recent trend toward "professional politicians." Challengers as well as incumbents would regard public service more as a contribution to the nation, and less as a personal career goal. What our country needs, as envisioned by the framers of the Constitution, are "citizen legislators" not "career politicians."

> Competition for public office would be enhanced. More people would be encouraged to run for office, many of whom may now feel as if they don't have a real chance to be elected when challenging a well entrenched incumbent.

> A limitation on service is a limitation on the power of incumbency; the power of incumbency can be stagnating, unreceptive to fresh ideas and new approaches to the nation's problems.

It would strike at the heart of the seniority system, the nature of which is such that all voters do not have equal representation in Congress. Powerful committee chairmen dictate hearings and schedule consideration of bills to which they are favorable. Rotating committee chairmanships would be assured by limiting terms of service.

Many politically volatile issues and long-range problems that require solutions and immediate attention often remain unattended in the face of continual reelection campaigns. Election interests may be nurtured at the expense of these solutions; consequently, we often fail to see the comprehensive legislative remedies that are so necessary. A limitation on terms may bring these remedies about.

Members may be prompted to take a closer look at legislation and regulations proposed while they serve in Congress if they knew that they would be obligated to leave Congress after a specified period of time to live with those laws and regulations implemented during their tenure.

By requiring new people to run for office after a certain interval of time, voters may be encouraged to look closer at the issues involved in a campaign, and less closely at simply the candidates' names.

At the Senate hearings on the term limitation proposal, one of the witnesses testified that he had just returned from a meeting with a large group of scholars of Congress. He polled this group and found that they were unanimously opposed to a constitutional amendment to limit the number of terms that members of Congress could serve. At the hearings, this particular congressional scholar was joined by two other leading students of the institution in voicing opposition to the resolution and demonstrating that such opposition comes not just from incumbent members of Congress with something to lose. The major arguments made by those opposing a limitation on congressional terms may be summarized as follows:[11]

Limited terms would deny voters the opportunity to return to Congress those Members whom they regard as worthy of office. The public should retain the ultimate power to expel from office those Members who are not performing their jobs, or to reelect as many times as it chooses those Members who are serving their constituencies well. Any limitation would be an arbitrary limitation on the public's ability to vote for the candidates of its choice.

Experienced, seasoned, capable lawmakers would be lost automatically, and perhaps prematurely, from public service if we were to limit the number of years they can serve in Congress.

Limited terms would create "lame-duck" Congressmen, similar to the lame-duck President created by the 22nd Amendment. Not only might a Member's legislative ability be impaired, but he/she may also feel less accountable to the public for his/her actions and decisions, causing him/her to disregard the constituency's wishes when voting.

A regular influx of new, inexperienced Members would result in a loss of cohesion and sensibility when scheduling or dealing with legislation. This would invite institutional instability and would make it difficult to formulate comprehensive policies with the Executive.

Congressional reforms, spurred by recently elected (post-Watergate) Members have already brought about changes in the seniority system; Members are now more likely to "speak up" and challenge their elders. Internal reforms can adequately address problems inherent in the seniority system; a Constitutional Amendment limiting terms of service would be "overkill."

Whether or not one supports a congressional term limitation depends on the relative emphasis one gives to the representational and lawmaking functions of Congress. Supporters of the Madisonian model discussed in Chapter 1 would be likely to support a term limitation on the grounds that it would make Congress more representative than it is today. But those who favor a Hamiltonian or Jeffersonian model would be likely to oppose a term limitation on the grounds that it would seriously weaken Congress as a lawmaking institution. The comments of Senator Alan Cranston, an opponent of the term limitation proposal, clearly show the lawmaking emphasis of his position:

John Sherman introduced the Sherman Antitrust Act in his twentieth year in Congress. Paul Douglas introduced the Voting Rights Act in his sixteenth year. Clinton Anderson introduced the

Medicare Act in his sixteenth year. Jacob Javits, a Republican, introduced the War Powers Act—a very significant piece of legislation in the post-Vietnam era—after serving more than a decade and a half in the Senate.[12]

Congress did not pass the congressional term limitation in the Ninety-sixth Congress (1979–1980), nor is it likely to do so in the foreseeable future. But it is the debate surrounding such a proposal, rather than the outcome, that is helpful in furthering our understanding of the politics of Congress. The debate on such fundamental reform proposals as this brings into the open the different values that people assign to the congressional goals of lawmaking and representation.

A key element in the debate surrounding this reform proposal, and indeed in any evaluation of Congress, is the meaning of the term *representation*. People may be referring to quite different things when they say that Congress is, or is not, the representative body it was intended to be. In this chapter we will have a closer look at some of the meanings of the term and apply them to the modern Congress. A useful starting point for this discussion is Hannah Pitkin's analysis in *The Concept of Representation*. She talks about four different dimensions of representation: formal, descriptive, symbolic, and substantive.[13] These four aspects of representation provide a framework for our investigation of how representative Congress really is.

FORMAL REPRESENTATION: ONE PERSON, ONE VOTE

Formal representation is the authority to act in another's behalf, gained through an institutional arrangement such as elections. The essence of representation is that the representatives are authorized in advance to act in behalf of their constituents, who agree to be bound by the representatives' collective decisions.[14] Emphasis is on the formal arrangements that precede the actual representative behavior. This notion of representation as a process requiring formal transfer of authority from many people to one delegate was a central part of Thomas Hobbes's conception of the state. In *Leviathan* (1651), Hobbes observed: "A multitude of men are made *one* person, when they are by one man, or one person, represented; so that it be done with the consent of every one of that multitude in particular." [15] It is the covenant between the people and the person selected to act in their behalf that establishes the latter as a representative. The formal arrangements of selection, not the behavior of the representative, define representation.

Recent political analysts have adopted the Hobbesian concept of formal representation. The remarks of a political scientist, Joseph Tussman, illustrate this:

> The essence of representation is the delegation or granting of authority. To authorize a representative is to grant another the right to act for oneself. Within the limits of the grant of authority one is, in fact, submitting himself in advance to the decision or will of another. . . .
>
> The fact that our rulers are elected does not make them any less our rulers. . . . To say that we send our representatives to Congress is not to say that we have sent our servants to market. We have simply designated the person or persons to whose judgement or will we have subordinated ourselves. Nor does the fact that at a later date we must redesignate a representative alter the fact that an act of subordination has occurred. [16]

Defining representation this way leads us to focus on the procedures for selecting representatives rather than on the representatives' behavior once in office. We can measure representation, in this sense, only by reference to the institutional procedures for selecting legislators. When the Seventeenth Amendment provided for direct election of senators, it made the Senate more representative than it had been when state legislatures were the electors. It is more representative simply because the people now use the more direct method for selecting senators. Another example of the use of formal representation as a criterion for evaluating Congress is found in discussions of reapportionment. Here again, the question of how representative Congress is is phrased in terms of the formal procedures of elections.

In 1960, when American voters were electing the first urban president in history, a common criticism of both state and national legislatures was that conservative rural interests were overrepresented in both Congress and state legislatures and that the conservative coalitions that dominated legislative proceedings ignored the needs of the majority of citizens, who lived in cities or suburbs. Malapportionment (the drawing of legislative district lines in such a way that a minority of citizens in a state or the nation could control a majority of votes in the legislature) was especially rampant on the state level. But because state legislatures determine the boundaries of congressional districts, rural overrepresentation in state legislatures also had an impact on Congress.

In 1964 nearly 1,000,000 constituents of Texas's Fifth Congressional District had to be content with a single representative, while the 177,000 residents of Michigan's Twelfth District also were entitled to a representative.[17] In the 1962 election, the largest congressional district in Texas had 951,527 residents, while the smallest had 216,371. The same situation was true of Michigan, which had 802,994 in its largest district and 177,431 in its smallest.[18] Because of this great variation in the size of constituencies, critics of Congress maintained that a majority in Congress did not necessarily reflect a majority in the country.

The Supreme Court, in a series of cases beginning in 1962, leaped into the political thicket of reapportionment. Chief Justice Warren outlined the Court's notion of representation:

> Legislators represent people, not trees or acres. Legislators are elected by voters, not farms or cities or economic interest. As long as ours is a representative form of government and our legislatures are those instruments of government elected directly by and directly representative of the people, the right to elect legislators in a free and unimpaired fashion is a bedrock of our political system.[19]

In *Wesberry* v. *Sanders* (1964), the Court ruled that Article I's statement "Representatives shall be apportioned among the states according to their respective numbers" and "chosen by the people of the several states" meant that "as nearly as is practicable one man's vote in a congressional election is to be worth as much as another's." The impact of *Wesberry* v. *Sanders* is shown in Table 2-1, where the pre-*Wesberry* variation in congressional district population is compared with the post-*Wesberry* variation in the ten states with the greatest malapportionment.

What Table 2-1 shows us, basically, is that the grossest discrepancies in the population of House districts were impressively corrected by state legislatures in compliance with Supreme Court dictates. But more important questions are still unanswered. Who is to gain by reapportioning districts to reflect population: Republi-

TABLE 2-1 The Impact of *Wesberry* v. *Sanders*

State	Before *Wesberry* (February 1964) Maximum Variation [a]	After *Wesberry* (September 1966) New Maximum Variation
Arizona	− 54.3%	− 7.8%
Colorado	− 55.4	+12.6
Florida	+ 60.3	+13.2
Georgia	+108.9	+16.4
Indiana	+ 64.6	−12.8
Maryland	+ 83.5	−14.9
Michigan	+ 84.8	− 2.1
Ohio	+ 72.1	−20.9
Tennessee	+ 58.2	+14.4
Texas	+118.5	+10.2

[a] The maximum variation is expressed in terms of the largest or smallest congressional district's population as a percentage of the average district's population.

Source: Congressional Quarterly Weekly Report, no. 37, September 16, 1966, p. 2006.

cans or Democrats? Liberals or conservatives? Cities or suburbs? The North, the South, or the West? Or would it make any difference?

The conventional wisdom of the 1960s was that *Wesberry* would produce a more liberal House attuned to the problems of the cities. But two studies by political scientists in the early 1960s suggested otherwise. Andrew Hacker and William Goss looked at a few representative bills of the Kennedy and Johnson administrations that divided the House along liberal/conservative lines (the 1961 expansion of the House Rules Committee, the 1962 proposal to create a Department of Urban Affairs, the 1964 Civil Rights Act, and the Economic Opportunity Act of 1964). They then compared the actual votes in the House on these measures with a weighted vote for each member that adjusted the value of his or her vote to reflect the actual population of his or her district. This procedure estimated the impact that perfect apportionment on the basis of population would have on vote outcomes in the House. The results were surprising. The weighted votes (those based on actual population of districts) produced support for the measures that was the same as or less than that which the bills had actually gained in the malapportioned house.[20]

The policy changes brought about by reapportionment are difficult to assess in broad liberal or conservative terms. An underlying difference between rural constituencies and urban or suburban ones is that the former tend to be producers of primary goods, especially agricultural products, while the latter tend to be consumers of goods and services. The sort of issues, therefore, that have gained support in a reapportioned house are consumer issues such as mass transit, antipollution measures, and education.

While it is difficult to assess the impact of reapportionment on policies emerging from the House, it is not difficult to see its impact on population characteristics of House constituencies and on party benefits. Table 2–2 shows the gains for suburbs from reapportionment that took place between 1966 and 1973. This population movement has resulted in two interesting aspects of congressional representation. First, the suburbs rather than the central cities have been the real beneficiaries of reapportionment. Second, the outward movement of normally Democratic voters from the city to the suburbs has undercut the edge that increased suburban representation was expected to give the Republican party.

Reapportionment during the 1980s, based on the census taken in 1980 rather than that of 1970, will continue the trend away from urban and rural areas and toward suburban ones. Nationally, the population movement away from the Midwest and Northeast and

TABLE 2–2 Changes in Population Composition of House Districts, 1966–1973

Population Composition	Number of Districts			Net Change, 1966–1973
	1966	1968	1973	
Urban	106	110	102	− 4
Suburban	92	104	131	+39
Rural	181	155	130	−51
Mixed	56	66	72	+16

Source: Adapted from *Congressional Quarterly Weekly Report,* April 6, 1974, p. 878.

toward the sun belt states of the South and West will give additional congressional seats to Arizona, California, Florida, Oregon, Tennessee, Texas, and Utah. States likely to lose at least one House seat are New York, Illinois, Michigan, Ohio, Pennsylvania, and South Dakota. All of these losses come from urban areas, and almost all of the gains are expected to be in suburban areas.[21]

DESCRIPTIVE REPRESENTATION: THEM AND US

Descriptive representation is the extent to which representatives reflect the characteristics of the people they formally represent. Characteristics such as ethnic background, social class, age, place of residence, and occupation are considered important. According to this measure, a representative legislature "should be an exact portrait, in miniature, of the people at large." [22] Representative Jim Wright of Texas illustrates the descriptive dimension of representation in remarking:

> Congress is the mirror of the people, and it reflects the aggregate strengths and weaknesses of the electorate. Its membership might include just about the same percentage of saints and sinners, fools and geniuses, rogues and heroes as does the general populace. Congress is a highly concentrated essence of the virtues and faults of the nation as a whole.[23]

Descriptive representation rests on a belief that a legislator acts in terms of his or her own social-economic background. A suburban district with a high percentage of professional people will be automatically represented by selecting a congressman or congresswoman who is typical of the people in that district. There will be no need to continually seek to influence the legislator's vote because he or she will be predisposed to vote the way most people in the district would want him or her to vote. A state legislator articulated this idea of descriptive representation:

> Basically you represent the thinking of the people who have gone through what you have gone through and who are what you are. You vote according to that. In other words, if you come from a suburb you reflect the thinking of people in the suburbs; if you are of depressed people, you reflect that. You represent the sum total of your background.[24]

To determine just how representative Congress is according to this definition, we can compare the characteristics of representatives and senators with those of the general population and those of other political leaders. Such a comparison brings to mind an exchange between F. Scott Fitzgerald and Ernest Hemingway. "The very rich are different from you and me," said Fitzgerald. Hemingway replied, "Yes, they have more money." Members of Congress, general speaking, are different from you and me because they possess certain background characteristics that add up to political money. These include family background, occupation, and education—all of which are generally intermingled with personality attributes and situational conditions that make the typical congressman or congresswoman quite different from the typical citizen, or voter.

In attempting to determine how representative Congress is, within the meaning of descriptive representation, we can look at certain background characteristics of members of Congress and compare them with those of the general population. Some of the measures commonly used in this type of analysis are education, occupation, age, religion, gender, and race. A related characteristic, one

TABLE 2–3 Educational Attainments of House and Senate Members and the General Population, 1977

Level of Education	House	Senate	General Population
No college	4%	1%	70%
Some college	11	8	14
Bachelor's degree (or equivalent)	19	14	⎫
Law degree	51	64	⎬ 16
Advanced degrees	15	13	⎭
Total	100%	100%	100%

Source: The figures on House and Senate members are from the *Congressional Directory*, Ninety-fifth Congress, 1977, and Michael Baron, Grant Ujifusa, and Douglas Matthews, *The Almanac of Politics, 1978* (E. P. Dutton, 1977). Those on the general population, for persons twenty-five years of age and older, are from the Department of Commerce, Bureau of the Census, Current Population Reports, Series P-20, no. 314, December 1977.

that ties in with the career legislator-citizen legislator dispute discussed earlier in this chapter, is previous political experience.

Education. In Table 2–3 the educational attainments of House and Senate members are compared with those of the general population. It is clear from this table that the typical House or Senate member is different from the typical American in terms of educational background. In 1977, only 16 percent of the general population had a college degree of some sort, whereas 85 percent of the House and 91 percent of the Senate had a bachelor's or advanced college degree.

Occupation. Table 2–4 shows the occupational background of House and Senate members in the Ninety-sixth Congress. The occu-

TABLE 2–4 Occupations of Members of the Ninety-sixth Congress, 1978–1979

	House		Senate	
Occupation	Percentage of Total Membership [a]	Number	Percentage of Total Membership [a]	Number
Law	47	205	65	65
Business or banking	29	127	29	29
Education	13	57	7	7
Agriculture	4	19	6	6
Journalism	3	11	2	2
Public Service/ Politics	9	41	12	12
Other [b]	6	25	4	4

[a] The percentages sum to more than 100 because many members listed several occupations.

[b] "Other" includes engineering, labor, law enforcement, medicine, the clergy, and science.

Source: Adapted from *Congressional Quarterly Weekly Report,* January 20, 1979, p. 81.

pational backgrounds of representatives and senators tend to over-represent high prestige professional and business jobs. Occupational groups such as factory workers, farmers, and human service workers consistently have been underrepresented in Congress. The most striking aspect of legislators' backgrounds, however, is the number of lawyers among them. While lawyers constitute about one-tenth of 1 percent of the total work force in the general population, the 270 representatives and senators who list law as their occupation constitute over 50 percent of the total membership of Congress.

This overrepresentation of the legal profession in Congress is not new. In 1790, 37 percent of the membership of the House were lawyers; in 1840, 70 percent; and in 1957, 54 percent.[25] The 1979 figure actually represents a decline in the number of lawyers in Congress. With only twenty-eight of the seventy-seven new House members elected in 1978 having a background in law, nonlawyers outnumbered lawyers in the House for the first time in thirty years. Fourteen of the twenty new senators elected in 1978 were lawyers, however, so that the great overrepresentation of lawyers in Congress seen in previous years continues.[26]

The lawyers' affinity for politics is explained not only by their expertise but also by the fact that lawyers are more able than other professionals to combine politics with their professional careers. While most professionals, such as doctors, educators, architects, scientists, and engineers, would find that running for office or serving in Congress hampered their professional knowledge, lawyers are able to take such a leave of absence and return with new contacts and information helpful for their law careers.

Business and banking constitute the second most common occupational background of representatives and senators. These occupations, combined with the law, account for about 85 percent of the total membership in the House and Senate. Still, there is something about all of those lawyers that catches the eye of congressional critics. The number of members in business and banking who avoid such criticism suggests that complaints about lawyers as representatives and senators are not just a reflection of antipathy toward the dominance of the upper classes in Congress. Many people feel that the abstrusity of most legislation and the difficulty of interpreting it are a direct result of having so many lawyer-legislators involved in drafting it. The basis of such criticism, which generally avoids conspiracy explanations, is that you need a lawyer to interpret most of the bills that pass through Congress. No one else can really understand their intricacies and legal nuances. If such legislation is drafted by institutions consisting primarily of lawyers, one is tempted to think that there is some professional, albeit unconscious, collusion taking place between those who are paid to make laws and those who are paid to interpret them.

A sunnier interpretation of the fact that there are so many lawyers in Congress is offered by those who point out the natural similarity between the roles of lawyer and legislator. One of the more perceptive observers of the American political scene contends that critics of the legal background of representatives and senators are "dead wrong." "No better training could be found for them." He continues:

> They, too, must struggle with each other yet be friends the next day; make maximum claims as bargaining points but aim at a compromise settlement; satisfy most people somewhat, rather than a few people fully; represent diversity by muting differences; be always more neutral than hostile; deal in increments and margins only, but deal constantly; always adjusting, hedging, giving in a little, gaining a little; creeping toward one's goals, not heroically striding there. Always leaving oneself an out, a loophole, a proviso—what [the political scientist] Willmoore Kendall used to call a "verbal parachute" —so that no allegiance is irrevocable, no opposition adamant.[27]

Age. "Critics of Congress often picture the institution as a collection of aging mossbacks waiting patiently for the seniority system to reward them with power," said one recent observer. "But whatever truth that stereotype might once have contained, the fact right now is that Congress is getting younger every year." [28] The average age of freshmen House members elected in 1978 was forty, and the average age of new senators elected that year was forty-three.[29] Table 2–5 shows that the age component of the 1978 election fits in with the general trend in recent years toward younger representatives and senators. In the House, the average age has been going down every two years since 1969, and in the Senate the decline has been steady since 1965. Between 1939 and 1977 there was at least one member of the House who was eighty years of age or older; since 1977 there have been no members in this age bracket.

Religion. Of the total general population of the United States, about 60 percent claim some religious affiliation. In Congress, more than 94 percent do. Whether this means that members of Congress

TABLE 2-5 The Changing Age Structure of Congress

| Year | Average Age of Members at Start of First Session | | |
	House	Senate	Congress
1949	51.0	58.5	53.8
1959	51.7	57.1	52.7
1969	52.2	56.6	53.0
1979	48.8	52.7	49.5

Source: Adapted from *Congressional Quarterly Weekly Report,* January 27, 1979, p. 154.

are more likely to attend a church or synagogue than are others or whether it is an indication that religious affiliation for elected officials is considered good politics is unclear. An executive of the National Council of Churches seems to think that the latter is the case: "People want to have a politician identifying himself with some denomination." [30]

Table 2-6 shows the affiliations of members of the Ninety-sixth Congress for the ten most common religions. Since the 1960s there has been a decline in the number of Protestant members, a group which has in the past dominated Congress, and an increase in the number of Catholic and Jewish members; these two groups are now represented in Congress in rough proportion to their numbers in the general population. Catholics make up 22 percent of the general population and 24 percent of the membership of Congress. About 3 percent of all Americans are Jewish, while Jews constitute about 5 percent of the membership of Congress. Episcopalians and Presbyterians, however, are still the most overrepresented religious groups in Congress. Less than 4 percent of the general population is Episcopalian or Presbyterian, but more than 24 percent of the members of Congress claim one or the other as their religious affiliation. [31]

Gender. If women were represented in Congress in equal proportion to their numbers in the general population, there would be more than 218 women members of the House (i.e., half of the total House membership) and more than fifty women senators (again more than half). But that is not the case. In the Ninety-sixth Con-

TABLE 2–6 Religious Affiliations in Congress

Religion	House	Senate	Congress
Baptist	10%	11%	10%
Episcopal	12	17	13
Jewish	5	7	5
Lutheran	4	4	4
Methodist	13	19	14
Presbyterian	12	12	12
Roman Catholic	27	13	24
Unitarian	2	4	3
United Church of Christ and Congregationalist	2	2	3
Unspecified Protestant	4	3	4
Other	8	8	8
Unaffiliated	1	0	0
Total	100%	100%	100%
(*n*)	433	100	533

Source: Adapted from *Congressional Quarterly Weekly Report,* January 20, 1979, p. 80.

gress (1979–1980), there were sixteen women members of the House and one woman senator. These figures represent a decline of two women in the House and one in the Senate from the preceding Congress. Of the eighteen women in the House in the Ninety-fifth Congress (1977–1978), three retired and two were defeated in elections. Of the thirty-one women challengers for a House seat in the 1978 election, only three were successful. Nancy Kassebaum of Kansas was the first woman to be elected to a U.S. Senate seat in twelve years when she won in 1978, but the actual number of women senators declined because of the departure of two women appointed to complete the terms of their late husbands.

More important than the gains and losses in particular elections is the fact that the number of women in Congress has remained between ten and twenty since 1950. "Until the number of women in the House hovers around 25 percent," says the executive director of the National Women's Education Fund, "you are just playing tiddlywinks over whether the number of congresswomen is eighteen or sixteen." [32]

Race. Blacks, like women, have consistently been underrepresented in Congress. In 1978, the defeat of the first black candidate for U.S. Senator since reconstruction left only the sixteen black members of the House of Representatives as congressional representatives of their race. For the proportion of blacks in American society to be reflected by the proportion of black representatives, however, the number of blacks in Congress would have to be fifty rather than sixteen.

The changing population characteristics discussed above in the section on reapportionment do not bode well for any substantial increase in the proportion of blacks in Congress after the 1980 census. A survey done in 1978 listed the fifty House districts that had lost 5 percent or more of their population since 1970. These are predominantly urban districts, and many of them will be subject to reapportionment after the 1980 census. All except one of the House districts then represented by a black were included in this list.[33]

We come away from this consideration of descriptive representation with two strong impressions. First, the notion of Congress as a microcosm of society as a whole—as one big mirror reflecting all of the traits of the citizenry—is not an accurate depiction of congressional representation. Second, unless we can systematically relate the background characteristics of legislators to varied patterns of behavior it does us little good to know how many x's and how many y's are in Congress. Coalitions in Congress change constantly, depending on the issue. Small town legislators join urban legislators, lawyers join nonlawyers, women legislators do not necessarily take the same side, and blacks join whites against other blacks and whites. Sometimes background characteristics do influence a legislator's vote, but often they are of no relevance in explaining congressional behavior.

While connections between an individual's social background and legislative behavior are often difficult to establish, the general array of backgrounds touched on in this section does permit some overall assessment of the representativeness of Congress. The general conclusion is that there is a difference between "them" and "us." When you add up the informal requirements of office, you do find a class structure in the pattern of legislative representation. A person's class is sometimes defined as the ceiling he or she puts upon expectation. Matthews suggested that less than 5 percent of the country's population could reasonably expect to serve in the Senate. Although there are occasional exceptions to the rule—the election, for instance, of a Rhode Island house painter to the House in 1974—political offices in the United States appear to be class ranked, with people of high social or political status holding the more important offices. An observation made in 1960 still serves as an appropriate and accurate summary of descriptive representation: "As long as the system of stratification in a society is generally accepted, one must expect people to look for political leadership toward those who have met the current definition of success and hence are considered worthy individuals. Voters seem to prefer candidates who are not like themselves but who are what they would like to be." [34]

Previous Political Experience. The underlying philosophy of those supporting a limit on congressional terms is that the nation would be better served by citizens who temporarily leave their normal occupation to serve as legislators than it is by career politicians whose real occupation is holding political office. Almost all members of the House and Senate will list their occupation as lawyer, businessperson, teacher, or some other nonpolitical profession even if the major part of their adult life has been spent in politics. Representatives and senators are obviously different from the average constituent by virtue of their holding an elective office, but not all of them are career politicians.

The background of the large, activist freshman class of 1974 in the House, collectively known as "the Watergate babies," showed somewhat of an aberration from the pattern of most representatives having had political experience. Only 49 percent of the seventy-five freshmen Democrats elected that year had previously held elective office. The two following elections, however, saw a return to the pattern of representatives coming to the House from another elective office. In 1976, 75 percent and in 1978, 65 percent of the freshmen Democrats elected had held office previously. "We're not so completely wide-eyed at everything. We're a more practical group. We came up through the process," is the way one member of the 1976 freshman class compared the 1976 group with the 1974 group.[35] House Speaker Thomas P. (Tip) O'Neill was pleased with the previous political experience of the 1978 freshmen: "This crowd will be easier to talk to. It's a real break when you get some people like that." [36]

Although 64 percent of the House freshmen and 70 percent of the Senate freshmen elected in 1978 had previously held political office, these figures actually represent a decline in the number of House and Senate members with previous political experience. In 1958, for instance, 94 percent of the new senators had previous political experience, and in 1962, 94 percent of the new House members had previous political experience.[37] Although recent classes elected to both the House and the Senate seem to provide enough politically experienced individuals to make the leadership happy, there seems to be a trend toward citizen legislators that should also please those supporters of the Madisonian model who agree with the goals of the term limitation reform proposals.

SYMBOLIC REPRESENTATION

Symbolic representation, unlike formal and descriptive representation, is not easily measured by looking at aggregate data such as population, ethnic background, occupation, and education levels. The essence of symbolic representation is not what the representative is but what he or she is perceived to be by his or her constituents. The real measure of symbolic representation is whether or not the constituents accept the officeholder as their representative. "The crucial test of political representation," according to this definition, "will be the existential one: Is the representative believed in? And the basis of such belief will seem irrational and affective because no rational justification of it is possible. Hence, political representation will be not an activity but a state of affairs, not an acting for others, but a 'standing for'; so long as people accept or believe, the political leader represents them, by definition." [38]

Representatives and senators perform two distinct types of symbolic representation, depending on whether the arena is Washington or the home district. In Washington, symbolic representation most often takes the form of introducing bills, or amendments to bills, that have little or no chance of becoming law but that stake out a position taken by the representative. Within the district, symbolic representation has more to do with the sort of person the representative is, or is perceived to be, by his or her constituents. Their perception is determined more by the nonverbal signals he or she gives off and the degree of trust he or she is able to evoke than by issue positions.

Washington-Style Symbolic Representation

Shortly after taking office, the man known to his columnist brother as the "sainted junior Senator from New York" remarked that he had been surprised at how many things happen in the Senate "for symbolic reasons" rather than practical reasons. He gave as an example the common practice of senators introducing amendments that they know haven't the slightest chance of passing.[39] Anyone perusing the "bills introduced" section of the *Congressional Record* in the week following the Supreme Court decision of January 30, 1976, which declared unconstitutional certain provisions of the campaign finance law of 1974, would have had a reaction similar to that of the newly elected senator. It seemed that every other member of the House and Senate, whether they served on the committees having jurisdiction over the issue or not, wanted to introduce a bill with their name on it that would revise the 1974 act in line with the Court's objections. What mattered most was not whether their bills were realistic or likely to become law but that by introducing legislation they had staked out a symbolic position on the issue of campaign financing.

David Mayhew provides both a working definition of Washington-style symbolic representation and an analysis of its causes and effects:

> It is probably best to say that a purely symbolic congressional act is one expressing an attitude, but prescribing no policy effects. An example would be a resolution deploring communism or poverty. But the term "symbolic" can also usefully be applied where Congress prescribes policy effects but does not act (in legislating or overseeing or both) so as to achieve them.
>
> . . . There is a special reason why a legislative body arranged like the United States Congress can be expected to engage in symbolic action. The reason, of course, is that in a large class of legislative undertakings the electoral payment is for positions rather than for effects.[40]

Mayhew provides characteristics of such symbolic representation and cites specific cases. One characteristic is the fact that the real audience for the measure is not the people directly affected but rather a different group (or groups) that will applaud the effort represented by the symbolic act but not follow up to determine its real impact. Civil rights acts in 1957 and 1960, for instance, were directed more toward liberal constituents in the North than toward politically emasculated blacks in the South. Similarly, the allocation of money to help the poor that was included in the Elementary and Secondary Education Act of 1965 had very little real impact on that economic class. Rather, it provided symbolic rewards to middle-class liberal constituents who could crowd under the halo of charity suggested by passage of the bill without having to concern themselves with its real impact. This separation of affected people and approving people seems to be one of the defining characteristics of Washington-style symbolic representation.

A second characteristic might be best summed up (if you will forgive my pun) in this aphorism: "It is not who wins or loses that counts, but how they play your name." The press coverage and constituency approval that come from staking out a position by introducing a bill or an amendment to a bill (whose futility of passage is recognized by both the introducer and his or her colleagues) are the real payoffs of symbolic representation. Mayhew provides some examples of this basic point: "In the Ninety-second Congress Senator Robert P. Griffin (R., Michigan) no doubt found it quite useful to be the ostentatious purveyor of an antibusing amendment, but did it make much difference to him whether it carried? Would Senators Mark O. Hatfield (R., Oregon) and George McGovern (D., South Dakota) have been any the more esteemed by their followers if their antiwar amendment had won rather than lost?" [41] The increasing flood of bills and amendments offered by representatives and senators who have no committee assignments or expertise related to the specific issue emphasizes this symbolic aspect of representation in Washington. Not only is there a distinction between affected constituencies and approving audiences, but there is also a separation between the introduction of legislation and concern whether or not such legislation would have, or does have, any real impact. Substance becomes overshadowed by form and style.

The focus here has been primarily on individual representatives and the way symbolic representation serves their purposes of reelection. Now is an appropriate time for mentioning an effect of symbolic representation that has broad consequences for the American political system as a whole. Murray Edelman, in *The Symbolic Uses of Politics*, contends that much of American politics is characterized by the dispensing of symbolic rewards (such as status or broad assurances regarding national security or law and order) to the inattentive mass public, while at the same time material rewards are handed out (in the form of direct government payments or contracts, tax breaks, or other economic benefits) to the attentive political elite in society. Symbolic politics in the aggregate, suggests Edelman, not only reflect a bias in American politics favoring the politically active upper and middle classes, but also help to maintain the stability of the political system by giving symbolic rewards to those who benefit the least economically from the system and are thus the most likely potential sources of disruption.[42] Washington-style symbolic representation seen in the congressional practices discussed in this section would seem to be a part of this larger pattern of symbolic politics discussed by Edelman. To the representative and his or her colleagues, such activity might seem to be simply a necessary part of the job of getting reelected. But when we look at the overall impact of symbolic politics, as Edelman did, we see that—like descriptive representation—it reflects more than a hint of a class bias in American politics.

Home-Style Symbolic Representation

One of the reasons for legislators' engaging in Washington-style symbolic representation is their responsibility to explain to the constituents in their district or state exactly what they have been doing in the halls of Congress. If a representative is able to say that he or she has introduced a bill or an amendment (or even cosponsored someone else's proposal) that attempts to deal with an issue of importance to constituents, the impression is given that he or she is representing them in Washington.

While there is an obvious connection between the representative's symbolic activities in Washington and those at home, there does seem to be a difference in the primary focus of home-style and Washington-style symbolic representation. In Washington, symbolic representation exhibits a policy focus, even when the position-taking action of such representation is likely to have no real impact on policy in that area. In the district, symbolic representation is most likely to focus not on issues but rather on the qualities of the person chosen to represent the people in that district.

To understand this dimension of symbolic representation, one has to look at the interaction between the representative and his or her constituents. Regardless of the nature of such encounters, the representative is obliged to present to his or her concerned constituents some picture of who he or she is and why they should continue to send him or her to Washington as their representative. During the early 1970s, Richard Fenno, a leading scholar of Congress, observed sixteen members of the House in their home districts. Fenno found that many of the ideas advanced in Erving Goffman's *The Presentation of Self in Everyday Life,* which deals with the nuances of everyday encounters between average human beings, are applicable to the interaction between the representative and his or her constituents in the home setting. The nature of this interaction captures the essence of home-style symbolic representation.

> In all such encounters, says Goffman, the performer will seek to control the response of others to him by expressing himself in ways that leave the correct impression of himself with others. His expression will be of two sorts—"the expression that he gives and the expression that he gives off." The first is mostly verbal; the second is mostly nonverbal. Goffman is particularly interested in the second kind of expression—"the more theatrical and contextual kind"—because he believes that the performer is more likely to be judged by others according to the nonverbal than the verbal elements of the presentation of self.
>
> Those who must do the judging, Goffman says, will think that the verbal expressions are more controllable and manipulable by the performer; and they will, therefore, read his nonverbal "signs" as a check on the reliability of his verbal "signs." Basic to this reasoning is the idea that, of necessity, every presentation has a largely "promisory character" to it. Those who listen to and watch the performance cannot be sure what the relationship between them and the performer really is. So the relationship must be sustained, on the part of those watching, by inference. They "must accept the individual on faith." In this process of acceptance, they will rely heavily on the inference they draw from his nonverbal expressions—the expressions "given off." [43]

This "acceptance on faith" idea agrees with Hannah Pitkin's theory (mentioned in the first paragraph of this section on symbolic representation) that the crucial test of symbolic representation is whether the representative is believed in by his or her constituents. Such belief is based more on the nonverbal signs a representative gives off than it is on specific policy positions. "People don't make up their minds on the basis of reading all our position papers," observes one of the congressmen in Fenno's study. "We have twenty-six of them, because some people are interested. But most people get a gut feeling about the kind of human being they want to represent them." [44] Another representative comments:

> My constituents don't know how I vote, but they know *me* and they trust me. . . . They say to themselves, "everything we know about him tells us he's up there doing a good job for us." It's a blind faith type of thing.[45]

The essential tie between the representative and his or her constituents that must be achieved by home-style symbolic representation is one of trust. The cumulative effect of all the nonverbal signals given off by the representative must be strong enough to allow constituents to make at least a minor leap of faith so as to accept that person as their representative.

Fenno goes on to specify some of the essential components of this feeling of trust. First, the representatives must assure their listeners that they understand the job of representative and have the necessary experience and intelligence to hold their own in a collegial body of verbal and ambitious people. Their constituents must believe that they are qualified to represent them. Second, the representatives must convey a sense of identification with their constituents. They must be assured that a representative is one of them, or at least thinks as they do. Descriptive representational characteristics mentioned above are an obvious way of conveying this impression. A third component, and one that can exist even in the absence of descriptive/identification ties, is empathy. Even if the representatives are quite different from most of their constituents in terms of background, they can sometimes capture the trust of people in their districts by convincing them that they think as they do or put themselves in their shoes to make decisions. Successful home-style symbolic representation builds on all three of these components and is manifested in a sense of trust that constituents have for the representative as a person.

Further clarification of home-style representation is perhaps best achieved by looking at the case of a specific congressman whose pattern of representational behavior demonstrates the chief points of Fenno's analysis. This congressman comes from the Northeast. He is a liberal Democrat who has occupied one of the two districts in his state specifically gerrymandered so as to be safely Republican. He first ran in 1970 and lost to the incumbent Republican congressman. In 1972, after the incumbent had retired, this congressman won by a margin of about 1,000 votes out of the total of about 235,000 cast. In 1974, he won with 75 percent of the total votes cast in the general election. The fact that his district was the only one in the state to go for the Republican presidential candidate in 1972 attests to its essential Republican character. To understand fully this phenomenon of a liberal Democrat holding a safe seat in an essentially Republican district, we would have to consider an endless array of circumstances and electoral factors. We will consider here only those practices of the congressman that, taken together, constitute home-style symbolic representation.

The key to this member's home style, and his vehicle for achieving symbolic representation, is his program of open meetings. He conducts meetings in every city and town in his district twice a year, with a total of about one hundred meetings being held yearly. Every postal patron in the area receives an invitation to come on down and "have at" their congressman. Sometimes fewer than five constituents will show up; at other times the school auditorium or town hall will be filled with up to 300 constituents. During these meetings, the representative responds to an endless array of questions as to why he voted the way he did on some particular bill or how he stands on more general issues that may not yet have come to the floor of the House for a vote. Many of these meetings become more than just an inquisition of the congressman by his constituents; they turn into a general debate among citizens about the issues of the day. As such they serve a positive function of education and democratic participation. To the incumbent congressman, however, the most immediate effect of the open meeting is that it permits him to present himself favorably, which has obvious reelection consequences. "Politically," he says, "these open meetings are pure gold." This is especially true given the nature of his district. Most of the people who show up at these open meetings are not the committed loyalist supporters of the incumbent but rather those who are curious to see what this new kid on the block is really like. Given the Republican coloration of the district, these meetings serve a function of continuous outreaching, allowing the congressman to build a personal following in what should be a hostile environment. "At first, in some of these towns, they didn't know what to say to a Democrat. They probably hadn't met one except for the people who fixed their toilets. In one town, they held a special town meeting to decide whether the congressman could use the town hall. They probably figured, 'He's not our congressman; he's a Demmycrat.' Finally, they said 'okay, but nothing political.' " [46]

While there is obviously a substantive element to the presentation and exchanges involved in these open meetings—they would not be effective unless the congressman himself was both knowledgeable about the issues and able to articulate his positions—our interest here is more with the expressions given off, the symbolic representation dimension. Fenno sums up the signals given off by the incumbent's performances in these open meetings: the congressman comes across as "an accessible, issue-oriented, communicative, antipolitician." [47] The sheer number of such meetings (in early 1976 he was beginning his seventh round of open meetings) confirms the accessibility of the incumbent to his constituents. The tone of the meetings firms up the issue-oriented signal. There is a minimum of glad-handing and a focus on policies that the national government is or should be pursuing. Because the incumbent is extremely articulate and because these meetings are not a one-way forum of speech-making but rather a true exchange of ideas, the representative gives off a clear impression of communicativeness. The antipolitician image, which was an important factor in his candidacy as an anti-Vietnam War spokesman in 1970 and 1972, is maintained by his continuing attacks on the political establishment, especially Congress, and by his conveying the impression that he is different from Them—meaning most other members of Congress and politicians. "I don't want to pat myself on the back, but there aren't too many congressmen who would do what I am doing here today. Most of them dig a hole and crawl in. . . . As you know, I'm one of the greatest critics of Congress. It's an outrageous and outmoded institution. . . . All Congress has done since I've been in Congress is pass the buck to the President and then blame him for what goes wrong. Congress is gutless beyond my power to describe to you." [48]

Not all congressional candidates follow the pattern of successful home-style representation described above. But this brief look at one case is instructive not only because it shows the key elements that make up home-style symbolic representation but also because it points out what seem to be some defining characteristics of symbolic representation. The discussion of Washington-style symbolic representation emphasized the separation between individual position-taking and the passing of legislation and the separation between policy enactment and policy implementation. The discussion of home-style symbolic representation suggests another distinction—

the one between the individual representative and the institution of Congress. This distinction was suggested by the remarks of the freshman congressman mentioned in the first chapter who noted that most of the freshmen elected in 1974 basically ran "against Congress" as an institution. This theme was repeated in our closer look at symbolic representation as manifested by the behavior of a specific congressman.

Symbolic Representation as Schizophrenia

Symbolic representation might best be understood as a mild form of schizophrenia. We applaud our representatives for taking superficial positions on policies even when there will not be any real policy effects. We continue to reelect members of Congress who campaign against the ineffectiveness of the institution in which they serve. We love our legislators enough to send them back to Washington, as reflected in the high rate of reelection of incumbents. At the same time, however, we exhibit a great disdain for the institution of Congress and its failure to deal effectively with the most pressing issues of the political system.

The gap between what people think of the institution of Congress and what they think of their own particular representatives in that institution shows the impact of symbolic representation, whether it be Washington-style or home-style. By introducing amendments or bills that have no chance of passage, a legislator is able to convey to his or her constituents the idea, "Well, you know, I tried to do something about this problem by introducing bill X or amendment Y—but those old sons of bitches that run everything in Congress wouldn't let it see the light of day." A neat distinction between Them (the people who control Congress) and Us (the representative and the good folks at home) is made, and it benefits the individual representative at the expense of the institution. Home-style symbolic representation achieves the same purpose. If the representative is successful at this, he or she, *as an individual* is believed in by constituents.

SUBSTANTIVE REPRESENTATION: DELEGATE OR TRUSTEE?

The three types of representation we have looked at so far fail to provide a complete picture of what the term means. Neither formal, descriptive, nor symbolic representation tells us how the representative actually behaves once in office. Substantive representation enters into the realm of action. It deals with how representatives must act rather than how they were elected, what their background characteristics are, or how they are perceived by their constituents. Hannah Pitkin provides a thorough definition of the term:

> Representing here means acting in the interest of the represented, in a manner responsive to them. The representative must act independently; his action must involve discretion and judgement; he must be the one who acts. The represented must also be (conceived as) capable of independent action and judgement, not merely being taken care of. And, despite the resulting potential for conflict between representative and represented about what is to be done, that conflict must not normally take place. The representative must act in such a way that there is no conflict, or if it occurs an explanation is called for. He must not be found persistently at odds with the wishes of the represented without good reason in terms of their interest, without a good explanation of why their wishes are not in accord with their interest.[49]

We may delineate two aspects of substantive representation: the representative's influence and the representative's orientation. A committee chairman may argue that his position and influence make him a more effective representative for his district or state than a less senior member would be. A representative's orientation refers both to how the representative perceives his or her legislative role and to his or her position on specific issues.

The influence a legislator has within the Congress may determine his or her success at representing the interests of constituents. A committee chairman is able to influence members on other committees because they know they may need a return favor from the chairman's committee in the future. Thus it is argued that a district's representation is maximized by having a representative or senator with great seniority. "And the worst thing a district can do for itself," observed the late Speaker Sam Rayburn, "if it's got someone here doing the job right, is to keep changing its congressman."[50]

Voters, however, are often unimpressed with this argument. In 1978, voters turned out the incumbent chairmen of the House Post Office and Civil Service Committee, the House Appropriations Transportation Subcommittee, and the House Commerce Transportation Subcommittee. All committee chairpersons share the electoral benefits of incumbency with their colleagues, but they do not seem to derive an electoral benefit from their leadership position. "People don't care," groused one senator after a bitter defeat in 1978. "The guy mowing his lawn, he doesn't give a goddamn whether some clown is chairman of some subcommittee on the Energy Committee." [51]

The idea that constituents do not generally understand that a legislator's influence affects his or her representative ability is also suggested by a congressman's comment:

> If there is one thing I have found my people care nothing about it is my attainments in Congress. I could say I was chairman of four standing committees. I think they relate that to being chairman of a PTA committee or a Lions committee. I defeated a good man who made much of the fact that he was chairman of a congressional committee, and people laughed about it. I had hundreds tell me, "Why you will be a committee chairman before you have been up there three months." [52]

The representative or senator's orientation is often perceived as a choice between the trustee or delegate role of representation. A trustee votes for what he or she considers to be in the best interests of his or her constituents, regardless of their expressed preferences. Edmund Burke captured the essence of the trustee role in observing: "Your representative owes you, not his industry only, but his judgement; and he betrays, instead of serving you, if he sacrifices it to your opinion." [53] As a trustee, the legislator is expected to vote in accord with his or her own judgment after studying the legislation carefully and determining that that vote will be in the interest of his or her constituents and the country as a whole.

Senate majority leader Robert Byrd articulated the Burkean concept of the legislator as trustee in the 1978 Senate debate over ratification of the Panama Canal treaties:

> There's no political mileage in voting for the treaties. I know what my constituents are saying. But I have a responsibility not only to follow them, but to inform them and lead them. I'm not going to betray my responsibility to my constituents. I owe them not only my industry but my judgment. That's why they send me here.[54]

Underlying this role is a belief that constituents' preferences and their interests are often quite different. It is pointed out that preferences fluctuate, even when interests do not. The true representative, it is argued, should consistently represent those interests and not change his or her position in accord with changes in public opinion. Supporters of the trustee role say that constituents do not have the information that the legislator has and therefore cannot really evaluate the legislation at hand. "I figure if they knew what I know, they would understand my vote," is the way one legislator put it. Another says:

> I am sent here as a representative of 600,000 people. They are supposed to be voting on all the legislation. I try to follow my constituents—to ignore them would be a breach of trust—but I use my judgment often because they are misinformed. I know that they would vote as I do if they had the facts that I have.[55]

The delegate role is the complete opposite of a trustee role. Instead of relying on his or her own judgment and conscience, a delegate is expected to vote in accordance with majority opinion in his or her constituency. Parke Godwin expressed a rather extreme conception of the delegate role in his *Political Essays:* "A representative is but the mouthpiece and organ of his constituents. What we want in legislation as in other trusts, are honest fiduciaries, men who will perform their duties according to our wishes." [56]

One of the differences between the trustee and delegate roles is the way they define the national interest. A trustee rejects the notion that he best serves the country's interests by always reflecting the wishes of his district. He will argue that by voting in accordance with his own evaluation of the national interest and by considering the cues given by the party or by the president he is being a more responsible representative. For the trustee, what is good for his district is not necessarily what is good for the nation. Since the welfare of the district is greatly dependent on the national welfare, the trustee feels he serves the former by voting for policies that help the country as a whole.

A delegate defines the national interest as being that which is best for a majority of the districts. The national welfare is seen as the sum of the individual districts' welfare:

> I'm here to represent my district. This is part of my actual belief as to the function of a congressman. What is good for the majority of districts is good for the country. What snarls up the system is these

so-called statesman-congressmen who vote for what they think is the country's best interest.[57]

Adoption of a particular representational role is related to a person's conception of the proper functions of the Congress. Those who emphasize an active, programmatic legislature that responds to national mandates see the trustee role as an integral part of the institution. Those holding to the Jeffersonian model suggest that members of Congress are being representative when they vote according to the national party program even when this runs counter to constituency opinion. The Hamiltonian model emphasizes the national interest over that of particular districts of states. The president is seen as a more important cue-giver for representatives' votes than the legislator's constituency.

A delegate role is more suitable to those models of Congress that emphasize representation rather than rapid decision-making. The Madisonian model requires that Congress represent a constituency different from that of the president. To achieve this situation, legislators are expected to be delegates reflecting district opinion in order to provide a check against the president, who represents a national constituency. Such delegate representation supports the Madisonian system by providing viable checks and balances and by assuring that interests not held by a national majority will nevertheless be represented by particular legislators. For pluralists, a delegate role maximizes the number of interests that have access to the lawmaking process. (The trustee role would not provide this variety of interest representation because of its focus on national interests.)

A major problem in discussing the role of representatives as that of either delegate or trustee is the fact that it oversimplifies reality. It is based on the assumption that the legislator knows what a majority of his or her constituents want. As V. O. Key once observed, "The question of whether a legislator should be a man and vote his mature convictions in the national interest or be a mouse and bow abjectly to the parochial demands of his constituents is irrelevant," because "generally, a legislator may hear from a few people on a few issues. He must always, as he votes, assume the risk of antagonizing some constituents, but he is rarely faced by the difficult choice of rejecting or accepting the mandate of his constituency, for he does not know what it is. And, indeed, there may be none." [58]

A solution to this problem is provided by a third representational role, that of politico. The politico role is simply a combination of the trustee and delegate roles. One reason for adopting this role is the realization that the legislator often does not have information as to constituency opinion on many issues. Although the legislator is essentially a delegate, he may feel that this lack of information requires him to adopt a trustee orientation on some issues. Abraham Lincoln, when running for reelection to the Illinois General Assembly, outlined this politico role based on limited information: "If elected, I shall be governed by their will on all such subjects upon which I have the means of knowing what their will is, and upon all others I shall do what my own judgment teaches me will best advance their interests." [59]

Another reason for adopting the politico role is provided by ranking issues in terms of importance. A legislator may feel that some issues are so important that he must vote against his constituents' wishes when he thinks they are wrong. On other issues he will go along with constituency opinion. This occurs regardless of the amount of information about constituency opinion that the legislator has. Senator William Fulbright of Arkansas reflected this type of politico role when he said:

> The average legislator early in his career discovers that there are certain interests, or prejudices, of his constituents which are dangerous to trifle with. Some of these prejudices may not be of fundamental importance to the welfare of the nation, in which case he is justified in humoring them, even though he may disapprove. The difficult case is where the prejudice concerns fundamental policy affecting the national welfare. . . .
> As an example of what I mean, let us take the poll-tax issue and isolationism. Regardless of how persuasive my colleagues or the national press may be about the evils of the poll-tax, I do not see its fundamental importance, and I shall follow the views of the people of my state. . . . On the other hand, regardless of how strongly opposed my constituents may prove to be to the creation of, and participation in, an ever stronger United Nations Organization, I could not follow such a policy in that field unless it becomes clearly hopeless.[60]

The politico role suggests that rather than saying a particular legislator is a delegate or a trustee, it is more accurate to say that on some issues he or she acts as a trustee and on others as a delegate. Because of the flexibility the politico role provides, it is the role most often chosen by members of Congress. A study of House members found that 46 percent chose the politico role, 28 percent the trustee, and 23 percent the delegate.[61]

The question is: Under what conditions and on which issues is the legislator likely to adopt a trustee or delegate role? Roger Davidson's study of House members in the Eighty-eighth Congress showed that representational role choices were related to the margin of victory in the previous election. Table 2–7 shows this relationship.

Table 2–7 suggests that members from marginal districts are more likely to adopt a delegate orientation and those from safe districts are better able to be trustees. This same pattern was found in a study that focused on the sources of information, or voting cues, for legislators who won by large margins and for those who came from marginal districts. The more vulnerable a member was at the polls, the more likely he or she was to listen to a wide range of opinions and suggestions.[62] One reason why legislators from marginal districts tend to be delegates is that they are afraid to alienate any voters who might have supported them in the last election. The small margin of victory in the last election must be maintained or improved upon. Because of the small margin, however, it is difficult to discriminate among supporters and nonsupporters, and the legislator must try to represent a broad range of interests from within the constituency. "That margin was sufficiently narrow that anybody in the state can come into this office and claim credit for my

TABLE 2–7 Margin of Victory and Choice of Representational Role

Role	District Type [a]	
	Marginal	Safe
Trustee	19%	35%
Politico	37	54
Delegate	44	11
Total	100%	100%
(n)	(32)	(52)

[a] Marginal districts are those in which the incumbent won by less than 60 percent of the vote in the 1962 election. Safe districts are those in which the congressman won by 60 percent or more of the vote.

Source: Roger Davidson, The Role of the Congressman (Pegasus, 1969), p. 128. Reprinted by permission of Bobbs-Merrill Co.

winning" was John Kennedy's observation after his close election to the Senate in 1952.[63] The typical trustee may be characterized as a member who comes from a safe district and thus has achieved leadership status as a result of his or her seniority. A delegate, on the other hand, is more likely to come from a competitive district and have low seniority and no leadership status.

Some later studies of congressional behavior suggest that there is more to the marginal-district–delegate-role syndrome than is indicated by the earlier studies of role behavior.[64] We will consider the newer findings after the following discussion of legislators' actual behavior, which may be different from their role orientation.

Thus far, we have looked at substantive representation as reflected in a representative or senator's adopting a delegate, trustee, or politico role. Such analysis is limited, however, because it tells us how the legislators say they behave or how they feel they should behave but not necessarily how they really do behave. Role analysis, in short, studies attitudes rather than actual behavior. In order to move beyond this level in studying representation, we must look at actual voting behavior and relate it to constituency opinion. The Survey Research Center of the University of Michigan conducted an extensive study of this sort after the election of 1958. Incumbent representatives and senators, their opponents, and a sample of constituents in 116 congressional districts were interviewed. In addition, roll-call votes of these legislators and the social and political characteristics of their districts were studied. The results of this study are presented in an article by Warren Miller and Donald Stokes called "Constituency Influence in Congress." [65]

Miller and Stokes found that the extent of policy agreement between legislators and their constituents varied a great deal from issue to issue. On the question of American involvement in foreign affairs, there was no connection between the views of constituents and those of their representatives (a correlation coefficient of –.09). There was more agreement on matters of social and economic welfare (correlation of .3), and a high level of correspondence between constituencies and their representatives on the question of civil rights (correlation of .6).

The existence of such correlations between constituency opinion and the legislator's attitude does not tell us how this linkage is achieved. Miller and Stokes looked at three requirements that must be met before we can say that the constituency influences or controls the behavior of its representative. (1) The legislator's votes in the House must agree substantially with his or her own policy views or his or her perceptions of the district's views and not be determined entirely by other influences. (2) The attitudes or perceptions governing the legislator's voting behavior must correspond, to some degree, to the district's actual opinions. (3) The constituency must consider the policy views of candidates when it votes.

The first condition was satisfied in the congressional districts studied. The legislator's attitude and his perception of constituency views can together serve to predict accurately his voting behavior. This study and a later one using the same data both suggest that the legislator's perception of constituency opinion is more important than his own attitude in determining how he votes.[66] That is, when there is a difference between the legislator's attitude and his perception of constituency views, he is more likely to vote according to his perception of constituency views or to change his attitude to fit this perception than he is to distort his perception of constituency opinion so that it fits with his attitudes. The importance of perception also suggests that constituencies do not influence voting behavior by selecting legislators whose attitudes jibe with theirs. Rather, they have control because legislators, in order to stay in office, alter their own attitudes to fit those of their constituents.

The second condition, that perceptions of constituency views correspond with their actual views, is not met as well as the first condition. The highest correlation between legislators' perceptions and actual constituency opinion was found on the issue of civil rights. On the issue of foreign involvement, there was almost no relationship between the legislator's perception of constituency opinion and actual constituency opinion. The legislator's perceptions and attitudes on welfare issues were found to correspond more strongly with the views of the electoral majority in the district than they did with the opinions of the constituency as a whole.

The third condition of constituency control, that voters consider the policy positions of the candidates, is not satisfied. The low level of information that voters bring to the polls is one of the most widely documented findings of political science. In the 1958 election sample, 46 percent of those *who voted* said they had neither read nor heard anything about either of the congressional candidates. Even those who knew something about one or both candidates tended to express what they knew in broad evaluative terms ("he's a good guy"). "Only about three comments in every hundred had to do with legislative issues of any description." [67] A 1965 Gallup survey found the same low level of political information among the general public: "Of the nationwide sample of adults, 57 percent did not know the name of their own Congressman; 41 percent did not know his party affiliation; 70 percent did not know when he next stood for reelection; 81 percent did not know how he voted on any major legislation during the year; and 86 percent could not name anything he had accomplished for the district." [68] In a book on congressional elections published in 1978, Thomas Mann discusses this continuing pattern of low-level voter information:

> Even on controversial issues such as abortion and gun control, 70 to 80 percent of the voters surveyed in 1976 did not know the positions of the candidates for Congress.
>
> Seven out of every ten voters in a congressional district represented by a very visible Republican member of the House Judiciary Committee did not know what position he had taken on the Nixon pardon, although most were aware of his views on impeachment.
>
> At the height of the busing controversy in the Detroit suburbs, two-fifths of the voters in one congressional district had no idea what position their congressman had taken on the issue and three-fourths were unaware of the challenger's position.[69]

The low level of policy-related information among the general public means that most legislators do not need to fear defeat at the polls due to constituent rejection of their position on specific legislative issues. On most issues the legislator is free to follow a trustee role without having to fear rejection by the voters. A word of caution should be interjected here. We are talking about most legislators most of the time not having to fear constituent issue voting on most issues. When a large proportion of the public is aware of an issue position or positions of congressional candidates, it means that the representative is no longer free to follow a trustee orientation. As John Kingdon remarks, "If constituents were better informed, it would probably be a mark of arousal over something that the congressman did which was out of keeping with strongly held beliefs." [70] Issues in recent elections that seem to tap strongly held constituent beliefs include busing, gun control, and abortion. The defeat of Senator Dick Clark of Iowa in 1978 provides an example of this type of strong voter concern over a particular issue, in this case, abortion. Polls showed that 54 percent of the people in Iowa opposed abortions. Senator Clark had voted for a bill giving federal aid for abortions to poor women under certain conditions and had indicated that he would not support a constitutional amendment banning abortions. After a very strong battle by Iowans for Life had made abortion a salient issue in the campaign, Senator Clark was defeated.[71]

Given the public's generally low level of information, however, we may ask, How important are issues in most congressional elections? A number of studies have shown that voters' evaluations of presidential performance and the state of the economy seem to be the dominant issues related to the overall outcome of congressional elections.[72] Voters' opinions on these issues were generally expressed in terms of voting for or against congressional candidates from the president's party. These earlier studies were looking at aggregate voting patterns and national trends, but a more recent study by Thomas Mann looked at public opinion and voting trends within approximately forty House districts in the 1974 and 1976 elections. Mann concluded that "a lion's share of the electoral change that occurred originated at the district level." [73] In other words, instead of viewing congressional elections as a referendum on national issues and the performance of the incumbent president, we are more correct in seeing elections as a reflection of local concerns and voters' evaluations of the job that the incumbent representative has been doing.

One reason for the low awareness of voters on issues in congressional elections seems to be a tendency by candidates to avoid taking a position on potentially divisive issues and to stress instead common goals. By being in favor of both reducing government spending and maintaining popular government programs, striving for full employment and reducing the rate of inflation, or solving the energy crisis and preserving the quality of the environment, congressional candidates can gain voter support without making the voters aware of the conflicts inherent in these goals. One can hardly expect the public to be informed about the positions of candidates on issues when such information is not a part of the campaign itself.[74]

The picture we get from studies focusing on linkages between constituency position on issues and representatives' actual voting is that voters rely on vague indications of positions on issues by their representatives and generally have very little information about how they actually voted on most issues before Congress. On some issues, such as civil rights in the Miller and Stokes study, there is a close link between constituency opinion and congressional voting. But in the normal pattern, where a representative casts a vote on an issue about which most constituents know or care little, legislators seem to enjoy a freedom to vote pretty much the way they want to or the way they think they should. Although most members of Congress tend to overestimate their visibility to the public, most of them are aware of how little the public actually knows about their voting record. Consider these comments made by representatives:

> The people back home don't know what's going on. Issues are not most important so far as the average voter is concerned. The image of the candidate plays a much greater role.[75]

> In my campaign last year I had ten or twelve joint appearances with my opponent and in not a one of them did he criticize a vote I cast. Most of the time he talked about state issues. And the people didn't seem to know which was the state issue and which was the federal issue.[76]

> I got myself on both sides of a critical and important issue: I voted for a bill that passed Congress and then voted to sustain the veto. I thought it would defeat me because I was in a ridiculous posi- tion. It was my first campaign for re-election and that is all my op- ponent talked about. Finally, though, I made hay out of it. I bought some radio time and said, "I want to talk about a very serious issue. This is one I am expert on because I am one of the few people who have been on both sides of it." [77]

> You know I am sure you'll find out a Congressman can do pretty much what he decides to do and he doesn't have to bother too much about criticism. I've seen plenty of cases, since I've been up here where a guy will hold one economic or political position and get along all right; and then he'll die or resign and a guy comes in who holds quite a different economic or political position and he gets along all right too. That's the fact of the matter.[78]

Given the low public visibility of legislative voting and the high rate of reelection of incumbents, we might expect to find a large number of policy innovators in Congress. After all, it would appear that a legislator had little to lose, in terms of constituency support, by generating new ideas on the business of government. What we find instead, however, is an extremely high level of concern with reelection and a general pattern of little or no real policy innovation. David Mayhew's *Congress: The Electoral Connection* provides an excellent analysis of both of these phenomena. Mayhew suggests that there is a difference between winning and winning big. A high rate of incumbents are returned to office, but most of them have gone through at least one election with an outcome close enough to provoke some concern about the strength of their hold on that seat.[79]

In the Ninety-third Congress (1973–1974), to use Mayhew's example, 58 percent of the representatives and 70 percent of the senators had, at some time in their careers, won a general election with less than 55 percent of the total vote. Seventy-seven percent of the House members and 86 percent of the Senate members had won at least one election with less than 60 percent of the total vote.[80] It is important to note here that Mayhew is talking about the vote margin in at least one election in a legislator's career and not the number of marginal (less than 55 percent of the vote) elections in any particular election year. If we look at the vote margins in any particular year, we are struck more by the relatively few congressional elections in which the vote was close than we are by any signs of electoral insecurity. In the 1978 election, for instance, only 17 percent of the 435 House elections and 33.3 percent of the thirty-three Senate elections were decided by margins under 55 percent.[81] Although Mayhew and other political scientists have discussed, at great length, the consequences of a trend toward a declining number of marginal seats in Congress, the important point here is that an incumbent representative or senator thinks in terms of his or her one close election at the same time that a political analyst, viewing the aggregate data, thinks in terms of the increasing number of what appear to be safe congressional seats.[82] Once you recognize that the only really relaxed, secure, and happy politician is the one who has just collected 101 percent of the vote (even then he or she might be looking ahead to the next election), it begins to make some sense that a lot of a legislator's time and attention are given over to matters of reelection.

Now let us consider Mayhew's explanation for the second phenomenon mentioned above, that of the basically conservative, or status quo–supporting, behavior adopted by most legislators. The fact that a member of Congress occupies a seat means that he or she was able to satisfy some combination, or coalition, of electoral forces in both the primary and the general election. If the member has been in office for more than one term, reelection means that his or her position on the issues and voting record are accepted or tolerated by a majority in the district. The rational strategy for any legislator to adopt, therefore, is to cling to those positions upon which his or her electoral success is based. Given the low information level of the general public and the complexities of issues in most campaigns, most successful candidates for office are not likely to know exactly what factors were most important in determining their electoral success. Because of this uncertainty, members of Congress are unlikely to adopt a strategy of policy innovation that might serve to undercut their successful electoral coalition. Rational behavior, at least in reelection terms, is basically a conservative one—to maintain that basis of support reflected in the last election.

If the majority of representatives and senators are following basically conservative patterns of behavior, the question then becomes: Where are we to look for policy innovation in Congress? To answer this question, we need to go back to a matter raised earlier in this section, that members of Congress from marginal districts (defined as districts in which the winner drew less than 55 percent of the vote) are more likely to adopt a delegate than a trustee role. When we get beyond this somewhat superficial level of expressed role orientation and look at actual behavior, we find that legislators from marginal districts are likely to perform an important function as policy innovators in the legislature.

The logic that turns marginal representatives and senators into policy innovators is the same as that which makes most incumbents follow a conservative policy. If the old swayback horse of electoral coalitions has provided success in the past and still seems to be capable of running and winning, you stay with it; if not, you find a new horse. An incumbent who sees the old electoral base crumbling, or a candidate whose polls show that he or she is not benefiting from adherence to present policy positions, is likely to resort to policy innovation, the introduction of radically new programs, as a vehicle for changing or expanding a losing or shrinking base of electoral support. At times, such marginal legislators seem to go in all directions. Generally speaking, however, their policy innovation reflects a rational strategy of reelection. Mayhew mentions several cases in which a close reelection led representatives to stake out new ground and develop issues and positions out of the mainstream in a desperate attempt to rescue an otherwise losing reelection cause.

Let us now turn to one last consideration about marginal legislators and actual representation. One school of thought, reflected in Table 2–7, is that candidates and representatives from marginal districts are most likely to adopt a center-of-the-road moderate position on issues. For example, a survey by the *Congressional Quarterly Weekly Report* of seventeen Democratic House incumbents and six Democratic Senate incumbents who faced stiff reelection battles in 1978 found that there was a dramatic move by these legislators toward moderating their previous support for liberal positions.[83] When you think about it, this seems to make sense. In a district where the likely party vote is split about evenly, a candidate has to go out of his or her way not to offend any potential supporters. The best way to do this is to adopt a middle-of-the-road position on all issues so as to maximize the chances of getting votes both to the left and to the right of the vital center. But another school of thought—reflected in the discussion above about marginal legislators and policy innovation—suggests that the rational strategy for any candidate in a marginal district is to emphasize the differences, the extremes or positions away from the center, between her- or himself and the other candidate. One way to test the validity of both hypotheses is to look at marginal congressional districts to see whether a change in representatives resulted in any real changes in policy positions taken by the new and the old representatives of that district. The centrist, moderation school would suggest little change, while the policy-innovation (show me the difference) school would suggest noticeable change in the policy positions represented by the new member. While both schools of thought make sense, the best evidence that we have to date suggests that the marginality-innovation, or real change, explanation is the more accurate one. Table 2–8 indicates why. If candidates in marginal districts were following the centrist, moderation position, we would find little difference in the voting patterns of representatives of that district, regardless of party, who happened to win the last election, and their predecessors. What Table 2–8 shows, however, is that there is a great difference between representatives' positions on issues (as measured in summary indicators of support for the conservative coalition and support for a larger federal government role) when there is a turnover. The focus of the changes reflected in Table 2–8

TABLE 2–8 Marginal District Changes in Representation as Reflected in Support for the Conservative Coalition and a Larger Federal Role

Congresses	Mean Change in Conservative Coalition Support	Mean Change in Larger Federal Role Support
88th–89th	60.5%	51.4%
89th–90th	54.7%	40.1%
Both	58.0%	46.5%

Source: Reprinted by permission of the publisher, from Morris P. Fiorina, *Representatives, Roll Calls, and Constituencies* (Lexington, Mass.: Lexington Books, D. C. Heath and Company, copyright 1974, D. C. Heath and Company), p. 103. A bit of explanation is called for here. Fiorina is looking at forty-two districts that changed hands from one party to the other between the Eighty-eighth and Eighty-ninth Congress and thirty-two districts that did the same between the Eighty-ninth and Ninetieth Congresses. By doing so, he quite correctly narrows the focus of study to those districts that can be classified as truly marginal and measures the policy differences that result from a change in party representation.

are the districts that underwent changes in party control between two congresses. Because they are perfect examples of marginal districts, they represent good test cases for the hypotheses about marginal districts and issue positions advanced above.

The information in Table 2–8 reinforces the notion of marginal legislators as policy innovators. Given the relative electoral safety of most members of Congress and the rational conservative policy strategy followed by most incumbents, those members who come from marginal districts seem to represent the lifeblood of new ideas in Congress.

This discussion of actual representation has focused primarily on the voting behavior of legislators. Before ending this chapter, however, we should take at least a brief look at another type of behavior that constitutes an integral part of actual representation.

Voting is not the only way in which a member of Congress is expected to represent his constituents. Regardless of how the legislator votes, he or she is expected to perform personal services for constituents who request them. A great deal of the legislator's work load consists of this casework for constituents. "The most pressing day-to-day demands for the time of Senators and Congressmen," noted the late Senator Hubert Humphrey, "are not directly linked to legislative tasks. They come from constituents." [84] A study of members' allocation of their time conducted in 1977 by the House Commission on Administrative Review supports Senator Humphrey's point. Less than 40 percent of the average member's time *in Washington* was spent on legislative activity on the floor and in committees and subcommittees. Most of the remaining 60 percent of their time was spent on constituency-related activities. The amount of time members give to constituency work is even greater when one considers that they give almost all of their time spent in the district every other weekend or more to constituency work.[85] Servicemen who want an early discharge, farmers who fear the proposed construction of a federal highway, students who want information on government scholarships, in short anyone wanting information on or aid in dealing with the federal bureaucracy is told to "write your congressman." It is the representative, more than anyone else, who is expected to provide a link between the citizen and the vast bureaucracy of the federal government.

Providing these services to his or her constituents can often be more important than how the legislator votes. A representative who fails to maintain contact by frequent visits to the constituency and a quick response to constituent's requests subjects her- or himself to campaign attacks. "Martha Doesn't Shop Here Anymore" was the title of a campaign song used to help unseat Kansas Representative Martha Keys in 1978. Another politician had this to say about the defeat of eight-term Congressman Fred Rooney of Pennsylvania in the same year: "Fred didn't pay any attention to home. He rarely came up to events in the county anymore. He always sent telegrams." [86]

Because voters know so little about the issue positions of legislators, the performance of members of Congress in maintaining contact with constituents and doing these errands may often be more important in a campaign than anything else. In the words of one representative:

> Unless you can keep constantly in contact with your people, serving them and letting them know what you are doing, you are in a bad way. My experience is that people don't care how I vote on foreign aid, federal aid to education, and all those big issues, but they are very much interested in whether I answer their letter and who is going to be the next rural mail carrier or the next postmaster. Those are the things that really count.[87]

If there is one point that all political scientists and representatives, be they conservative Republicans or liberal Democrats, will agree on, it is that an important part of actual representation is to be found not in voting but in dealing with casework. The representative and senator's role here is to be an amateur lawyer, to represent the client's (constituent's) case before an executive agency or regulatory commission to the best of his or her ability.

Although just about everyone will agree that an awareness of constituent problems is a prerequisite for members of Congress to be effective representatives, there is concern among both scholars and members, a concern that was discussed in Chapter 1, about casework representation cutting into time that should be spent on policy representation. There is also concern about the low congressional turnover, which seems to be related to incumbent senators and representatives' effective use of resources to serve constituents. Substantive representation is predicated on some congressional turnover based on policy considerations, just as policy innovation in Congress seems to depend on the existence of marginal congressmen. Should the current trend of a decline in marginal seats continue, important questions would certainly be raised about how representative Congress is in the sense of substantive representation as discussed in this chapter.[88]

NOTES

1. Quoted in Spencer Rich, "Baker on Congress—Mingle More, Work Less," *Boston Globe*, April 3, 1977, p. 19.

2. *Congressional Quarterly Weekly Report*, January 15, 1977, p. 64. The term recess was maintained for the annual August break.

3. Richard Fenno, *Homestyle: House Members in Their Districts* (Little, Brown, 1978), p. 35.

4. Richard Lyons, "Indiana Freshman Reviews Nine Months on Capitol Hill," *Washington Post*, October 29, 1975, p. C1.

5. Richard Bolling, U.S. Congress, House, *Hearings Before the Select Committee on Committees*, Ninety-third Congress, first session, volume 3, September 21, 1973, p. 215. Richard Fenno also discusses the lawmaking-representational conflict in *Homestyle: House Members in Their Districts*, pp. 244–245.

6. Ann Cooper, "Congressional Term Limits Get More Support, but Still Unpopular on Hill," *Congressional Quarterly Weekly Report*, February 25, 1978, p. 534.

7. Ibid., p. 533.

8. John C. Gartland, testimony in U.S. Congress, Senate, *Congressional Tenure, Hearings Before the Subcommittee on the Constitution of the Committee on the Judiciary,* Ninety-fifth Congress, second session, March 16, 1978, p. 106.

9. Cited in Tom Wicker, "Halting the System: II," *New York Times,* July 28, 1978, p. A23.

10. The arguments here are from Catharine W. Trauernicht, "Pro and Con Arguments for Limiting Congressional Terms," Foundation for the Study of Presidential and Congressional Terms, Washington, D.C., correspondence to the author, February 26, 1979. Additional information on all these points may be found in U.S. Congress, Senate, *Congressional Tenure, Hearings Before the Subcommittee on the Constitution of the Committee on the Judiciary,* and Ann Cooper, "Congressional Term Limits Get More Public Support, but Still Unpopular on Hill," p. 534.

11. Ibid.

12. U.S. Congress, Senate, *Congressional Tenure, Hearings Before the Subcommittee on the Constitution of the Committee on the Judiciary,* appendix, part 2, p. 189.

13. Hannah Fenichel Pitkin, *The Concept of Representation* (University of California Press, 1967). For another discussion of the different dimensions of representation see Malcolm Jewell and Samuel Patterson, *The Legislative Process in the United States* (Random House, 1977), pp. 21–26.

14. Pitkin, *The Concept of Representation,* p. 43.

15. Thomas Hobbes, *Leviathan* (Collier Books Edition, 1962), p. 127.

16. Joseph Tussman, "The Political Theory of Thomas Hobbes" (Ph.D. diss., 1947), quoted in Pitkin, *The Concept of Representation,* p. 43.

17. Daniel Berman, *In Congress Assembled* (Macmillan, 1964), p. 387.

18. Congressional Quarterly Service, *Politics in America* (1969), p. 103.

19. *Reynolds* v. *Simms,* 377 U.S. 533 (1964).

20. Andrew Hacker, *Congressional Districting: The Issue of Equal Representation* (The Brookings Institution, 1964) and William Goss, "Measuring the Impact of Congressional Representation," cited in Nelson Polsby, ed., *Reapportionment in the 1970s* (University of California Press, 1971), p. 233.

21. *Congressional Quarterly Weekly Report,* July 29, 1978, p. 1933.

22. John Adams, "Letter to John Penn," quoted in Pitkin, *The Concept of Representation,* p. 60.

23. Jim Wright, *You and Your Congressman* (Coward-McCann, 1965), p. 15.

24. Quoted in John Wahlke, Heinz Eulau, William Buchanan, and Leroy Ferguson, *The Legislative System: Explorations in Legislative Behavior* (John Wiley and Sons, 1962), p. 253.

25. George B. Galloway, *History of the House of Representatives* (Thomas Y. Crowell, 1968), p. 35.

26. *Congressional Quarterly Weekly Report*, January 13, 1979, p. 43.

27. Gary Wills, "Hurrah for Politicians," *Harpers*, September, 1975, p. 49.

28. Alan Ehrenhalt, "Congress Is Getting Younger All the Time," *Congressional Quarterly Weekly Report*, January 27, 1979, p. 154.

29. Ibid., and Steven V. Roberts, "Senate's New Class Reflects Changing Political Standards," *New York Times*, November 15, 1978, p. A18.

30. Quoted in Alan Ehrenhalt, "Most Members of Congress Claim Religious Affiliation," *Congressional Quarterly Weekly Report*, January 20, 1979, p. 80.

31. Ibid.

32. Quoted in Christopher Buchanan, "Why Aren't There More Women in Congress," *Congressional Quarterly Weekly Report*, August 12, 1978, p. 2108. See also John W. Soule and Wilma E. McGrath, "Ideology and Socialization: Women in the U.S. House of Representatives," a paper prepared for delivery at the 1978 annual meeting of the American Political Science Association, New York, N.Y., August 31 to September 3, 1978.

33. *Congressional Quarterly Weekly Report*, July 29, 1978, p. 1935.

34. Donald R. Matthews, *U.S. Senators and Their World* (Vintage, 1960), p. 45. For an interesting discussion, and a sort of science fiction proposal, on the biases of representation discussed in this section see Dennis C. Mueller, Robert D. Tollison, and Thomas D. Willett, "Representative Democracy via Random Selection," *Public Choice*, vol. XII (Spring, 1972), pp. 57–68.

35. Quoted in Mary Russell, "New House Democrats Called More Restrained," *Washington Post*, December 2, 1976, p. A4.

36. Quoted in Elizabeth Drew, "A Reporter at Large (Washington, D.C.)," *The New Yorker*, April 9, 1979, p. 111.

37. The figures for 1978 are computed from data in the *Congressional Quarterly Weekly Report*, December 30, 1978, pp. 3508–3535 and Steven V. Roberts, "Senate's New Class Reflects Changing Political Standards," *New York Times*, November 15, 1978, p. A18. The data for 1958 and 1962 are from Roberts, "Senate's New Class Reflects Changing Political Standards" and Randall B. Ripley, *Congress: Process and Policy* (W. W. Norton, 1978, second edition), p. 98.

38. Pitkin, *The Concept of Representation*, p. 102.

39. Richard L. Madden, "Buckley after 100 Days in Washington: At Ease in Senate Role," *New York Times,* May 2, 1971, p. 20.

40. David R. Mayhew, *Congress: The Electoral Connection* (Yale University Press, 1974), p. 132.

41. Ibid., pp. 117–118.

42. Murray Edelman, *The Symbolic Uses of Politics* (University of Illinois Press, 1967).

43. Fenno, *Homestyle: House Members in Their Districts,* pp. 54–55.

44. Ibid., p. 95.

45. Ibid., p. 152.

46. Ibid., p. 98.

47. Ibid., p. 97.

48. Ibid., p. 97.

49. Pitkin, *The Concept of Representation,* pp. 209–210.

50. Booth Mooney, *Mr. Speaker* (Follett, 1964), p. 166.

51. Former Senator Floyd Haskell, quoted in Robert G. Kaiser, "No Sore Loser: Senator Foresees 'A Lot of Other Things To Do,'" *Washington Post,* December 4, 1978, p. A1.

52. Quoted in Charles Clapp, *The Congressman: His Work as He Sees It* (Brookings Institution, 1963), pp. 121–122. Copyright © 1963 by the Brookings Institution.

53. Edmund Burke, "Speech to the Electors of Bristol," *Writings and Speeches of Edmund Burke* (Little, Brown, 1901), vol. 2, pp. 93–98.

54. "Senate Debators Call Canal Treaty Unpopular Issue," *Boston Globe,* February 10, 1978, p. 5.

55. Both quotes are from Charles O. Jones, "The Agriculture Committee and the Problem of Representation," in Robert Peabody and Nelson Polsby, *New Perspectives on the House of Representatives* (Rand McNally, 1977, third edition), p. 181.

56. Quoted in Alfred de Grazia, "The Representative Ought to Consult the Majority," in Neal Riemer, ed., *The Representative* (D. C. Heath, 1967), p. 38.

57. Quoted in Lewis Anthony Dexter, "The Representative and His District," in Peabody and Polsby, *New Perspectives on the House of Representatives,* pp. 5–6.

58. V. O. Key, Jr., *Public Opinion and American Democracy* (Alfred A. Knopf, 1964), pp. 482–483.

59. Quoted in T. V. Smith, "Congress Must Follow the Popular Will," in Neal Riemer, ed., *The Representative,* p. 44.

60. Center for the Study of Democratic Institutions, *The Elite and the Electorate* (1963), p. 6.

61. Roger Davidson, *The Role of the Congressman* (Pegasus, 1969), p. 117.

62. David Kovenock, "Influence in the U.S. House of Representatives: Some Preliminary Statistical Snapshots," paper delivered at the annual meeting of the American Political Science Association, New York City, N.Y., 1967, p. 17.

63. Theodore Sorenson, *Kennedy* (Harper & Row, 1965), p. 74.

64. See, for instance, James E. Campbell, "Electoral Competition and the Congressional Connection: The Marginality Hypothesis Reconsidered," a paper prepared for delivery at the 1978 annual meeting of the Northeast Political Science Association, Tarrytown, N.Y., November 9–11, 1978.

65. Warren Miller and Donald Stokes, "Constituency Influence in Congress," *American Political Science Review* (March, 1963), pp. 45–56.

66. Miller and Stokes, "Constituency Influence in Congress," in Peabody and Polsby, *New Perspectives on the House of Representatives*, p. 44; Charles Cnudde and Donald McCrone, "Constituency Attitudes and Congressional Voting: A Causal Model," in Edward Dryer and Walter Rosenbaum, eds., *Political Opinion and Electoral Behavior* (Wadsworth, 1967), pp. 407–411.

67. Miller and Stokes, "Constituency Influence in Congress," in Peabody and Polsby, *New Perspectives on the House of Representatives*, p. 48.

68. AIPO Survey, November 7, 1965. Cited in Roger Davidson, David Kovenock, and Michael O'Leary, *Congress in Crisis: Politics and Congressional Reform* (Wadsworth, 1966), p. 49.

69. Thomas E. Mann, *Unsafe at Any Margin: Interpreting Congressional Elections* (American Enterprise Institute for Public Policy Research, 1978), p. 46. Mann's study of the campaigns and elections in approximately forty congressional districts did lead him to the conclusion that voters are more aware of congressional candidates than the political science literature on the subject would have us believe. See his discussion in chapters three and six.

70. John Kingdon, *Congressmen's Voting Decisions* (Harper & Row, 1973), p. 40.

71. Douglas E. Kneeland, "Clark's Defeat in Iowa Laid to a Single Issue," *New York Times*, November 13, 1978, p. A18.

72. Edward R. Tufte, "Determinants of the Outcomes of Midterm Congressional Elections," *American Political Science Review* (September, 1975), pp. 812–826 and James L. Sundquist, *Politics and Policy* (The Brookings Institution, 1968), pp. 456ff.

73. Mann, *Unsafe at Any Margin: Interpreting Congressional Elections*, p. 92.

74. Ibid., p. 45.

75. Clapp, *The Congressman: His Work as He Sees It*, p. 421. Copyright © 1963 by the Brookings Institution.

76. Ibid., p. 423. Copyright © 1963 by the Brookings Institution.

77. Ibid., p. 426. Copyright © 1963 by the Brookings Institution.

78. Dexter, "The Representative and His District," in Peabody and Polsby, *New Perspectives on the House of Representatives*, p. 5.

79. David R. Mayhew, *Congress: The Electoral Connection* (Yale University Press, 1974).

80. Ibid., p. 33.

81. The margins of victory are taken from the *Congressional Quarterly Weekly Report,* March 31, 1979, pp. 573, 576–582.

82. For an analysis and discussion of the literature see Morris P. Fiorina, *Congress: Keystone of the Washington Establishment* (Yale University Press, 1977).

83. Laura B. Weiss, "Tough Election Fights Forced Some Members to Moderate Their Stands," *Congressional Quarterly Weekly Report,* June 2, 1979, pp. 1062–1066.

84. Hubert H. Humphrey, "To Move Congress Out of Its Ruts," *New York Times Magazine,* April 7, 1963, p. 39.

85. Commission on Administrative Review, U.S. Congress, House, *Administrative Reorganization and Legislative Management,* Ninety-fifth Congress, first session, September 28, 1977, volume Two, pp. 17ff. For a discussion of allocation of time in the district see Fenno, *Homestyle: House Members In Their Districts.*

86. Rick Rood, "Complacency Helps Untrench 15-Year House Member," *Washington Post,* November 13, 1978, p. A3.

87. Clapp, *The Congressman: His Work as He Sees It*, p. 58. Copyright © 1963 by the Brookings Institution.

88. For an interesting discussion that looks at the representativeness of Congress as an institution rather than the representativeness of individual members vis-à-vis their constituencies see Robert Weissberg, "Collective vs. Dyadic Representation in Congress," *American Political Science Review* (June, 1978), pp. 535–547.

LAWMAKING I:
PARTIES AND STAFF

ONE IMAGE of the member of Congress is that of a salesperson out in the provinces continually pitching a product. Much of this activity involves the salesperson selling her- or himself; but as any encyclopedia salesperson will tell you, the product must also be worth peddling. In the congressional instance, the product is legislation—or the attempts at, or appearance of, legislation. Representational activities exert a centrifugal force on the legislative body. Salespeople need to know their territory, and this requires that they spend a lot of time in that district selling their wares. But in order to have a product to sell, someone must be back home minding the factory. This is where we get into those aspects of congressional activity that help to produce some legislative product worth peddling. In this chapter and the next, we will be looking at some of the structures of Congress that provide a centralizing force, that help to produce a legislative product in this basically decentralized institution. This chapter will focus on party organization and staff; the next on committees and subcommittees. The underlying thinking here is that all of these structures perform an important lawmaking function. Without them Congress would resemble nothing more than an annual convention of salesmen coming together to swap stories (there are, of course, critics of Congress who say this is exactly what it is). To the extent that there is some concentrated, or centralized, congressional focus on fashioning legislation, the party organization, staff, and committee structures can be said to play key roles.

It often happens that seemingly trivial events best illustrate important aspects of political behavior and that the real impact of important congressional structures can be most fully appreciated when the absence of those structures leads to unusual and surprising outcomes. A case in point is the "Great Magna Carta Fiasco," which took place in the spring of 1976. This event illustrates what happens when there is a breakdown of informational services normally provided by party leaders and congressional staffers, showing that much legislative voting (the ultimate fashioning of the product to be peddled by representatives) often takes place in an environment of low information and high uncertainty.

On March 9, 1976, the House of Representatives considered a resolution calling for twenty-four members of Congress to go to London to accept the loan of an original copy of the Magna Carta, one of the great documents of Western civilization and individual liberty. The Senate had already approved this resolution; all who knew about it thought it a fitting part of the 1976 bicentennial celebration (the document was to be put on display in the Capitol). The party leadership, assuming easy passage of the resolution, brought it up under unanimous consent, in which one member's objection could bring a halt to the whole process. That one member appeared in the form of a conservative Republican congressman from Maryland. In objecting to the unanimous consent proposal, the congressman observed:

> As I read this concurrent resolution it allows a sort of Bicentennial junket of twenty-four Members of the House and the Senate to go to England and bring back a copy of the Magna Carta for display in Washington. They will have apparently unlimited expenses and travel being paid out of the contingent funds of the House and Senate, which means the taxpayers' pockets. Staff travel is also authorized.
>
> I am surprised that a gentleman of Irish ancestry (the Democratic majority leader) would be here before us pleading for expenditure of the taxpayers' funds to go to London to see the Queen. What is the necessity for this? I think we all know why we had the recent unpleasantness with Great Britain two centuries ago. . . .
>
> I would say to the gentleman [the majority leader] that based on the travel records I have seen published, on any given day the gentleman could probably find twenty-four Members of the U.S.

Congress in London. I do not see why we must have a special delegation of twenty-four Members on a Government-paid junket over there to carry this important document back.[1]

The House eventually took a roll-call vote on the matter, and the resolution was defeated, 219 to 167. As members arrived on the floor to vote, most of them were told that the issue at hand was another government boondoggle or congressional junket, an issue that does not sit well with voters in an election year. After the vote, floor leaders from both parties apologized for not informing members that Great Britain had actually requested the formal party of twenty-four members to accompany the transfer of the document. The resolution represented a polite response to that government's request rather than a congressionally originated junket. The following week the same issue came to the House floor—this time under the more formal auspices of a rule from the House Rules Committee rather than the unanimous consent procedure—and it passed.

The earlier vote on this matter is more instructive because it represents what one commentator describes as "a perfect and horrible example of what can happen when members do not understand what they are voting on." He goes on to note:

> House members frequently do not really know what they are voting on. Some legislation is too complex for any but experts and has to be taken on faith. Also, during floor debate explaining a bill or amendment most members are at committee hearings or in their offices talking with constituents. When the bells ring for a vote they rush to the floor and ask an aide or trusted colleague what the issue is about.
>
> But some customary protective backstops were missing in the Magna Carta disaster.
>
> Usually, the legislative program is announced in advance. Legislation is explained in committee reports and in daily or weekly digests from the party whip and other sources. Legislative assistants keep their bosses abreast of what's coming up. Then issues are debated on the floor. None of that happened Tuesday [the day of the House vote].[2]

While this particular case may seem to represent an anomaly, the central issue remains. Members of Congress rely heavily on the party organization and their own staffs to provide them with sufficient information to avoid the embarrassment of ignorant voting as reflected in the Magna Carta debacle. Party organizations and congressional staffs provide important centralizing forces that help draw together enough legislators to perform lawmaking functions. Their ability to do this is seriously challenged by the many decentralizing forces influencing Congress. This conflict is perhaps most evident in the case of political parties.

One of the models of Congress outlined in the first section of this book was the Jeffersonian, or party government, model. The first chapter brought out some of the key elements of this model, suggesting some differences between the American system and the British system that serve as the basis of comparison. Perhaps the key difference is the American emphasis on district, or geographic, representation and its lack of sanctions against party deviants. To evaluate the impact of political parties on congressional behavior, we have to look at three different aspects of the political process: the role that parties play in congressional elections, the role parties play in legislative voting, and party organization in Congress.

In the present system there are a number of factors working against the fulfillment of a genuine party government model. There is the fact that a number of people hold the representational function of Congress to be more important than the lawmaking function. Reforms that would tighten national party control over legislators' voting would weaken the strong geographic representation that the present system favors. When such changes reach the point where many members of Congress feel that following the national party in their voting threatens their reelection, then the idea of party voting to reflect national electoral mandates becomes unsatisfactory. This emphasis on geographic representation permeates all discussions of the possibility of achieving a party government system in Congress. It sets the limits within which American parties may attempt to influence legislative voting.

The essential irony of political parties in the American legislative system is this: while party identification is perhaps the most important determinant of voting behavior in elections (as well as legislative voting), the sort of unified, efficient party organization that would seem to be a necessary part of such a system is lacking at both the electoral and the legislative level. In order to explain this system we have to look at the way parties influence electoral and legislative voting in spite of this lack of a strong organization and at the way the legislative party organization is able to exert influence within the limits set by the system's emphasis on geographic representation.

PARTIES AND VOTERS

Anthony Downs, in *An Economic Theory of Democracy*, outlined the way in which a perfectly rational human being would go about voting.[3] A rational voter is defined here only in terms of means; he or she seeks efficiency by either maximizing output for a given input (casting a vote in such a way that it has the greatest impact in bringing about policies he or she favors) or by minimizing input for a given output (not spending scarce resources such as time and money on gathering information in order to cast an "informed" vote that really will not make any difference in the political system).

To cast a rational vote for every candidate, the individual citizen would have to spend most of his or her working hours evaluating the policy positions of all candidates. Such behavior, while insuring an informed voting decision, would be grossly inefficient in terms of payoffs the voter would receive. The likelihood that his or her one vote will elect the chosen candidates and produce the desired policies is not great enough to justify the tremendous costs of gathering the information. A rational solution to this problem is to delegate the evaluation and analysis of political information to another person or agency.

If citizen A has a friend who knows about economics and has similar political goals, then it makes sense to rely on his friend's analysis of which candidate would be more likely to help achieve those goals in the economic sector. By relying on the superior information his friend has in this area, citizen A greatly reduces his own costs of gaining information to cast a rational vote. Similarly, if the voter knows that one political party is committed to particular groups or segments of the electorate, he may cast a rational ballot by voting strictly in terms of party labels. Again, the voter is able to support candidates who share his policy goals without having to expend a great deal of time and energy on the information gathering process itself. The most important requirement of such delegation of analysis and evaluation is that the delegated agency share the policy goals of the delegating individual. It is irrational to delegate such analysis to a political party if that party is likely to change its base of group support or policy goals in order to broaden its political appeal.

We noted in Chapter 2 the low level of political information voters bring to the polls. Because the average voter knows so little about the candidates and their issue positions, it is difficult to say that he or she casts a rational vote. By voting in terms of party, however, even an uninformed voter may cast a ballot in line with his or her own interests. In studying the American electorate, political scientists have found great consistency in citizens' identification with one party or the other.

Table 3-1 shows such a pattern for the period, 1952–1978. Before analyzing the trend indicated in Table 3-1, we will consider a few points about the concept of party identification. Political scientists first started to employ the concept of a person's self-described affiliation with one party or the other in studying elections in the 1950s. In retrospect it seems that this same period was one in which the importance of the effect of party identification on electoral outcomes was greatest. A person's identification with the Democratic

TABLE 3-1 Party Identification of the American Public

Year	Democrat	Republican	Independent
1952	49% [a]	28%	23%
1956 [b]	45	30	24
1958	51	29	20
1960	46	30	24
1962	48	30	22
1964	52	25	23
1966	46	25	29
1968	46	24	30
1970	44	25	31
1972	41	24	35
1974	40	23	37
1976	42	18	37
1978	44	23	33

[a] The percentages have been rounded off.
[b] There was no survey in 1954.

Source: Election Studies, Inter-University Consortium for Political and Social Research, Institute for Social Research, University of Michigan.

or Republican party was found to be a remarkably stable phenomenon that he or she acquired early in life.[4] This early established party attitude was found to act as a perceptual screen through which all political stimuli were given meaning. Information about issues and candidates generally took on meaning as it was related to party identification. Most important, party identification was found to be the single most significant variable in predicting electoral outcomes. This last point is one to keep in mind as we look at changes in the importance of party identification for voters in more recent years. Even after a decade of what many observers consider to be a terminal decline of American political parties, a book published on the subject in 1979 was able to conclude that "although partisan affiliation has declined, it is still the most stable predictor of the electorate's voting behavior."[5]

One trend that is clearly evident in Table 3–1 and that has drawn a lot of attention is the great increase in the percentage of the population that defines itself as independent rather than affiliated with either party.[6] Although this trend is seen by many as the clearest indication of the decline of political parties as a cue for voters, in a number of studies political scientists have found that many of these self-described independents regularly vote along party lines. A close analysis of the actual voting behavior of these partisan independents for the period 1956–1976 showed that "the percentage of people who generally vote along party lines has remained about the same over the twenty year period."[7] It is really the stability of partisan affiliation and voting, in other words, rather than the rise of independents that is important in the 1970s. At the level of presidential voting, this stability was reflected in Carter's party victory in 1976, in which Democratic identifiers who had massively defected from party ranks in 1972 returned home. At the congressional level, this stability is reflected in the fact that the Democrats won a national majority in twenty-four of the twenty-six congressional elections between 1932 and 1978.[8] Since we are concerned here with congressional elections, I have included Table 3–2, which shows the trend of party line voting in House elections for the two decades, 1956–1976. While a 10 percent drop shows a clear trend of declining party line voting during this period, the table also shows that about three-fourths of the vote in House elections was party line voting.

One factor that helps to account for the stability of party identification is its group base. Certain religious, racial, income, educa-

TABLE 3–2 Party Line Voting in House Elections

Year	Party Line Voters	Defectors	Independents
1956	82%	9%	9%
1958	84	11	5
1960	80	12	8
1962	83	12	5
1964	79	15	5
1966	76	16	8
1968	74	19	7
1970	76	16	8
1972	73	17	10
1974	74	18	8
1976	72	19	9

Source: Thomas E. Mann, *Unsafe at Any Margin: Interpreting Congressional Elections* (American Enterprise Institute for Public Policy Research, 1978), p. 14.

tion, age, and residential groups traditionally associate with the Republican or Democratic party, and one's membership in these groups is generally a stable phenomenon (with the obvious exceptions created by time, money, or moving). Indeed, the basic difference between the two parties is often expressed more as a difference in the groups represented by each than as a difference in ideology.[9] Tables 3–3 and 3–4 illustrate the group bases of the two parties as they are reflected in constituency characteristics associated with Democratic and Republican congressional districts and in patterns of group voting in congressional elections.

As the tables indicate, groups traditionally associated with the Democratic party are voters with lower incomes, those who rent rather than own their own homes, blacks, Catholics, younger voters, and those with no college education. City dwellers and blue-collar workers are two additional groups, not included here, which have traditionally been associated with the Democratic party. The Republican group base, conversely, is made up of higher income, home-owning, Protestant, white, older, college-educated, white-collar, and suburban voters.

TABLE 3-3 Constituency Characteristics and Party, Ninety-third Congress (1973–1974)

Characteristic	Percentage of All Democratic Seats ($n = 243$)	Percentage of All Republican Seats ($n = 192$)
Median Income in District		
Under $7000	14	4
$7000–$9999	54	43
$10,000 and over	32	53
Percentage of Owner-Occupied Housing Units in District		
Under 50%	19	3
50%–69%	56	49
70% and over	25	48
Black Population— Percentage in District		
Under 10%	53	83
10%–19%	19	11
20% and over	28	6
Median Years of School Completed (Adults, 25 Years and Over)		
Under 10	10	2
10–12	45	24
Over 12	45	73

Source: Data were compiled from *Congressional District Data Book,* Ninety-third Congress (U.S. Government Printing Office, 1974).

There are, of course, many exceptions to these general patterns of group affiliation and group voting. Short-term forces, such as the law and order issue in 1968 or a candidate's personality, may produce defections of certain groups from their traditional party in presidential elections. And the electoral attraction of incumbency in congressional elections may lead to many traditionally Republican voters supporting a Democratic incumbent and vice versa.[10] But the traditional alliance of certain groups with either the Democratic or the Republican party does help to explain both the stability in party identification and party voting seen in congres-

TABLE 3–4 Group Voting in Two Congressional Elections

	1970		1978	
Group	Percentage Voting Democratic	Percentage Voting Republican	Percentage Voting Democratic	Percentage Voting Republican
Race				
White	52	48	52	48
Nonwhite	83	17	84	16
Religion				
Protestant	48	52	50	50
Catholic	63	37	62	38
Sex				
Men	53	47	53	47
Women	55	45	57	43
Age				
18–29 years	61	39	58	42
30–49 years	55	45	54	46
50 and over	51	49	54	46
Education				
Some College	44	56	46	54
High School	57	43	56	44
Grade School	60	40	70	30

Source: The Gallup Poll, December 17, 1978. The figures are based on personal interviews with 1,564 likely voters out of a total sample of 2,844 adults aged eighteen years and older.

sional elections and the fact that in the five congressional elections in the 1970s the Democratic party won an average 54 percent of the vote.[11]

The affiliation of a group with a particular party would be meaningless unless members of that party consistently sought policies that would favor the group. In spite of the great slack in the American party system and the existence of "wayward freaks" who almost always vote against their party, it is possible to discern a consistent difference between Democratic and Republican policy emphases. More congressional Democrats favor policies providing benefits to the less educated, to the blue-collar worker, and to the city dweller. More congressional Republicans will favor policies benefiting the groups that provide the bulk of G.O.P. support.

The lack of a strong national party organization, however, means that party labels are often misleading as indicators of policy preferences. A Republican, Javits of New York will consistently support policies favorable to traditionally Democratic groups, more often than will Democrats Stennis or Eastland of Mississippi. Being a Republican senator from Connecticut is quite different from being a Republican senator from Florida or California. But if we are to speculate how a voter with little interest in, or information about, politics might cast a rational vote in terms of his or her own interests, the importance of party labels cannot be overlooked. Knowing the party of a congressional candidate requires the expenditure of little or no time or effort by the voter. It provides a cue that enables the individual to vote in his or her own general interests even though the voter may know nothing about the particular candidates running or their policy positions. It is as a cue-giver, rather than as an organization controlling the selection and behavior of legislators, that the political party most directly affects congressional elections.

PARTIES AND LEGISLATORS

When we move from the setting in which a voter makes a decision to that in which a legislator acts, we are struck by obvious differences. The average voter cares little about politics; a legislator's entire life centers around it. While most voters do not have much information on which to base a voting decision, legislators are flooded with information provided on every issue by the press, interest groups, executive agencies, and their own staffs. It would seem, therefore, that the process by which a member of Congress makes up his or her mind about a legislative vote would be quite different from that of the voter in elections. The party cue would not seem to be such a reliable basis for casting a rational vote. The legislator not only has information available, he or she also has a great interest in using this information to cast a knowledgeable vote. The costs of casting uninformed votes are great enough to the legislator to justify his or her assuming the costs of gathering information.

These differences between the citizen's voting decision and the legislator's voting decision seem not so great, however, when we consider the number and scope of decisions legislators must make. A voter makes a political decision every two years; a legislator is constantly called on to make such decisions. In the House alone, the number of roll-call votes increased from 93 in 1958 to 233 in 1968 to 834 in 1978.[12] The introduction of the electronic voting system in the House in 1973 led to an even greater increase than that seen previously. Table 3–5 provides a brief summary of the impact of the electronic voting system in the House and shows how the number of recorded votes also increased in the Senate, although not at the same rate as in the House.

This increase in the number of recorded floor votes represents only a fraction of the total number of decisions that must be made by each representative. Added to this total are the great number of unrecorded decisions the legislator makes on the floor, in committees and subcommittees, in his office, and simply through answering constituent mail. Even decisions about a stand on an issue require some minimal information, which must be supplied by the normal cue sources of party leadership, interest groups, colleagues, and staff.

The scope of these decisions is mind boggling. In its final legislative day on October 15, 1978, the Ninety-fifth Congress dealt with the following subjects: energy legislation, a major tax bill, a full-employment bill, airline deregulation, endangered species legislation, creation of a wilderness area in Minnesota, regulation of

TABLE 3–5 Increase in the Number of Roll-Call Votes

Year	House	Senate	Total
1971	320	423	743
1972	329	532	861
1973	541	594	1,135
1974	537	544	1,081
1975	612	602	1,214
1976	661	668	1,349
1977	706	635	1,341
1978	834	516	1,350

Source: *Congressional Quarterly Weekly Report,* October 21, 1978, p. 2999.

banking practices, maternity coverage for health insurance programs, federal funding of abortions, federal water projects, price supports for sugar, federal aid for middle-income families with college students, aid for elementary and secondary education, federal housing assistance, highway and mass transit funding, school busing, White House staff size, veterans' pensions, meat import quotas, and textile tariff levels.[13] Because of the number and variety of issues that arise, legislators often find themselves in a decisional situation with a low level of information, not unlike the voter. One House member, on his way to the chamber to cast his fourth roll-call vote in about an hour, paused and had this to say about the bill he was to vote on: "I don't know a goddamn thing about the Amateur Sports Act of 1978. So I'll just have to ask someone on the floor. And frankly, I couldn't care less." [14] Two other representatives' comments:

> I have to vote on 150 different kinds of things every year—foreign aid, science, space, technical problems, and the Merchant Marine, and Lord knows what else. I can't possibly become an expert in all these fields.

> It's not uncommon for me to go on the floor with the bells ringing, votes being taken, and it's on a bill or issue that I have never heard of before. I haven't the remotest idea of the issues involved. You've got to make up your mind; you can't vote "maybe" and you can't vote "present"—you don't want to. So you have to make a decision on the best basis you can.[15]

Members of Congress seek to make rational decisions in voting on issues about which they know little. Because of the number and scope of decisions, it is impossible for the legislator to avail her- or himself of the technical information needed to cast an informed, independent vote on the merits of every issue. Two students of Congress, Donald Matthews and James Stimson, have suggested that the normal process of congressional decision-making follows a low-information strategy of seeking cues from fellow members and from limited external sources of information.[16] These cues serve the same function for the legislator as they do for the voter in elections. They permit the decision-maker to make rational voting decisions without having to incur great costs of gathering information. The sources of these cues will vary a great deal from member to member and from issue to issue. They may include state delegations, parties, subject matter experts, the president, those who come from similar districts, and other members with whom the legislator has apolitical, informal ties (such as playing squash or drinking bourbon).

By building a network of cue-givers for different issues, the legislator assures her- or himself of fairly reliable information on how to vote without having to expend a great deal of time and effort arriving at an independent decision. Instead of trying to determine the impact on his or her constituency of a proposed tax reform bill by extensive research on constituency opinion, the legislator may simply follow the advice of a Ways and Means Committee member whose district is similar. A legislator might find it more reasonable to vote with the other members of his or her state delegation than to run the risk of notoriety that comes with being "the only congressman from Illinois to vote against the interests of her citizens."

The most extensive study of the cue network in Congress is that of Matthews and Stimson, done in 1975 and reported in *Yeas and Nays: Normal Decision-Making in the U.S. House of Representatives.* The authors distinguish between two important types of cue-givers: initial and intermediary. The legitimacy of initial cue-givers is based on their technical expertise. This is developed by serving on the committee reporting the bill to be voted on or by tapping the expertise of the executive branch. While there is never much doubt about the reliability of the technical expertise of initial cue-givers, members may sometimes question their underlying value preferences. The second set of cue-givers, the intermediaries, consists of groups of members who have examined the technical information supplied by the initial cue-givers and arrived at a collective decision as to how to vote on the issue at hand. A representative looking to these groups for cues as to how to vote puts trust in the value preferences he or she shares with them and in their having attained some modicum of technical information about the bill from initial cue-givers. In their study, Matthews and Stimson asked members to indicate the sources of information or cues they would turn to when called upon to vote on a matter about which they knew nothing. Table 3–6 shows what they found.

Table 3–6 shows the importance of the political party in the cue network of congressional voting. Even if we write off partisan committee leaders, on the grounds that their basis for serving as a cue-source relies more on the expertise that comes from serving on

TABLE 3–6 The Relative Importance of Cue Sources in the House

Cue-Givers	Number of Mentions	Percentage of All Mentions
Initial		
Chairman of Relevant Committee	34	13
Ranking Minority Member of		
Relevant Committee	29	11
President	35	14
Intermediary		
State Party Delegation	44	18
Party Majority	19	7
Majority of the House	9	4
Democratic Study Group or		
Wednesday Club	32	13
"Conservative Coalition"	12	5
Not Classified a		
Party Leaders	40	16
Total	254	101

a Party leaders are put in the "not classified" category because they play both an initial and an intermediary role as cue-givers.

The data on which this table is based come from interviews with 100 representatives. Members were asked: "Suppose you had to cast a roll-call vote and could know only the position of three of the people or groups on this list?" They were then handed a card that listed ten groups: the majority of the member's state party delegation, the majority of the member's party, the president, the Democratic Study Group, the Wednesday Club (the conservative Republican equivalent of the liberal DSG), the "Conservative Coalition," the chairman of the reporting committee, the majority of all members, and the leadership of the member's party. Not all members chose to list a total of three of these groups; that is why the total number of mentions is 254 rather than 300.

Source: Donald Matthews and James Stimson, *Yeas and Nays: Normal Decision-Making in the U.S. House of Representatives* (John Wiley and Sons, 1975), p. 94. Copyright © 1975 John Wiley and Sons, Inc., reprinted by permission.

the committee than it does on party differences, we find that the legislative party occupies a dominant position in the legislative cue network. The most frequently cited sources of cues are colleagues from the member's party who come from his or her state and congressional party leaders. If we combine the three party cue sources (state party delegation, party majority, and party leaders), we find that 41 percent of the total cue sources cited by members of Congress are party ones. Matthews and Stimson looked at initial cue sources in greater detail and concluded that party leaders represent the single most important source of initial cues for members involved in a low-information decision.[17]

It is clear that the political party occupies a central position in the cue-seeking network within Congress. This influence is achieved both through the party leadership's control over certain kinds of information (such as the number of pro and con voters on an issue before it comes to the floor) and through the attachment the legislator has to the party label. The impact of party leadership and the party organization as an intelligence network will be discussed below. Here we are more interested in the way the party acts as a cue for the legislator's vote.

Members of Congress indicate a desire to support their party even when other pressures, such as constituency opinion or ideology, lead them to oppose their party in floor votes. A survey by Randall Ripley in the Eighty-eighth Congress found 94 percent of the Democratic representatives interviewed and 96 percent of the Republicans responding affirmatively to the question: "Do you want to act in accord with your party's position?" Seventy-four percent of the Democrats and 72 percent of the Republicans indicated that this was generally their first consideration in determining their position.[18]

The impact of party as a major cue source is reflected in voting on the floor. Numerous studies of roll-call votes in Congress have found that party is the single most important predictor of roll-call behavior.[19] Studies by the *Congressional Quarterly Weekly Report* throughout the 1970s consistently measured both the incidence of partisan voting in Congress (defined as votes in which a majority of one party is arrayed against a majority of the other) and party loyalty (defined as the percentage of the time the average Democrat and Republican voted with his or her party majority in partisan votes). Although the 1978 figures showed a slight decline in both the incidence of party voting and the average member's party loyalty, the percentages for party loyalty demonstrate the importance of party as a cue source on roll-call votes. For Congress as a whole, the average Democratic member voted with the party on 64 percent of the partisan votes, and the average Republican member voted with the party on 67 percent of the partisan votes.[20]

An extensive study of roll-call votes over fourteen years found that the importance of the party cue varies from issue to issue. Conducted by political scientist Aage Clausen, the study covered the years 1953–1964 and (to check whether those earlier years were atypical) the years 1969–1970. Clausen found that there were five general policy dimensions along which legislators were arrayed in terms of their roll-call voting behavior. These five dimensions, which included a wide range of specific issues and roll-call votes, were civil liberties, international involvement, social welfare, agricultural assistance, and government management. The study showed that the member's political party was basically irrelevant to his or her position on issues of civil liberties and international involvement, while it was a relatively strong indication of how the member would vote on social welfare, agricultural assistance, and government management issues.[21] Issues relating to government management—such as government ownership and/or regulation of economic enterprises, spending on public works as opposed to private business incentives, public versus private development of natural resources, business regulation, distribution of the tax burden, interest rates, and a balanced budget—were found to be those that most clearly differentiated congressional members of the two parties. It would be incorrect to say that a legislator's party identification always signals how he or she will vote on every issue. Clausen's study clearly showed that the importance of party varied from issue to issue. The underlying importance of the issues raised by the government management dimension and the fact that party is found to be such an important determinant of voting on that dimension tend to reinforce the importance of the party cue for congressional voting.

More recently, a study by Jerrold Schneider of ideological coalitions in Congress during the 1970s found a great deal of consistency in members' voting on foreign policy, economic policy, racial policy, and civil liberties issues. Schneider's findings portray a Congress that is much more regularly ideological than the pluralist picture of shifting coalitions described by earlier voting studies. Although the impact of parties on congressional voting was not a major concern in this study, the author does note that "the ideological character of congressional parties, or factions within them, was implicitly confirmed by the findings of this study." [22]

The Clausen study fits in with other studies of roll-call voting in Congress that suggest party is an important component of the individual legislator's decision but that the influence of party identification will vary from issue to issue and will also be affected by the nature of procedural matters attending the voting process.

Most of these studies indicate that in the absence of strong pressures from constituency or from committee leadership, the average legislator is predisposed to support his or her party's position on issues. The party cue becomes less important when the party position runs counter to the legislator's own electoral or ideological interests. A study of Democratic party leadership in the House by Lewis Froman and Randall Ripley outlines six conditions that help to create a situation in which most legislators will follow their party's leadership.[23]

1. *Party leadership is committed and active.* By terming a particular issue a party vote, by disseminating information as to the importance of the vote through the interpersonal cue-giving networks, and by polling legislators so as to gain information and a commitment, the legislative party leaders can make it more difficult for a member of Congress to vote against his or her party.

2. *The issue is procedural rather than substantive.* Parties achieve their greatest cohesion on the most procedural measures such as the election of a Speaker and the greatest number of defections on narrowly substantive measures such as votes on conference committee reports and amendments to bills.

3. *The visibility of the issue is low.* The more complex an issue and the less play it gets in the news media, the more likely it is to produce a vote along partisan lines. This is a direct result of the fact that members of Congress are more likely to support their party position in the absence of strong conflicting pressures. The complexity and low visibility of an issue reduce these outside pressures.

4. *The visibility of the action is low.* The most visible type of activity, roll-call votes on the floor, produces the greatest number of party defections. Voice votes, division votes, and unrecorded teller votes generally produce more cohesive partisan voting patterns. This results from the fact that legislators may support their party against conflicting pressures when it is unlikely that those agents urging a defection from the party will be aware of how the legislator voted.

5. *There is little counterpressure from constituencies.* While the average northern Democrat in the Senate supported the Democratic party on 75 percent of the roll-call votes in 1978, the average

southern Democratic senator supported the party on only 48 percent of these votes. The same pattern held in the House, with northern Democrats supporting their party on 71 percent of the votes, and southern Democrats supporting it on 46 percent of the votes.[24] The low party support by southern legislators is generally explained by their coming from constituencies different from those of the northern Democrats. Indeed, most deviations in party votes are explained in terms of constituency factors.

Lewis Froman suggests that differences between northern Democrats and northern Republicans are a function not just of party but also of the different types of constituencies they represent. Looking at such variables as percentage owner-occupied dwellings, percentage nonwhite population, average population per square mile, and percentage urban, Froman found that Democrats tended to represent constituencies that were more urban, were more racially mixed, had a lower percentage of owner-occupied dwellings, and had more people per square mile than Republican constituencies.[25] In supporting the programs of Democratic presidents, these northern Democrats were able to represent their constituents best. Table 3–3 shows these differences in constituency characteristics for the Ninety-third Congress.

A legislator's party interests and constituency interests are not always the same, and when they are different, much deviation in party voting occurs. Republicans in both the House and the Senate who had the lowest party loyalty scores for 1978 came primarily from northeastern states and districts with high urban populations. Democrats with the lowest party unity scores for the same period came primarily from southern states and districts with a low proportion of urban constituents.[26] To support consistently their party positions in Congress, these legislators would have had to go against what they considered the interests of their constituencies and would thus have risked electoral defeat. The legislative party is more likely to receive support on issues in which there is no conflict between constituency interests and party interests.

6. *State delegations are not engaged in collective bargaining.* Members of Congress from the same party and the same state are an important reference group for legislators. State delegations are a primary socializing agency for freshmen legislators and continue to play an important cue-giving role throughout their tenure in the legislature. Voting in line with party colleagues from the same state provides a member with an automatic rationalization for his

vote. He need only point out to those who challenge his position that every member of his party from his state voted the same way. By acting in unison the state delegation can be an effective bargaining agent in winning concessions from the party leadership. The party leadership may be forced to meet the demands of a state delegation in return for needed votes.

As a potent source of cues conflicting with the legislative party, then, the state delegations may weaken the effectiveness of the party in much the same way that constituencies do. About half of the state delegations in the House meet on a regular basis and seek unified issue positions. This represents about half of the total membership of the House. Roll-call analyses show that state delegations are most influential on two quite different sorts of issues: "tough questions, controversial both within the party and within the House," and "matters of trivial or purely local importance." [27] The party's strength as a cue-giver is greatly enhanced when state delegations either have been co-opted to support the party leadership position or are not separated from the party position on the issue.

The congressional party, then, is most correctly conceived as an effective source of voting cues within a complex network of competing cue sources. At times, the constituency cue or state delegation cue will be more important in determining the legislator's vote. But in a great number of issues voted on, the party is one of the most consistent sources of legislative cues. This helps to explain its importance in determining legislative outcomes in spite of its lack of a cohesive national and legislative organization.

PARTY ORGANIZATION

This is that part of any book on Congress that usually presents amusing anecdotes about Lyndon Johnson's prowess as Senate majority leader in the 1950s or the backroom techniques of power employed by Speaker Sam Rayburn during his seventeen-year reign in the House. Discussions of this sort are often instructive in terms of highlighting the possibilities available to party leaders seeking to maximize their hold over the legislative process. But times change, and Congress changes, and the old stories no longer portray an accurate picture of party leadership and its impact on the congressional process. Not only has there been a change in the personalities running the party organization but there has also been a great change in the institutional setting. Party leaders in both chambers face a much more decentralized and individualistic membership structure than that of the Johnson and Rayburn days. Even the strong party leaders who assumed control in 1977, House Speaker Thomas P. (Tip) O'Neill and Senate majority leader Robert Byrd, now talk more about the limits on congressional leadership than about restoring the power of party leaders to what it was in the 1950s. This section will outline the structure of the party organizations in the House and the Senate, with particular emphasis on the Democratic organization, which as the majority party has organized both chambers over the past two decades.

House Leadership

The four key elements of the Democratic organization in the House of Representatives are the Speaker, the whip organization, the Democratic Steering and Policy Committee, and the House Democratic caucus. The Republican equivalents, who are charged with organizing the opposition rather than the business of the House, are the minority leader, the Republican whip organization, the Policy Committee, and the Republican Conference.

When Congressman Tip O'Neill was elected Speaker in 1977, he followed six years of what most members considered to be the weak leadership of Speaker Carl Albert.[28] O'Neill's election came at a time when the office of Speaker had been strengthened by a series of reforms designed to correct what many saw as a leaderless House. The changes brought by O'Neill's leadership of the Ninety-fifth Congress led one observer to comment that the trains now run on time but that sometimes it is hard to know where they are going.[29] Just getting the trains to run on time, organizing the House so that it operates on a regular schedule, is the result of a strong personality exercising the new powers granted to the Speaker by the reforms that began in 1973. Even with these powers, however, the contemporary Speaker is unable to impose party loyalty on members who feel that they owe the party little or nothing.

Specific reforms that have increased the powers of the Speaker include two reforms of 1973 that made the Speaker the chairperson of the Committee on Committees and created a new Steering and Policy Committee, in which ten of twenty-four members are appointed by the Speaker. In 1975, the Speaker's discretion in referring bills to committee was broadened by permitting him or her to send a bill to two or more committees concurrently or sequentially, to divide a bill and send different sections to different committees, to create ad hoc committees for considering a particular matter, and to set time limits on committee consideration of a bill. Also, in the Ninety-fourth Congress (1975–1976), the Speaker was given the power to nominate Democratic members and the chairperson of the House Rules Committee, and the Democratic Steering and Policy Committee was given the power to make all committee appointments. The Ninety-fifth and Ninety-sixth Congresses (1977–1978 and 1979–1980) saw a continuation of this trend toward a stronger Speaker in a number of procedural rules changes that made it easier for the leadership to control floor proceedings and prevent delaying actions by the minority. All of these centralizing reforms have given the modern Speaker a wide range of tools for exercising party leadership, but they in no way guarantee success. Even after fervent pleas for support by Speaker O'Neill in May, 1979, for example, the leadership lost crucial votes on a standby gasoline rationing plan and an initial budget resolution when 106 of the 258 House Democrats in the first instance and 152 of the 258 House Democrats in the second instance voted against their party leaders.

The Democratic whip organization is presided over by the House majority whip who, like the Speaker and the majority leader, is elected by all of the Democratic House members who together constitute the Democratic caucus. The majority whip is one of the three top officials in the House. Also included in the whip organization are one chief deputy whip, three deputy whips, ten at-large whips, and twenty-two zone whips. The zone whips are elected by Democratic members from the geographic area included in a particular zone, while the deputy and at-large whips are chosen by the Democratic leadership (Speaker, majority leader, and majority whip). The primary function of the whip organization is the collection and dissemination of information relevant to floor consideration of a bill. The whip organization disseminates information by issuing whip notices, which summarize the major issues involved, on all important bills and by informing all Democratic members of the upcoming legislative schedule. The collection of information is conducted primarily by the zone whips through whip checks in which all Democratic members are asked "Will you vote for" the bill that is scheduled for floor consideration. This tally is then used as a guide by party leaders in their attempts to persuade enough members to support the party position.[30]

The Democratic Steering and Policy Committee was created as part of the broad reforms adopted in 1973. The Committee has twenty-four members: the Speaker, majority leader, majority whip, chief deputy whip, three deputy whips, chairperson of the Democratic caucus, four at-large members appointed by the Speaker, and twelve members selected by regional caucuses. The Speaker acts as chairperson and, as mentioned earlier, accounts for ten of the twenty-four members of the committee. While the Speaker obviously will have a great impact on Steering and Policy Committee decisions, the Committee is intended to function not simply as an extension of the Speaker but rather as an independent and representative formulator of party policy. Calling this committee "the key to the success of the overall move to party government," one political scientist said that the Steering and Policy Committee "provides the best arena in which the spirit of party cooperation and a representative direction to party efforts can be fashioned, while at the same time constraining and guiding the Speaker." [31] Beginning with the Ninety-sixth Congress (1979–1980), the Democratic Steering and Policy Committee put more effort into the earlier stages of legislation than it had previously by working with subcommittees and committees in the formulative stages of legislation. In addition to its policy role, the Democratic Steering and Policy Committee serves as the Democratic Committee on Committees, a function it was given in 1975. These committee assignment decisions, however, must be ratified by the House Democratic caucus.

The House Democratic caucus is made up of all Democratic representatives meeting as a group to discuss procedural matters such as reviewing committee assignments, voting on committee chairpersons, electing party leaders, and recommending changes in House rules and procedures. Unlike the Steering and Policy Committee, the caucus is supposed to concern itself with procedural rather than policy matters. As we shall see, however, this is not always the case.

During the 1970s the Democratic caucus emerged as a major force in the House both as an instigator of sweeping reforms that changed the structure of the House and as an important check on theretofore independent committee chairpersons. Two rules adopted in 1969, one requiring monthly caucus meetings and the other giving any member the right to bring an issue before the caucus for debate and possible resolution of a policy position, laid the ground-work for this development. Reforms in 1971 and 1973 gave the caucus the power to review nominations for committee chairpersons coming from the Committee on Committees, and in 1975 the caucus deposed the chairmen of three major committees. This influence over the committee system gives the caucus an obvious, but indirect, toehold in the policy process. A more direct policy rule was exercised by the caucus when it instructed the Rules Committee to permit a House vote on the oil depletion allowance in 1975 and passed a resolution opposing military aid to Cambodia and Vietnam in the same year. The strong negative reaction of both policy opponents and the House leadership to these caucus policy votes led to the caucus backing off from its new policy role. It did not have another direct vote on a policy matter until 1978, when it passed a resolution opposing a Social Security tax increase.[32] While the caucus continues to be an important element of House deliberations, the emergence of an activist, responsive Democratic leadership under Speaker O'Neill has somewhat diminished the role of the caucus as the only instrument available to House progressives and reformers as it was seen in the early 1970s.

The structure of the Republican organization in the House roughly parallels that of the Democrats. The official House Republican leaders in the Ninety-sixth Congress (1979–1980) are the chairman of the Conference, vice-chairman of the Conference, secretary of the Conference, floor leader, whip, and chief deputy whip. In addition to these officers, the chairpersons of the Policy Committee and the Research Committee and the ranking minority member of the House Rules Committee can be said to be important figures in the House Republican leadership. The more diffused structure of the House Republican leadership fits well with what is perceived to be its most important function: to maximize representational values and to develop alternatives to Democratic legislative proposals. This function has consistently led to Republican opposition of those House procedural reforms designed to facilitate lawmaking and to their seeking full debate and representation in policy development. Their minority status for the last quarter century obviously has limited the ability of House Republicans to affect congressional lawmaking, but their advocacy of full representation does prevent members from forgetting that lawmaking is not the only function of Congress.

Senate Leadership

A membership of 100 rather than 435 makes a big difference in the structure of party leadership in the Senate. The fact that an estimated 10 percent of all senators at any given time are seriously pursuing higher office in the form of the presidency or vice-presidency means that a large number of them are more interested in leading than they are in being led.[33] These differences in size and members' goals help to account for the Senate party leadership's being a smaller, more informal, more collegial structure than that of the House. The key elements of the Senate party leadership are the majority leader or floor leader, the majority whip and assistant whips, the party Conference (which includes all senators of that party), the Policy Committee, and the Steering Committee. Except for the lack of a Steering Committee, the structure of the minority party is the same as that of the majority (there is a Republican Steering Committee, but it is a coalition of conservative Republican senators organized on ideological grounds rather than a part of the formal party structure). Although this discussion, like the preceding one, will focus on Democrats because of their long-standing majority status, the much closer party split in the Senate (59 Democrats and 41 Republicans after the 1978 election) means that the Democrats' maintaining the majority in the Senate throughout the 1980s is not nearly the sure thing that it seems to be in the House.

The majority leader in the Senate might be considered the equivalent of the House Speaker in the sense that they both are responsible for controlling floor proceedings. The Senate majority leader, however, is not a constitutional officer as the Speaker is, nor does he or she preside over the Senate. The majority leader serves as chairperson of both the Policy Committee, which is responsible for scheduling legislation, and the Steering Committee, which is responsible for majority committee assignments. The ascendancy of Senator Robert Byrd to the majority leader's position in 1977 showed certain parallels to Congressman Tip O'Neill's becoming House Speaker the same year. Byrd, like O'Neill, showed a concern for strengthening the lawmaking abilities of Congress after a period when leaders in both chambers seemed to stress representational values. Senator Byrd's success in 1979 in getting the Senate to change its filibuster rule, discussed in Chapter 1, is one indication of this commitment to lawmaking.

While many parts of the Senate's party leadership correspond to those of the House's party leadership in either name or function, this does not mean that they are of the same importance in both chambers. Although the majority whip in the Senate is an important member of the collegial group running that chamber, the Senate whip organization is very much a staff operation; the Senate leaders themselves rely more on their informal contacts with members for the same information that in the House is gathered through the whip structure. The Steering Committee, chaired by the majority leader, makes committee assignments, but Senate leaders have far less control over members' committee assignments than House leaders do.[34]

As Senator Byrd's emphasis on changing the filibuster rule indicates, the major responsibility of party leadership in the Senate is to control the floor. This necessitates the majority leader's working through the Policy Committee and the minority leadership to schedule floor consideration of legislation in a way that gives all senators the opportunity to speak and vote yet does not turn the Senate into a debating society that never produces legislation.

Party Leadership

The primary responsibility of party leaders and the chief function of the party organization in both the House and the Senate is to see that policy proposals favored by the majority party are passed by Congress. To achieve that goal, the party organization must first organize both party mechanisms and the chamber as a whole so that it is capable of conducting its legislative business. Once organized, the party leadership's major functions are gathering and disseminating information relevant to the policies under consideration, scheduling the business of the House and the Senate, and controlling the floor proceedings of both chambers. Party leaders in both the House and the Senate have gone about meeting these responsibilities in a variety of ways. Underlying this great variety is the fact that any party leader has an established source of resources from which he or she can draw in order to bring forth party programs in the legislative process. All party leaders dip from this same pool of resources, but the specific techniques of leadership that party leaders employ depend upon widely varying factors such as personalities, the legislative structure as changed and shaped by reforms, the party occupying the White House, and the general political climate. Rather than going through a long list of party leadership techniques and cases illustrating such techniques, let us close this section with a quick look at the general sources of leadership party leaders have at their disposal as they attempt to provide some centralizing force and reliable cue network in Congress.

Randall Ripley, one of the leading scholars of the role of political party leadership in Congress, suggests that all successful tactical maneuvers and leadership ploys are connected to four basic sources of party leadership influence. These four resources are the leaders' ability to use congressional rules to their own advantage because of their expertise in such matters; the power to bestow or withhold tangible rewards such as appointments to special committees and commissions, office space, and material support for reelection campaigns; the ability to affect an individual member's standing in the informal and unstated hierarchy in each chamber and thereby determine his or her position in the cue network of that chamber; and control over the intelligence and communications network in Congress.[35] Structural reforms in recent congresses, the personal style of elected leaders, and the political variables related to the larger political system all affect the relative importance of each of these resources. But taken together, these four sources of power represent a stable base from which all party leaders draw whatever influence they have over the legislative process.

A quick rundown of the impact of these resources on congressional behavior includes the following observations. The first resource (ability to use rules effectively) works primarily to the advantage of the majority party. The minority party leadership can employ chamber rules to obstruct passage of unwanted legislation, but the majority party—because it has total control over scheduling (i.e., when and under what conditions a bill will be brought to the floor)—can exercise great influence in pushing legislation safely through Congress. This is particularly true in the House. Structural controls over the floor are more important there. The rules in the House facilitate quick passage of noncontroversial legislation under procedures such as "suspension," which are designed to maximize the lawmaking function and thus enhance the party leaders' control over the floor proceedings. My emphasis on majority party leadership rather than on the activities of minority leaders reflects the inherent advantage the majority party enjoys in the use of congressional rules to provide an essential centralizing force.

The remaining three sources of leadership power (control over tangible rewards, ability to affect each member's informal position, and control over the communications network internal to Congress) have all been affected by sweeping reforms that took place in the

1970s. When it comes to horse trading, party leaders find that they have little of the control over dispensing the tangible rewards, such as a public works project or guaranteed passage of a program designed to help particular states or districts, that they had prior to the reforms of the 1970s. "You have a hunting license to persuade—that's about all you have," is the way House majority leader Jim Wright described the situation in a recent interview.[86] This persuasion can be facilitated by a party leader's promise of assistance in gaining a sought after committee assignment or of scheduling help to move along a member's bill, but what strikes most observers of the modern Congress are the limited resources for horse trading that party leaders now have.

The party reforms brought about in the last decade can be said to have cut in two directions. First, they enhanced the potential power of the party leadership by seriously cutting down challenges to leadership control that had existed for so long in the form of the independent committee leadership system. Second, the reforms opened up the congressional process, greatly reducing the number of decisional arenas in which party leaders were able to gain compliance because members were not subject to counterpressures from constituency and lobbying groups. The balance of power created by these reforms seems, on the whole, to have strengthened party leadership. This was done chiefly by reducing the influence of the independent committee leaders. But the nature of party leadership in the new system is one that must rely more than ever on cooperation and consensus rather than on a system of centralized control over tangible rewards that permits party leaders to manipulate individual members. Successful party leadership can still act as a powerful centralizing force in the Congress. The basis of such leadership, given the many reforms of the 1970s, is closely tied to recognizing and respecting the representational functions of Congress.

Political parties provide a centralizing force in helping Congress to carry out its lawmaking and representation functions. Let us now turn to another congressional structure that contributes to the lawmaking function, the congressional staff.

CONGRESSIONAL STAFFS

A close observer of the Washington scene once noted:

> Someday a U.S. congressman will vanish from this town and nobody will know it. The congressman will still deliver speeches for the

Congressional Record; he will still be quoted on the evening news; his mail will be answered, his views made known, his legislation introduced and his coffee poured. But he will be gone, laughing from a gazebo on the Rhone or testing the waters off the Bahamas. . . .

The Fifth Estate is what makes such a happening quite possible. There are only 535 senators and representatives, but the Fifth Estate consists of the more than 30,000 people whom they employ. First, there are the aides or assistants, 10 to 30 of them depending upon the legislator's committee assignments and his personal wealth. Then there are the office workers, letter-writers, secretaries, memo readers and campaign staffers. The several dozen congressional committees have staffs of up to 40 each.

This commentator states that some congressmen show up in Washington as rarely as possible, and most of them spend Mondays or Fridays at home. "Meantime, their speeches are inserted in the record, their committee votes made by proxy, and press assistants see to it that they are quoted on public issues just as though they were in their offices." [37] While admitting that the congressional staffers making up this "Fifth Estate" do play important roles in the complex political and congressional system, the columnist quoted above sees a bit of irony in the fact that the recent and rapid expansion in the size of this congressional bureaucracy has come at a time when most members of Congress are denouncing the growth in the federal government bureaucracy in general.

There is a great deal of variation from office to office and from committee to committee in the roles played by congressional staff. Some critics of this huge congressional bureaucracy suggest that its sheer massiveness does more to create problems for congressional decision-making than it does to aid legislators in those decisions. "Everybody is working for the staff, staff, staff; driving you nutty. In fact, they have hearings for me all of this week," complained one senator. A colleague of his agreed: "If we would fire half the Senate employees we have, fire half the staff and not permit a paper to be read on the floor of the U.S. Senate, we would complete our business and adjourn by July 4th. When you get more staff and more clerks they spend most of their time thinking up bills, resolutions, amendments. They write speeches for Senators, and they come in here on the floor with Senators. Unanimous consents are obtained for so-and-so to sit. He is there prodding, telling the Senator how to spend more money." [38] Other students of the legislative process, however, suggest that the expanded size of congressional staffs has greatly improved the ability of Congress to function in an increasingly complex world. Two political scientists who conducted an extensive study of congressional staffs in the 1970s had this to say about the importance of staff to the congressional process:

> Our contention is that staffs perform much of the congressional work: They perform almost exclusively the constituent-service function; do most of the preliminary legislative research; help generate policy ideas; set up hearings, meetings, and conferences; carry out oversight activities—program evaluations, investigations, etc.; draft bills; and meet and talk with executive, interest, and constituent groups on substantive matters.[39]

Whatever their positions on the matter, all students of Congress can agree on the fact that there has been a tremendous growth in the size of this Fifth Estate over the last decade. This fact is sharply brought home to the thousands of college students who volunteer to work in congressional offices *(for free)* during school vacations. The students are told that there is no room for them because the paid staff and limited numbers of interns occupy every inch of office space available to that particular member. Experienced civil servants and political scientists taking part in various fellowship programs that provide free labor to congressional offices and committee staffs are similarly shocked to discover that their long experience and impressive resumes do not automatically lead to their being welcomed with open arms. There is simply no office space for them, and for the most part the regular staff adequately covers all policy areas of interest to the legislator or committee member.[40] Table 3–7 provides a graphic summary of the growth in congressional staff from 1930 to 1978.

The increases reflected in Table 3–7 are seen in other measures of the growing congressional bureaucracy. Between 1970 and 1975 consumer prices rose by 39 percent. During that same period Congress increased staff salaries by 71 percent, stationery allowances by 116 percent, and allowances for renting district office space by 275 percent. Appropriations for simple operations of the congressional branches (excluding joint committees, the Capitol architect, and similar operations) came to $102 million in 1966, to $171 million in 1971, and to $325 million in 1976.[41] In 1979, this figure was $491 million, out of a total $1.12 billion for all legislative appropriations.[42]

By any sort of measure, it is clear that the congressional bu-

TABLE 3–7 Number of Congressional Staff Members, 1930–1978

Year	Senate Committee	Senate Personal	House Committee	House Personal
1930	163	280	112	870
1935	172	424	122	870
1947	290	590	193	1,440
1957	558	1,115	375	2,441
1967	621	1,749	589	4,055
1972	918	2,426	783	5,280
1976	1,534	3,251	1,548	6,939
1978	1,612	5,248	2,453	7,346

Source: The 1978 figures are from the *Report of the Secretary of the Senate,* Ninety-fifth Congress, second session, November 21, 1978, and from the clerk-hire payroll for a selected month, U.S. House of Representatives, Office of the Clerk of the House, 1978. The figures for earlier years are from Harrison W. Fox, Jr., and Susan Webb Hammond, *Congressional Staffs: The Invisible Force in American Lawmaking* (Free Press, 1977), appendix, p. 171.

reaucracy has greatly increased. The question is: What do all of those people do? Some critics of the role of the congressional staff suggest that too much staff time is directed toward campaigning and reelection efforts and that public money is really being spent in shoring up the advantages of incumbents in their reelection efforts. Certainly, the advantages of incumbency discussed in the previous chapter include staff allowances, free mailing, and district offices. In response to criticism about incumbents using staff and mailing allowances for reelection purposes, however, Congress voted in 1977 to ban the use of free mailings during the sixty days preceding a primary or general election. One effect of this was that the House folding room, which distributes these newsletters and other mass mailings for incumbents, had to add more staff members to handle the big rush in mailings before the sixty-day deadline in the election year 1978.[43] While electoral challengers and critics of Congress decry use of staff, public funds, and other resources by incumbents for what seem to be campaign purposes, defenders of the system point out that what others call campaigning is really a part of the legislator's job as representative and handler of constituent prob-

TABLE 3–8 Increasing Use of District Offices

Parameter	1960	1967	1974	1977
Percentage of total House personal staff members assigned to district offices	14	26	34	40
Percentage of House members with more than one district office	4	18	47	61

Source: The 1977 figures are from the June, 1977, survey by the House Commission on Administrative Review, reported in U.S. Congress, House, *Administrative Reorganization and Legislative Management, Commission on Administrative Review,* Ninety-fifth Congress, first session, September 28, 1977, and from the *Congressional Staff Directory, 1977.* Earlier figures are from Morris P. Fiorina, *Congress: Keystone of the Washington Establishment* (Yale University Press, 1977), p. 58.

lems. One measure of the district orientation of congressional staffs is the increasing percentage of the total staff that is located in the home district rather than in Washington. Table 3–8 shows this increase for House staffs since 1960.

Looking at the pattern shown in Table 3–8, one can see different things. Certainly, the increasing importance of the legislator as ombudsman, a trend discussed in Chapter 1, is reflected in the increasing proportion of House staff that is allocated to district offices. For it is the district office rather than the Washington office that is responsible for the bulk of the casework handled by most members' offices. One congressional staffer sees in this outflow of staff from Washington to the district a purpose that is directed more toward the reelection campaign than it is toward the objective handling of casework: "Everyone who's running has guys in his state office working on politics during his campaign—and not just during the campaign, but all year round, every year, all the time, for crying out loud." [44] The expanded allowances for district and state offices and for staff clearly provide one answer to the question of what this growing number of congressional staff members do— they help to reelect incumbents.

Our attention is now directed to the Washington-based staff, and the question is again asked: What do they do? Even with this

Washington focus, one is struck by how much of the congressional staff activity is oriented toward constituency casework or legislative solutions to problems that arise from the requests or demands of individual constituents. One reason given for the great increase in congressional staffs is the fact that more and more citizens are calling on their representatives in Congress for solutions to their own problems stemming from current government policy. A rough measure of this phenomenon is provided by the volume of mail received by members of Congress. One study showed that the amount of mail received by House members increased from about 14 million letters in 1971 to 43 million letters in 1975, or about 32,000 letters per office every year.[45] Members estimate that their casework load has doubled in the last ten years. A survey in 1977 by the House Commission on Administrative Review found that the average workload in a member's office was 10,000 constituent cases a year.[46]

A number of studies of congressional staffs have measured the relative importance of staff activities related to legislation and staff activities related to representation and constituent casework. John Saloma's study of the Eighty-ninth Congress (1965–1966) found that about 41 percent of the average staff work week was devoted to answering the mail, 25 percent to constituent service, and 14 percent to legislative activities.[47] In 1977, the House Commission on Administrative Review found a similar pattern of emphasis on constituent service. The average House office had just under sixteen employees. Of these, four were caseworkers, three were clerical workers, two were office supervisers, two were legislative researchers, one a legislative correspondent, one a communications specialist, and one a personal secretary.[48] Another study, published in 1977, found that professional staff members in Senate offices, most of whom were hired to perform legislative duties, also devoted a great deal of their time to constituency service such as federal projects and casework.[49] Taken together, these studies suggest that the bulk of the work done by congressional staffs in members' offices has more to do with assisting the representative or senator to perform representational duties than it does with assisting a member in lawmaking activities.

The fact that so much of the work of congressional staffs is constituency-oriented should not lead us to ignore the legislative or lawmaking functions, which staff members also perform. As Table 3–7 indicates, the growth in committee staffs accounts for a great deal of the overall increase in congressional staffs shown in that

table. The work of committee staff members—doing legislative research, scheduling hearings, and assisting members in drafting legislation—is obviously directed to assisting members to perform their
lawmaking function. In addition, when one looks closely at the increase in staff positions on members' personal staffs, one finds that
the greatest increase has come in the number of aides performing
legislative work or who, at least, have a job title such as legislative
assistant or legislative aide.[50]

On the basis of this increase in the number of legislative aides,
we would expect to find that legislators depend a great deal on staff
members for information relevant to lawmaking. A study done in
1969 by Donald Matthews and James Stimson, however, found that
legislators relied on their individual staffs only occasionally for legislative cues. Close to 30 percent of those interviewed said that they
never relied on staff for legislative research tasks. The authors cite
as typical the remarks of one congressman:

> We have a staff meeting and at that time my legislative assistant
> will report on the legislation that is coming up in the week, and
> will give a brief description of it. In all candor I must say that this
> does not often influence my thinking on the bill.
>
> If it hasn't come up at our (state party delegation) breakfast,
> I'll run to a guy on the floor just about the time the bill is being
> considered and say, "Hey, what is this all about and what does it
> do?" And frequently we'll check with the doorkeeper—who has a
> pipeline into the leadership and into those committee members who
> are responsible for it.
>
> I'd much rather be able to answer that my staff thoroughly briefs
> briefs me on pros and cons in the quiet of my office, and that's how
> I make up my mind, but that is not true. I think that is really
> natural. A staff member is reading the cold lifeless reports. They
> have not been exposed to the various pressure groups or the "gut"
> arguments for or against something. I think the congressman himself
> involved in that area, who's been on the firing line, can give you a
> much better capsule than the more isolated staff man.[51]

A more recent study of House members gives us a quite different
picture. In 1977, the Commission on Administrative Review sur-
veyed 151 House members and asked the questions: "Where do
you turn to get what you need to know to handle your committee
work—who do you really rely on for this kind of information?";
"Where do you turn to get what you need to know to vote on the

floor on bills which don't come through one of the committees on which you sit?"; and "Where do you turn to get what you need to know to be knowledgeable about public issues and policies about which you, as a public person, are expected to be knowledgeable?" Members' responses covered a wide range of information sources, including personal and committee staff, executive agencies, party groups, colleagues, congressional support agencies (such as the Congressional Research Service and the Congressional Budget Office), interest groups and lobbyists, sources in the district, personal reading and study, and universities and private research groups. The information source that was listed by members more than any other, however, was the congressional staff. Sixty percent of the members mentioned personal staff, and 61 percent mentioned committee staff in response to the first question (committee work); 57 percent of the members mentioned personal office staff in response to the second question (bills from other committees); and 49 percent of the members mentioned personal staff in response to the third question (public issues).[52] For all of these issue areas, then, the congressional staffs were found to be the single most important source of information relevant to legislators' performing their lawmaking duties.

While recognizing that a great part of the work done by the expanded congressional bureaucracy is geared toward district and constituency problems, we should not lose sight of the important legislative support role that is played by committee and personal staffs. We should also recognize that it is difficult to draw clear-cut lines between what is a legislative support activity and what is a constituency service or correspondence function. Letters coming in complaining about the same problem are routinely answered by the staff. But in the act of answering those letters, staff members are going to dig into that problem and convey to the member the fact that a lot of letters have been coming in concerning that matter. Most likely, they will be in a position to offer some advice as to possible legislative action to correct the problem. The bulk of time spent in such a case might quite naturally be regarded as constituency service or correspondence, yet there is certainly a legislative offshoot—both in the fact that staff members have acquired some knowledge in that particular area that might be useful at a later time to the member and in the fact that the legislator has been alerted that there exists a problem area that might be subject to legislative solution. The point here is that much of the legislative staff activity does have an overall effect on the lawmaking capabilities of members of Congress.

We have been discussing legislative staffs in this section by focusing primarily on the role of personal staffs of House members. This focus has been at least partially a result of the focus of existing studies on congressional staffs. Within the general category of legislative staffs there is a great deal of variety. Committee staffs in both the House and the Senate tend to be more professional and to have a longer tenure than do personal staffs of individual members. The same sort of differences in longevity of staff exist between personal House staffs and personal Senate staffs. There is a changeable but fairly clear hierarchy among committee, subcommittee, and personal member staffs within and between the two chambers.

Differences between staffs of the two chambers were summed up in the following comment by a Senate staff member: "Staff on the Senate side are more pompous than those on the House side. You have a system of layers here—the Senators only talk to Senators, the administrative assistants to administrative assistants, the legislative assistants to legislative assistants, etc. On the House side, you find out what was going on in forty-five minutes by going from group to group in the cafeteria. Over here, I go down to the cafeteria and eat alone." [53] Within each chamber there is a similar hierarchy, or system of layers, extending down from full committee staff to subcommittee staffs to individual staffs.

Perhaps the best way to understand this hierarchy among different staff levels and to close in on the answer to the question of what congressional staffs do is to conceptualize the legislative system as a communications network. We did this earlier in looking at the party cue within this network. Contrary to popular notions about the limited or inferior information systems available to Congress (especially when compared with those available to executive agencies), both legislative committees and individual members of Congress are continually bombarded with information. Constituents, interest groups, executive agencies, legislative colleagues, congressional committees, the news media, and legislative support systems such as the Congressional Research Service, the General Accounting Office, and special legislative committees or commissions provide a constant source of information on every legislative topic.

The problem faced by individual legislators is generally not one of obtaining enough information but rather one of filtering out information not relevant to the immediate decision and reconstituting information so that it can most efficiently be employed by the decision-maker. The real impact of congressional staffs on the legislative process is probably best understood within these terms of the communications and information networks of Congress. Committee and subcommittee staffs are able to maintain their superior positions over staff members of individual legislators by closely guarding and controlling the dissemination of information crucial to the decision-making of individual committee members. Effective personal staff members are often those who channel off enough of the flood of information directed to the member to permit him or her to participate actively in the colleague-oriented cue system on Capitol Hill. At times this will be manifested in simply dealing with constituency demands at the submember level so as to free more of the legislator's time for dealing with colleagues on issues on the floor or in committee. At other times, effective staff work will mean providing the member with crucial information (that the member could not otherwise obtain through his or her normal cue networks) in an understandable form that permits the member both to employ that information in arriving at his or her own decision and to establish a position as a cue source on the issue for colleagues.

Like the congressional party, then, congressional staffs can exercise an important centralizing and organizing force on Congress. The demands of representation and reelection are constantly pulling legislators' attention toward the district or state. When in Washington, though, representatives and senators are expected to make rational decisions on a vast array of issues about which they may know very little. By processing information and transmitting it to members so that they can effectively employ it in their decision-making, both committee and personal staffs play an important, and growing, role in the legislative process.

NOTES

1. *Congressional Record*, vol. 122, no. 33, March 9, 1976, p. H1715.
2. Richard Lyons, "The Magna Carta Disaster," *Washington Post*, March 11, 1976, p. A3.
3. Anthony Downs, *An Economic Theory of Democracy* (Harper & Row, 1957).
4. Fred Greenstein, *The American Party System and the American People* (Prentice-Hall, 1970), p. 36. Also see his *Children and Politics* (Yale University Press, 1965), Chapter 4.

5. Ruth K. Scott and Ronald J. Hrebenar, *Parties in Crisis: Party Politics in America* (John Wiley and Sons, 1979), p. 142.

6. For the general trend of declining party affiliation expressed in terms of weak partisans, strong partisans, and independents, see *Congressional Quarterly Weekly Report*, March 18, 1978, p. 717.

7. Vera E. McCluggage, "From Apathy to Involvement: Redeeming the Independent Partisan," unpublished manuscript (Yale University, March, 1979), p. 28.

8. For an analysis of the actual vote and the normal vote expected on the basis of party identification, see Bruce A. Campbell, *The American Electorate: Attitudes and Action* (Holt, Rinehart & Winston, 1979), p. 266.

9. Theodore Lowi, *The End of Liberalism* (W. W. Norton, 1969), p. 72.

10. Albert D. Cover, "The Advantage of Incumbency in Congressional Elections," Ph.D. dissertation, Yale University, 1976; Robert S. Erikson, "The Advantage of Incumbency in Congressional Elections," *Polity*, vol. 3 (Spring, 1971), pp. 395–405; John A. Ferejohn, "On the Decline of Competition in Congressional Elections," *American Political Science Review*, vol. 71 (March, 1977), pp. 166–176; and Candice J. Nelson, "The Effect of Incumbency in Congressional Elections, 1964–1974," *Political Science Quarterly* (Winter, 1978–79), pp. 665–678.

11. For the pattern of Democratic dominance in the national vote for Congress in the 1970s, see the *Congressional Quarterly Weekly Report*, March 31, 1979, p. 575.

12. The source for the 1958 and 1968 figures here was the *Congressional Quarterly Almanac* (Congressional Quarterly, 1968), p. 19.

13. Richard L. Lyons, "Marathon Adjournment Session Leaves Members Groggy," *Washington Post*, October 16, 1978, p. A8.

14. Quoted in Ann Cooper, "House Use of Suspensions Grows Drastically," *Congressional Quarterly Weekly Report*, September 30, 1978, p. 2693.

15. Donald R. Matthews and James A. Stimson, *Yeas and Nays: Normal Decision-Making in the U.S. House of Representatives* (John Wiley and Sons, 1975), pp. 18 and 25. Copyright © 1975 John Wiley and Sons, Inc., reprinted by permission.

16. Ibid.

17. Ibid., p. 103.

18. Randall B. Ripley, *Party Leaders in the House of Representatives* (The Brookings Institution, 1967), p. 141.

19. Julius Turner, *Party and Constituency: Pressures on Congress* (The Johns Hopkins University Press, 1951), revised edition by Edward V. Schneier, Jr., 1970; Duncan MacRae, Jr., *Dimensions of Congressional*

Voting (University of California Press, 1958); David B. Truman, *The Congressional Party* (John Wiley, 1959); Lewis Froman, Jr., *Congressmen and Their Constituencies* (Rand McNally, 1963); and Lewis Froman and Randall Ripley, "Conditions for Party Leadership: The Case of the House Democrats," *American Political Science Review*, vol. 59 (March, 1965), pp. 52–63. For a recent summary of this literature see Scott and Hrebenar, *Parties in Crisis: Party Politics in America*, pp. 255ff.

20. Bob Livernash, "Party Unity Down in House, Up in Senate," *Congressional Quarterly Weekly Report*, December 16, 1978, pp. 3447–3449.

21. Aage R. Clausen, *How Congressmen Decide: A Policy Focus* (St. Martin's Press, 1973), pp. 93ff.

22. Jerrold E. Schneider, *Ideological Coalitions in Congress* (Greenwood Press, 1979), p. 199.

23. Froman and Ripley, "Conditions for Party Leadership: The Case of the House Democrats."

24. *Congressional Quarterly Weekly Report*, December 16, 1978, p. 3448.

25. Froman, *Congressmen and Their Constituencies*, p. 92.

26. *Congressional Quarterly Weekly Report*, December 16, 1978, p. 3448.

27. Ripley, *Party Leaders in the House of Representatives*, p. 169. Also see Richard Born, "Cue-Taking within State Delegations in the U.S. House of Representatives," *Journal of Politics*, vol. 38 (February, 1976), pp. 71–94.

28. For a good comparison of Albert and O'Neill as Speakers in the Ninety-fourth and Ninety-fifth Congresses, respectively, and an analysis that is sympathetic toward the limits faced by any Speaker, see Sidney Waldman, "Leadership in the House of Representatives: The 94th and 95th Congresses," a paper prepared for delivery at the 1977 annual meeting of the American Political Science Association, Washington, D.C., September 1–4, 1977.

29. Rachelle Patterson, "Mediator O'Neill's First Two Years," *Boston Globe*, October 16, 1978, p. 1.

30. Ann Cooper, "House Democratic Whips: Counting, Coaxing, Cajoling," *Congressional Quarterly Weekly Report*, May 27, 1978, pp. 1301–1306.

31. Larry Dodd, "Emergence of Party Government in the House of Representatives," *DEA News Supplement*, American Political Science Association (Summer, 1976), pp. 2–3.

32. For a good discussion of the caucus policy role see Waldman, "Leadership in the House of Representatives: The 94th and 95th Congresses," pp. 32–36 and Ann Cooper, "Democrats Still Arguing Over Party

Caucus Role on Legislative Matters," *Congressional Quarterly Weekly Report,* April 15, 1978, pp. 868ff.

33. The 10 percent estimate is that of Robert L. Peabody in *Leadership in Congress* (Little, Brown, 1976), p. 321.

34. Ibid., p. 349.

35. Randall B. Ripley, *Congress: Process and Policy* (W. W. Norton, 1978, second edition), pp. 215–218.

36. Quoted in "Eroding Loyalty Weakening House Leaders," *Quincy Patriot Ledger,* June 7, 1979, p. 10.

37. Tom Braden, "The Hidden Fifth Estate," *Washington Post,* March 20, 1976, p. A15.

38. Senators Ernest Hollings and Herman Talmadge, respectively, both quoted in Harrison W. Fox, Jr., and Susan Webb Hammond, *Congressional Staffs: The Invisible Force in American Lawmaking* (Free Press, 1977), pp. 4–5. For an interesting critical discussion of the growth in the congressional bureaucracy, see Milton S. Gwirtzman, "The Bloated Branch," *New York Times Magazine,* November 10, 1974, pp. 31ff.

39. Fox and Hammond, *Congressional Staffs: The Invisible Force in American Lawmaking,* p. 143.

40. See U.S. Congress, House, *Administrative Reorganization and Legislative Management, Commission on Administrative Review,* Ninety-fifth Congress, first session, September 28, 1977, vol. 2, pp. 126ff for a discussion of office space limitations. The average work area available to a staff member in Congress was found to be 36–40 square feet. In the executive branch and in private industry, the average space per employee considered minimal for effective functioning was 120–150 square feet.

41. William Taaffee, "The Costs of Keeping Congress Exceed Other Inflation," *Washington Star,* November 12, 1975, p. 1. Also see Stephen Isaacs, "Growth in Senate Staff Opposed as Costly," *Washington Post,* February 4, 1976, p. A8 and Martin Tolchin, "Congress Expenses Show a Sharp Rise," *New York Times,* January 16, 1977, p. 16.

42. *Congressional Quarterly Weekly Report,* September 30, 1978, p. 2699.

43. Ann Cooper, "Elections Plus Reforms Equals More House Employees," *Congressional Quarterly Weekly Report,* April 29, 1978, p. 1044.

44. Spencer Rich, "Staff Election Role Troubles Hill," *Washington Post,* January 25, 1976, p. A2.

45. "A Concise History of Hill Staffs and Hill Staffers," U.S. Congress, House, *Staff, Commission on Information and Facilities,* Ninety-fourth Congress, first session, no. 1, p. 3, and U.S. Congress, House, *Adminis-*

trative Reorganization and Legislative Management, Commission on Administrative Review, p. 41.

46. *Administrative Reorganization and Legislative Management,* p. 41.

47. John Saloma, *Congress and the New Politics* (Little, Brown, 1969), p. 185.

48. The figures do not add up to sixteen because of rounding. For the precise figures, see Thomas E. Cavanagh, "The Two Arenas of Congress: Electoral and Institutional Incentives for Performance," a paper prepared for delivery at the 1978 annual meeting of the American Political Science Association, New York, N.Y., August 31 to September 3, 1978, pp. 30–31.

49. Fox and Hammond, *Congressional Staffs: The Invisible Force in American Lawmaking,* pp. 92–99.

50. Ibid., p. 25.

51. Matthews and Stimson, *Yeas and Nays: Normal Decision-Making in the U.S. House of Representatives,* pp. 23–24. Copyright © 1975 John Wiley and Sons, Inc., reprinted by permission.

52. *Administrative Reorganization and Legislative Management,* pp. 56–57.

53. Harrison W. Fox, Jr., and Susan Webb Hammond, "The Growth of Congressional Staffs," in Harvey C. Mansfield, *Congress Against the President* (Proceedings of the Academy of Political Science, 1975), vol. 32, p. 122.

LAWMAKING II: SUBCOMMITTEES, COMMITTEES, AND THE BUDGET PROCESS

ON MONDAY, APRIL 12, 1976, at 10:00 in the morning, the Senate Foreign Relations Committee began hearings on the topic, "Foreign Policy for the 70's—Do People Really Care?" The four witnesses appearing before the committee and reading prepared statements were Norman Lear, television producer (responsible for such successful television programs as "All in the Family," "Sanford and Son," and "Mary Hartman, Mary Hartman"); Studs Terkel, popular radio talk show host and author of *Hard Times* and *Working;* Lerone Bennett, author and senior editor of *Ebony* magazine; and J. Saunders Redding, a Cornell University professor of American studies and author of several books, including *On Being Negro in America.* The hearings were part of a continuing self-education program through which the Senate committee sought to find out what particular issues of foreign policy the average American citizen was interested in. The senators were concerned with charges that the public was generally not included in debates about U.S. foreign policy and that they paid little attention to the debates on foreign policy issues that supposedly take place in the Senate and House chambers all the time.

Norman Lear began to read his statement. "Mr. Chairman, members of the committee," he said, glancing up at Chairman John Sparkman of Alabama, his eyes slowly passing over the fifteen empty committee chairs on both sides of the lone senator in attendance. "I see that nobody but Claude Rains is present." Lear's reference to Claude Rains (star of a 1933 movie entitled "The Invisible Man") was intended to highlight the absurdity of holding a hearing where fourteen of the sixteen committee members failed to appear (one other member joined Sparkman after an hour had gone by). The hearing ran for one hour and forty minutes, with the witnesses addressing a semicircle of empty chairs, or, in the words of Studs Terkel, "talking to leather."

The chairman of the committee tried his best to reduce the embarrassment of all involved. "Monday is a terrible day for a committee meeting," he said at the outset. After an hour had gone by and all four witnesses had completed their prepared statements and it seemed that there was little more to be said, Sparkman tried some words of encouragement: "I've just been told that Senator Percy will be here very soon. Senator Biden is coming down from Wilmington by train, but I don't know what time the train gets here. (Pause) Oh, here comes Senator Percy. I'm sure he'll have a lot of questions to ask you." Shortly after Senator Percy arrived, Senator Sparkman excused himself to attend another meeting. Percy's first question was whether the witnesses thought ordinary Americans were "able to relate foreign policy issues to their own outlook on life,"—in other words, whether people cared about foreign policy. One can empathize with the stifled groans of the witnesses who were being asked to start the discussion on foreign policy all over again. After another forty minutes, the hearings were, mercifully, recessed.[1]

My purpose in relating this story is to raise the question: Is this sparse attendance by committee members at such information-gathering hearings more the rule than the exception for Senate and House committees and subcommittees? Sparkman was right in noting that Monday mornings are not the best time to schedule any sort of committee meeting. (Chairpersons in both chambers generally adapt committee schedules to fit in with the legislators' desire to be in their districts and states for long weekends. Most of the important committee work is done between Tuesday and Thursday.) There is another reason why only two of the sixteen committee members showed up for that particular hearing. Ten of the sixteen members of the Foreign Relations Committee had other, conflicting committee or subcommittee hearings or meetings going on at the same time. Many of these other committee sessions were almost as sparsely attended since each of those ten members had to decide which of the two simultaneous committee meetings was more important. A list of some of these conflicting hearings and their topics indicates why some members of the Foreign Relations Committee felt compelled to attend the hearings of the other committees on which they serve. They included: an Appropriations subcommittee hearing on the Department of the Interior budget estimates for the fiscal year 1977; a Banking, Housing, and Urban Affairs Committee hearing on a bill to establish a government corporation known as the Energy Independence Authority; a Commerce subcommittee hearing on proposals to change the regulatory structure of the air transport industry; an Interior subcommittee hearing on the alleged use of his public position for private gain by the president's former campaign manager; and a Judiciary Committee hearing on increased funding for the Civil Rights Commission.[2] Given these other important responsibilities, it is easy to see why many members of the Foreign Relations Committee might have decided not to attend the hearing, knowing that everything that was said was being recorded by stenographers and would be available in printed form. They were also aware that no crucial votes would take place at the committee session and decided to go to another committee hearing where their presence might be more important.

The "Foreign Policy for the 70's—Do People Really Care?" hearing attracted press attention because of the irony of seemingly uncaring senatorial no-shows and because of some of the celebrities involved. It by no means represents a unique or even uncommon event or nonevent in the committee rooms of Congress. Four months after this foreign policy hearing a Senate Appropriations subcommittee supposedly held hearings on budgets for the fiscal year 1977 for the Department of Labor and the Department of Health, Education and Welfare. The eight volumes of hearing records, totaling 4,500 pages, showed twelve days of hearings—complete with senators' and witnesses' remarks—but the hearings never actually took place.[3]

First-time visitors to the House or Senate galleries are often shocked at how few members are on the floor when supposedly important business is being considered. Their knowing companions or guides are often quick to reassure them that the most important legislative business is not conducted on the House or Senate floor but rather in committees and subcommittees. Imagine the surprise of these visitors when they attend a committee or subcommittee hearing and find impressive witnesses appearing with prepared statements, every chair in the audience taken, and only one or two out of the fifteen to twenty legislators on the committee present. Picture yourself as an expert in some subject area who has been called to testify before a congressional committee or subcommittee. After months or years of preparation, you are ready to deliver your very considered opinion on some legislative proposal and to answer any and all questions. Instead of the klieg lights and television cameras and the packed gallery of eager committee members listening to your words and considering your data, you are faced with an almost empty committee bench with only the committee or subcommittee chairperson and ranking minority member present. You might conclude, after such an experience, that all this talk about committees and subcommittees being so important to the legislative process is just that—talk.

To put all of the foregoing discussion into context, it should be emphasized that committee hearings and meetings can take quite different forms. The level of member attendance is often greatly dependent on the type of hearing or meeting in progress. Two different types of committee or subcommittee sessions are likely to draw the most members. The first involves *markup* of an important bill being considered by that subcommittee. The markup stage occurs when the legislators are fashioning the committee or subcommittee version of a particular piece of legislation out of the many similar bills (including the executive's bill) brought before it. Important amendments are accepted or rejected, crucial language changed, and often close votes taken. Any committee member wishing to play a responsible lawmaking role must be present at these markup sessions, and the general level of attendance is high.

The second type of committee gathering that is likely to draw a high attendance is one that promises wide media exposure. The reason members attend such sessions is clearly not to make laws. There are those who maintain that if you organize a crowd, a politician will appear out of nowhere to address it; if you flash a flashbulb often enough, a politician will show up to have his or her picture taken; and if you bring in CBS/ABC/NBC cameras and reporters, a politician will be there to help make the news or to comment on it. One way to boost attendance at committee or subcommittee hearings is to guarantee national television coverage. In the mid-70s, the House International Relations Committee was notorious (but not unique) for its low attendance at committee meetings. Committee staffers found that the only time they could arrange to have the annual official committee picture taken, and to count on most members being there, was when the picture taking coincided with the appearance of some "star"—such as Secretary of State Henry Kissinger. Kissinger's appearance meant the presence of all three national networks and possible media exposure for any committee member asking the most penetrating, the most embarrassing, the funniest—in short, the most newsworthy question. Committee sessions with such high media coverage are more likely to occur in the Senate than in the House. But in both chambers, the level of attendance at committee meetings is likely to be at its highest when there is media coverage.

If the markup and the media event occupy one end of the scale (guaranteeing the highest levels of turnout of members), then the preliminary, fact-finding, not-immediately-legislative hearing represents the other end of the scale. Given the number of conflicting engagements each committee member has, and given the fact that everything that is said by witnesses will shortly be available in printed form, it does seem to make sense for most committee members to spend their tightly allocated time elsewhere. The only physical presences required in such sessions are those of the witnesses, the stenographer, and at least one legislator (almost always the committee or subcommittee chairperson and/or ranking minority member).

The absence of bodies, the lack of interchange between members and witnesses, and the irregular character of such proceedings do not mean that no lawmaking function is being performed. *Building a record* is the term used on Capitol Hill for these preliminary, fact-finding, sparsely attended committee and subcommittee sessions. It is useful for a committee member to have this record of expert opinion to fall back on as a source of the legitimacy of a position when the member does have to make a decision in committee markup or must convince a noncommittee member to vote his or her way. The record is built, whether there be one or twenty-one legislators present. The committee hearing record serves as a fundamental basis of rational decision-making by both committee and subcommittee members (whether they were actually present at these record building sessions or not) and for their colleagues who rely on them for voting cues.

In this chapter we are once again concerned with the lawmaking function of Congress. This leads us to focus on the centralizing forces that bring together the 535 members of Congress. The chief concern of these individuals seems to be representation and reelection. They want a legislative product that not only "sells in the provinces" but also makes some contribution to the overall governing of the nation.

Because of the many changes and reforms of the 1970s, we can no longer focus only on committees as the major force of centralization and lawmaking. We must also look at the effects of the proliferation and the growing importance of subcommittees (a generally decentralizing force) and the impact of the new congressional budget process established in 1974 (a clearly centralizing force). This second chapter on lawmaking is organized in terms of an ascending level of centralization and control, going from subcommittees, to committees, to the budget process. All are concerned with lawmaking. Committees and subcommittees are the nuclei of lawmaking activities, while the new budget committees and the budgetary process provide an innovative centralizing force to congressional decision-making.

SUBCOMMITTEES

One of the most important and comprehensive congressional reforms passed by Congress in the last half century was the Legislative Reorganization Act of 1946. It was a grand scheme to democratize and modernize Congress and to redress the imbalance of powers. During the war years powers that once belonged to Congress had slipped to the executive branch. The key to streamlining and modernizing Congress to make it more efficient was to eliminate minor or inactive committees and to merge committees whose areas of jurisdiction seemed to be similar or overlapping. The Legislative Reorganization Act reduced the total number of standing committees in the House from forty-eight to nineteen and those in the Senate from thirty-three to fifteen.[4] The 1946 reorganization was clearly intended to improve the lawmaking functions of Congress by consolidating and centralizing legislative power. With fewer independent committee fiefdoms, it was expected that party leaders would be able to exercise a tighter control and more efficiently bring forth a cohesive legislative program.

There was one side effect to this legislative reorganization that served to undercut the centralizing influence—the continuation and expansion of the number of subcommittees in both chambers. In 1945 there were 106 House subcommittees and 68 Senate subcommittees; in 1968 there were 139 House subcommittees and 104 Senate subcommittees.[5] Table 4–1 shows the number and distribution of subcommittees in the Ninety-sixth Congress (1979–1980): 147 House subcommittees and 100 Senate subcommittees. The centralization sought under the 1946 Reorganization Act has been effectively circumvented by the proliferation of subcommittees. Prior to the 1946 Act there were 81 standing committees and 174 subcommittees in Congress; in the Ninety-sixth Congress there were 37 standing committees and 247 subcommittees. "Reforms have created something approaching a subcommittee government in Congress," one observer noted. The same observer commented on the policy implications of this when the Carter Administration's hospital cost containment bill died in Congress in July, 1978: "A decade ago, Carter's bill would have gone to one committee in the House and one in the Senate. Last year (1978), it went to two committees in each chamber and subcommittees in each committee. Each of the four subcommittees would get to take a crack at Carter's bill. And then each of the four parent committees would have its turn. That made eight major station stops. The bill reached seven of the eight stations but at each of the stops it ran into peculiar problems of politics, power and personalities." [6]

There are a number of explanations for this increase in the number and importance of subcommittees in Congress. First, this proliferation of subcommittees and the concomitant increase in specialized expertise represent a rational attempt by the legislative branch to keep pace with the increasing specialization and decentralized autonomy of executive agencies. A Senate Finance Committee Social Security Financing Subcommittee and a House Ways and Means Social Security Subcommittee are clearly in a better position to oversee and legislate in their particular area than the full committees that are also dealing with other major policy areas.

Second, we can look at the proliferation of subcommittees in terms of the party leaders' control over tangible rewards for members. Committee and subcommittee assignments are one of the most effective ways in which party leaders are able to manipulate their members. A high rate of return of committee incumbents and a fixed number of committees can limit the available resources for party leaders in this area. It is only natural that leaders would want to expand their resource base by increasing the size of committees and the number of subcommittees.[7] The proliferation of

TABLE 4–1 Subcommittees in the Ninety-sixth Congress (1979–1980)

Committee	Number of Members	Number of Subcommittees
House of Representatives		
1. Agriculture	42	10
2. Appropriations	54	13
3. Armed Services	45	7
4. Banking, Finance and Urban Affairs	43	10
5. Budget	25	8
6. District of Columbia	17	3
7. Education and Labor	37	8
8. Foreign Affairs	34	9
9. Government Operations	39	7
10. House Administration	25	8
11. Interior and Insular Affairs	43	7
12. Interstate and Foreign Commerce	42	6
13. Judiciary	31	7
14. Merchant Marine and Fisheries	39	6
15. Post Office and Civil Service	25	7
16. Public Works and Transportation	48	6
17. Rules	16	1
18. Science and Technology	39	7
19. Small Business	39	6
20. Standards of Official Conduct	12	0
21. Veterans' Affairs	32	5
22. Ways and Means	36	6
Subcommittee Total		147
Senate		
1. Agriculture, Nutrition, and Forestry	18	7
2. Appropriations	28	13
3. Armed Services	17	8

TABLE 4–1   Continued

	Number of	
Committee	Members	Subcommittees
4. Banking, Housing and Urban Affairs	15	8
5. Budget	20	0
6. Human Resources	15	8
7. Foreign Relations	15	9
8. Government Affairs	17	6
9. Rules and Administration	10	0
10. Energy and Natural Resources	18	5
11. Commerce, Science, and Transportation	17	7
12. Judiciary	17	10
13. Environment and Public Works	14	6
14. Veterans' Affairs	10	3
15. Finance	20	10
Subcommittee Total		100

Source: Congressional Quarterly Weekly Report, January 27, 1979, and April 14, 1979.

subcommittee seats available no doubt decreases the value or scarcity of such leadership resources. At the same time it increases the base of rewards from which party leaders are able to draw.

Third, we have the notion of *politics as property* as advanced by Norman Mailer in *Miami and the Siege of Chicago.* The central idea here is that committee and subcommittee positions represent a type of political property of value to the holder of that position. That value may be primarily symbolic and only have consequences in terms of the members' prestige and chances of reelection. Or, it might represent an important position from which the member is able to affect policy outcomes. David Mayhew sees credit-claiming as one of the primary activities or goals of legislators. In noting that the existence of a great number of subcommittee positions means that "every member can aspire to occupy a part of at least one piece of policy turf small enough so that he can claim personal responsibility for some of the things that happen on it," Mayhew illustrates the importance of subcommittees to legislators.[8] The chairman of the House Commission on Administrative Review, Representative David Obey of Wisconsin, had this third explanation in mind when he said:

> The problem right now is, everyone around this place is badge-happy. If you get to be a subcommittee chairman, you get to have an extra staffer, maybe even an extra secretary. So you have great pressure to expand subcommittees, the number of subcommittes; the numbers show it.
>
> We do not have an expansion of subcommittees because we have so many interesting subjects. We have expansion of subcommittees because we have a lot of people, number one, who want a badge and, number two, who want the ability to get an extra staffer.[9]

This proliferation of subcommittees, and the number of people with badges, led another representative to chuckle: "When you walk down the halls and you don't know a member's name, if you say 'Hello, Mr. Chairman' you come out right one out of three times."[10] Once members are given a piece of legislative property, in the form of a subcommittee position, it becomes difficult to take it away from them for the sake of a more efficient Congress.

All three explanations for the increase in the number of subcommittees make sense. The additional consideration of the representational function served by these multiple points of access for citizens and expanded number of podiums for articulating different viewpoints should not be ignored. But to really appreciate the lawmaking functions now being performed by subcommittees, we have to look at some of the reforms of the 1970s.

Between 1971 and 1975, a series of changes in House rules and in positions adopted by the controlling House Democratic caucus drastically altered the relative power of committees and subcommittees and their leadership. The overall impact of these changes was to reduce greatly the power and authority of committees and their chairpersons and to enhance greatly the independence and real policy roles of subcommittees. A summary of these rules includes the following:[11]

1. No House member can be chairperson of more than one legislative subcommittee. This rule was adopted at the beginning

of the Ninety-second Congress and had an immediate impact on the legislative structure. Sixteen new subcommittee chairmen were brought in through this reform in 1971 with positions on such important committees as Banking, Currency and Housing, Foreign Affairs, and Judiciary. The reform opened up subcommittee leadership positions to middle-level and junior Democrats who previously had been frozen out by conservative senior Democrats on many of these committees. One study showed that the new chairmen of the subcommittees had an average seniority in 1971 of about seven years of service, while the men they replaced had an average seniority of almost eighteen years of service.[12]

2. The Democratic caucus adopted a series of new rules in 1973 known collectively as the Subcommittee Bill of Rights. These new rules require committee chairpersons to share most of their powers with other Democrats on the committee, who are formally organized into a committee Democratic caucus. The committee caucus has the power to select subcommittee chairpersons, establish subcommittee jurisdictions, provide full subcommittee budgets, and guarantee that all members be given a major subcommittee assignment whenever vacancies occur. Giving the committee caucus the power to establish subcommittee jurisdictions means that committee chairpersons can no longer follow their long standing practice of arbitrarily assigning bills to select subcommittees that will do what the chairperson wants. A final rule requires the committee chairperson to refer bills to subcommittees within two weeks after their referral to the full committee. This eliminates the chairperson's power of quietly vetoing proposed legislation by simply not referring it to a subcommittee.

3. All House committees having more than twenty members are required to have at least four subcommittees. As Table 4–1 indicates, only the District of Columbia Committee, the Rules Committee, and the Standards of Official Conduct Committee have fewer than twenty members. (Because of their special centralizing role in the legislative process the Budget committees in both chambers have no subcommittees.) The House Ways and Means Committee, which had operated without subcommittees for over fifteen years under the tight control of former Chairman Wilbur Mills, was the chief target of this new subcommittee requirement. Ways and Means now has six relatively autonomous subcommittees organized in terms of distinct policy areas within the full committee's juris-

diction. The six subcommittees are: Health, Oversight (as of 1975, every committee is required to have an oversight subcommittee),[18] Public Assistance, Social Security, Trade, and Unemployment Compensation.

4. All subcommittee chairpersons and ranking minority subcommittee members are authorized to hire one staff person who works directly with them on their subcommittee work. On a committee such as Foreign Affairs, which has nine subcommittees, this means that there is now a subcommittee staff bureaucracy totaling twenty professionals. By making subcommittee leaders less dependent upon full committee staff (which is under the direction of the full committee leadership), the autonomy and independence of the subcommittee is further enhanced.

5. Committees are required to have written rules. These rules have the effect of reducing or eliminating the great discretionary power that chairpersons were able to exercise in the absence of written committee rules, and to provide another step in the institutionalization of subcommittees. (Aspects of these written rules are connected with the formal relationships between the committee and its subcommittees.)

6. In December, 1974, the Democratic caucus voted to restrict senior Democrats to membership on only two of a committee's subcommittees. This rules change was directed primarily at the Appropriations Committee, where multiple subcommittee memberships permitted a handful of senior Democrats to dominate subcommittees handling funding for such important areas as defense, agriculture, labor, health, education, and welfare appropriations. The thrust of this rules change is to open up subcommittee positions to younger and middle-level members.

7. A final reform measure, adopted at the beginning of the Ninety-fourth Congress, requires that chairpersons of all of the Appropriations subcommittees be approved by the full House Democratic caucus. The prime sponsor of this reform, Representative David Obey of Wisconsin, ranked twenty-second out of the thirty-seven Democrats on the Appropriations Committee during the Ninety-fourth Congress. He saw these subcommittee reforms as being absolutely crucial to loosening the control of conservative chairman George Mahon of Texas and the *college of cardinals* (the con-

servative subcommittee chairmen) over the full Appropriations Committee.[14] It is Obey's contention that this single reform might have the greatest long lasting effect of all of these reform measures because of its opening up and restructuring the appropriations process, which affects all aspects of congressional behavior.

One immediate effect of these reforms was an increase in activity at the subcommittee level. Studies made shortly after most of the reforms were enacted showed an increase in the number of hearings conducted by subcommittees in which new leadership had been brought in under these reforms.[15] This increase is reflected in the total number of committee and subcommittee meetings. In the Ninetieth Congress (1967–1968) there were 4,386 committee and subcommittee meetings in the House, in the Ninety-second Congress (1971–1972) there were 5,114, and in the Ninety-fourth Congress there were 6,975. Subcommittee meetings account for about 80 percent of the total number of meetings.[16] Another effect (though not necessarily intended) was to increase the number of resignations at the upper end of the congressional hierarchy. In the spring of 1976, the number of retirements from Congress reached a new high as fifty-two members announced that they were not running for reelection. The retirement list included eight senators and forty-four House members. Eighteen of those House retirees were running either for the Senate or for governor in their states. The list of retirees also included six House full committee chairmen: Henderson of Post Office and Civil Service, Jones of Public Works and Transportation, Morgan of International Relations, Patman of the Joint Economic Committee, Randall of the Select Committee on Aging, and Sullivan of Merchant Marine and Fisheries. One of the reasons offered for this high rate of committee chairpersons' retirement was that "being a chairman isn't all that great now that House rules changes have spread power around and left the chairman with little but a gavel and an administrative headache." [17] As we noted in Chapter 1, the number of voluntary resignations increased again two years later, with a total of fifty-nine senators and representatives opting out of the system.

The greatest effect of these reforms was to shift the site of most congressional lawmaking from the full committee to the subcommittee level. The increased number of subcommittee hearings and the ability of the subcommittees to dig deeper into narrow areas of policy has created a level of expertise unmatched by full committees. The increasing importance of subcommittees is summed up by a full committee chairman:

> I didn't pay much attention to subcommittee chairmen before—I did it all myself. Now, the subcommittee chairmen handle bills on the floor. They know that when they're answering questions on the floor they had better know what they're talking about. They really study the legislation now: they're much better prepared and more knowledgeable. Now we go to conference and they do the talking—the Senators never open their mouths. Their staffs are the only ones who know anything. So we're more effective with the Senate.[18]

It is clear that subcommittees in the House have come into their own as new centers of power. They once again seem to represent "the inner circle of an inner circle," a phrase used to describe congressional subcommittees in the last century.[19] Supporters of these subcommittee reforms will argue that their more intense particularization and specialization make for more effective lawmaking by Congress. Yet there are those who suggest that the increased decentralization reflected by this increase in subcommittees makes it more difficult to provide the coordination required for effective lawmaking. One case cited to show the effects of this decentralization was that of the twenty-eight different committees and subcommittees in Congress that had jurisdiction over sections of the 414 energy bills and resolutions introduced in Congress in 1973.[20]

The Senate has long relied on subcommittees to provide tangible rewards to its members and to enable senators to perform their most important representational functions. The real work of crafting legislation was generally left to the House, with its more centralized and coordinated legislative committees. With the increasing democratization of House procedures and the growing autonomy of subcommittees, the House is now seen by some critics as giving up its traditional role of chief lawmaker. One influential member of the House complained:

> We're going the way of the Senate. We've spread the action by giving subcommittees more power and by making it possible for members to play more active roles on them. But there's nothing at this point to coordinate what all these bodies are doing and to place some checks on their growing independence.[21]

This feeling that the many democratizing reforms may have gone too far in creating subcommittee government in Congress has led both chambers to make more recent changes to stem the flow of *all* power to the subcommittee level. About two years after the House member quoted above was complaining about that chamber's going the way of the Senate, a committee reorganization plan was adopted by the Senate. The reorganization plan, adopted in February, 1977, reduced the number of standing committees from thirty-one to twenty-one by the Ninety-fifth Congress and limited each senator to service on no more than three committees and eight subcommittees. It also provided that no senator could chair a total of more than three committees and subcommittees. The Senate committee reorganization plan was clearly aimed at reversing the decentralizing trend of growing subcommittee power in the 1970s. Recent actions in the House followed the same pattern. When the Democratic caucus met in late 1978 to consider rules changes for the Ninety-sixth Congress, there were a number of proposals for limiting subcommittee power. These included a limit of five subcommittee assignments for each member; a requirement that subcommittee chairpersons who had been convicted of a felony, reprimanded, or censured by the House be approved by the full Democratic caucus rather than just the full committee for them to hold their seats; and a restriction stating that full committee chairpersons could not also chair a subcommittee. The caucus adopted the subcommittee assignment limit, exempted subcommittee chairpersons who were only reprimanded from the full caucus approval proposal, and defeated the proposal to prevent committee chairpersons from also chairing subcommittees.

It is important to understand that these latest reforms in both chambers did not represent a step backward to a Congress completely dominated by a few powerful chairpersons, nor did they continue to advance a trend toward a Congress sometimes described as being all minnows and no whales. "The main message this week," noted Representative Morris Udall of Arizona after the House had acted on these reforms, "has been that people realize that it's time to tie up loose ends. There's still major work to be done. But you can't restructure everything every two years. Now and again you have to slow down and fine tune and modify." [22] The purpose of this fine tuning was not to roll back the earlier reforms and remove all the power now placed in the hands of subcommittees. Rather, the goal was to provide some coordination among subcommittees and some cohesion in policy-making. The obvious institution for coordinating subcommittees, in addition to the party leadership, is the full committee. Let us now turn to a consideration of the full committee as one of the chief forces for lawmaking in Congress.

COMMITTEES

One of the rather morbid games congressional staffers play whenever an incumbent announces plans for retirement or dies in office might be called "musical committees." When news of the impending or immediate vacancy on a committee is announced, the alert staffer will reach for the list of committee memberships to see what the new opening means in terms of his or her boss's committee and subcommittee seniority standing and whether a move to a more prestigious or more valuable committee might now be in order. ("Musical committees" is played simultaneously with another game, called "musical offices." When a senior member dies or retires, a spacious suite of offices opens up that has been the envy of cramped junior members and their staffs for years.) "Musical committees" is only one of the many ways by which members express their feelings about the importance of committees in the congressional process. A member's entire career may be structured by the committee or committees to which he or she is initially assigned. The ability to serve constituency needs, to be reelected, to begin developing the expertise needed for advancement in the congressional hierarchy, and to gain a forum providing the exposure necessary for a national or senate campaign all depend on the committee to which the legislator is assigned.

Political scientists and other students of Congress have long shared members' appreciation of the importance of committees in the legislative process. Writing in 1884, Woodrow Wilson observed: "It is evident that there is one principle which runs through every stage of procedure, and which is never disallowed or abrogated—the principle that the Committee shall rule without let or hindrance. And this is a principle of extraordinary formative power. It is the mould of all legislation." [23]

Almost eighty years later, Representative Clem Miller described Congress as "a collection of committees that come together in a chamber periodically to approve one another's actions." [24] However, discussions of congressional committees that talk about seniority, patterns of interaction, and the chairperson's power, as though all committees are all alike, tend to be misleading. Not only do House and Senate committees perform different functions in their respective chambers, but also, there is great variety in the role each committee plays within the chamber.

House and Senate differences about the relative emphasis put on representation and lawmaking affect the roles the committees play in each chamber. Senate committees tend to maximize representational goals; House committees are geared more to decision-making. House members can spend more time developing expertise relevant to the one or two committees on which they serve, while senators would find such a task impossible because they serve on many committees. Committees are generally more important to individual House members than to senators, for they represent the member's only means of achieving power and policy goals within the lower chamber. House committees are also more important in determining the chamber's policy outcomes than are Senate committees because of House norms that tend to reinforce the acceptance of committee decisions on the floor. For these reasons, most of the following discussion will deal with House committees rather than their Senatorial counterparts.

There are many ways to classify committees. Some students of Congress focus on the pecking order and rank committees by their prestige. By looking at which committees members most consistently transferred from and to over a period of time and at the most commonly listed committee assignment preferences of newcomers, congressional scholars have been able to construct a relatively stable hierarchy of committees in both the House and the Senate.[25] But the reorganization of committees in the Senate in 1977 and the introduction of Budget Committees in both chambers in 1974 make any such listing of these old committee hierarchies not suitable for describing the modern Congress. A few committees that headed the old lists, however, remain today as the premier committees in each chamber. In the House the big three, or top-ranked, committees are Rules, Ways and Means, and Appropriations. In the Senate, the Foreign Relations, Appropriations, Finance, and Judiciary Committees would be at the top of any list of most-sought-after committees by members. The rules in both chambers recognize some committees as being more important, or at least more time-consuming, than others and limit the other committee assignments which members of these exclusive committees can have. As we shall see below in the more detailed discussion of Ways and Means and Appropriations, the chamber rules also recognize the relative importance of committees in the ways different committees' bills are considered on the floor. Although there is general agreement about which committees are the top committees, there is a great deal of variation in the attractiveness of particular committees among different members. While a senator or representative from Iowa might naturally find an assignment to the Agriculture Committee to his or her liking, a colleague from New York City might consider such an assignment to be punishment for past sins. One member, who thrives on the din of ideological battles, might consider a seat on the Education and Labor Committee to be a wonderful position for influencing policy on great national issues, while another member might regard the insistent demands made by antibusing forces, educational interest groups, and labor unions to be the sure cause of a heart attack.

With the exception of the few top committees that are always everyone's favorites, the prestige or attractiveness of particular committees is likely to ebb and flow with the tides of public opinion on national issues. In the years immediately after the "Watergate Summer" of 1974, for example, an assignment to the House Judiciary Committee was considered a plum because of the high prestige that committee had gained by its conducting the hearings on impeachment of President Nixon. The visibility and importance of war-limitation legislation in the early 1970s gave a similar aura of prestige to the House Committee on Foreign Affairs. But at the beginning of the Ninety-sixth Congress in 1979, both the Judiciary and the Foreign Affairs Committees had barely enough applications to fill the existing vacancies on the committee lists. That it would have to deal with such hot political issues as gun control, busing, and abortion made the Judiciary Committee, in particular, a body on which few members chose to sit. The most popular committees at the start of the Ninety-sixth Congress, as measured by members' preferences, were Appropriations, Budget, and Commerce. Responsibility for energy policy and oversight of the federal bureaucracy were said to be the attractions of Commerce, whereas the public mood of cost-cutting and government economy made the money committees of Budget and Appropriations a favorite of many legislators. "These Democrats want to get on here and embellish their reputation as economizers," is the way one member of the House Budget Committee explained the committee's popularity in

1979.[26] Although the particular standing any committee has in this hierarchy of committees is likely to change over time and vary from member to member, there definitely is a ranking of committees; they are not all equal. Awareness of this variety is useful because it prevents our falling into the trap of thinking that one can make general statements about *all* congressional committees with any degree of accuracy.

Committees may also be classified by type of policy they deal with. Donald Matthews's study of the Senate combined committee preferences and policy to come up with a fourfold typology of committees. These are: "top" committees (Foreign Relations, Appropriations, Armed Services, and Finance); "interest" committees (Agriculture, Banking and Currency, Interstate and Foreign Commerce, Judiciary, and Labor); "pork" committees (Interior, Post Office and Civil Service, and Public Works); and "duty" committees (Rules and Administration, Government Operations, and District of Columbia).[27] George Goodwin used a similar classification scheme, based on the scope of issues handled by the committee, in constructing a typology of national issue committees, clientele-oriented committees, and housekeeping committees. Some examples of each type are (1) national issue committees: Appropriations, Armed Services, House Ways and Means, and Senate Finance; (2) clientele-oriented: Agriculture, Banking, and the Commerce Committees in both chambers; and (3) housekeeping committees: District of Columbia, Government Operations, and Administration Committees in the House and Governmental Affairs and Rules and Administration Committees in the Senate.[28] Classification of committees by the type of policy they handle makes possible comparisons of committees and their counterpart institutions in other branches of government. When we compare committees classified by prestige with committees classified by the scope of the issues handled, we find that the most prestigious committees are those concerned with broad policy issues. But again, such a classifying scheme may often hide important differences among committees. Even though Education and Labor and Interior are both placed in the same category of clientele-oriented committees, they represent opposite extremes in terms of the degree of conflict found in committee activity. Whereas Education and Labor is consistently the scene of intense partisan and ideological conflict, Interior is best characterized by one of its members as "a neutral processing machine." [29]

Richard Fenno, in a book that seeks to provide a framework for comparative studies of congressional committees, suggests that a key factor in explaining the differences among committees is the goal a member wishes to accomplish by being on that committee. A member seeking internal influence in the House or Senate is drawn to different committees than a member who seeks to maximize constituency service or to draft good public policy. The difference between Interior and Education and Labor can be explained by the fact that members on the first want a low-conflict committee that can provide projects for home districts, while Education and Labor members are more concerned with drafting good legislation and are willing to engage in intense battles to do so.

Fenno studies six House committees by focusing on the following variables: committee member goals, environmental constraints, strategic premises, internal structure, and output. Committee members will organize the committee so as to achieve their individual goals. They are limited in doing so by other groups inside and outside of Congress who have particular expectations of that committee. To meet both individual goals and environmental expectations, members work out particular strategies that satisfy both groups. These strategies then become the bases on which committees are organized and determine the type of policy coming from committees.[30]

Members may have different reasons for being on the same committee. For most committees, however, there is some consensus as to why a legislator should seek appointment to that committee and what he or she can expect to get from it. On the basis of these shared member goals, we can classify committees as power committees, policy committees, and constituency committees.

Power Committees

Members seeking to maximize their influence within the House or Senate are naturally drawn to prestigious committees such as Appropriations, Ways and Means, and Rules. An overwhelming majority of the Appropriations and Ways and Means members in the Fenno study said that they sought power, prestige, or importance in joining that committee. One Ways and Means member sums up this attitude in discussing why he wanted to be on this committee:

> Ways and Means is powerful around here because it's interpreted as being powerful. Power is interpretation around here; it's all inter-

pretation. . . . The only way I can describe what I want to be is power. I don't know what I'd do with it when I got it, but I want to have it where I can reach out and use it when I want to.[31]

The fact that both committees deal with important money matters is obviously related to the members' preferences. But the essential drive for membership is influence, not policy. If committees with totally different subject matter were to assume this position of importance in the chamber, then these members would easily shift their attention and aspirations to the other committees. Most members of these committees hold relatively safe seats, and they do not need to worry a great deal about serving constituency interests. They are free to devote most of their time to the committee work that maintains their power.

There are four prominent groups of noncommittee members who often seek to influence committee behavior: members of the parent chamber, the executive branch, clientele groups, and party leaders. The relative importance of each of these groups will vary from committee to committee and from issue to issue.

Since members of Ways and Means and of Appropriations are most concerned with their influence in the House, the environmental group they are most concerned with is other House members. The importance of the money committees within the House is directly related to the fact that these functions are the fundamental legislative powers that determine the importance of Congress in the larger political system. All legislators want these committees to be powerful because the relative importance of Congress depends on it. In order to permit these two committees the independence deemed necessary for maintaining their influence, the House provides them with procedural rights denied other committees. Major bills from Ways and Means are brought to the floor under a closed rule that precludes amendments; Appropriations is allowed to hold hearings in secret executive sessions; and both committees are provided with large staffs.

In return for the great autonomy granted to these committees, they are expected to be responsive to House desires. The primary means for assuring this responsiveness is control over assignment to the committee. Party leaders are very active in determining who will sit on these committees. They will seek out legislators who have demonstrated a "responsible legislative style" emphasizing moderation and respect for the House as an institution.[32]

In seeking responsiveness, House members are more concerned

with matters of style than they are with substantive policy questions. This means that other groups in the environment play a role in providing cues on substantive policy matters. Coalitions seeking to influence Appropriations decisions tend to be dominated by executive groups, while those trying to influence Ways and Means are more likely to be party leaders. The nature of the budgetary process dictates that clientele group demands be channeled through executive agencies. By the time these demands reach the Appropriations Committee they are chiefly executive requests. Although revenue matters also heavily involve executive groups, a key difference between these issues and questions of funding is the fact that revenue matters are regarded as having greater electoral impact. Basic disagreements on the issues of taxation, social security, medicare, and trade have long characterized American political parties. Because of the electoral importance of these issues, party leaders seek to have some influence over the substantive content of Ways and Means decisions.

Strategic premises for Appropriations members must meet the twin demands of influence and responsiveness. To maintain the influence that all House members desire, the committee must establish policy independence from the executive branch. To do this, the committee has adopted as a major strategic premise the idea that any and all budgets submitted by executive agencies should be cut. Fenno's earlier study of the Appropriations Committee led him to this description:

> The workaday lingo of the Committee member is replete with negative verbs, undesirable objects of attention, and effective instruments of action. Agency budgets are said to be filled with "fat," "padding," "grease," "pork," "oleaginous substances," "water," "oil," "cushions," "avoirdupois," "waste tissue," and "soft spots." The action verbs most commonly used are "cut," "carve," "slice," "prune," "whittle," "squeeze," "wring," "trim," "lop off," "chop," "slash," "pare," "shave," "fry," and "whack." The tools of the trade are appropriately referred to as "knife," "blade," "meat axe," "scalpel," "meat cleaver," "hatchet," "shears," "wringer," and "fine-tooth comb." Members are hailed by their fellows as being "pretty sharp with the knife." Agencies may "have the meat axe thrown at them." Executives are urged to put their agencies "on a fat boy's diet." Budgets are praised when they are "cut to the bone." And members agree that "You can always get a little more fat out of a piece of pork if you fry it a little longer and a little harder." [33]

If Appropriations were to carry this norm of budget cutting too far it would fail to meet the other requirement the parent chamber places on it: responsiveness. Support for Appropriations' budget-cutting depends on the committee's providing adequate funding for programs the House has authorized. This second strategic premise of adequate funding suggests that the committee must constantly search for a balance: cutting the budget enough to maintain its independence and influence, yet providing adequate funding to maintain the support of members interested in particular programs.

Ways and Means members are faced with a similar need for keeping their influence. To do this, members emphasize the technical complexity and political importance of their legislation and their need for independence so as to be able to deal adequately with such measures. Since the influence of Ways and Means would be greatly diminished by floor defeats, a major strategic premise is to write a bill that is not only technically sound, but one that will also pass the House.

John Manley's study of Ways and Means suggested to him that "a good bill that cannot pass the House is a contradiction in terms for most members of Ways and Means." [34] Since the other environmental group of concern to Ways and Means members consists of party leaders, their second strategic premise is to follow partisan policy choices when they are relevant. This is done, not with an eye toward committee influence, but rather to satisfy party leaders who were instrumental in each member's being on the committee and who seek to have clearly drawn partisan positions for electoral purposes.

The internal structure of committees may be analyzed in terms of partisanship, degree and types of participation/specialization (as reflected in subcommittee structure), and patterns of leadership demonstrated by committee and subcommittee chairpersons. Fenno measured internal partisanship by looking at committee reports on major legislation, measuring the number of reports on which there was recorded disagreement, and then measuring the number of recorded disagreements on which a majority of one party was in opposition to a majority of the other.

Ways and Means and Education and Labor are clearly the most partisan committees in this study. But there is a key difference. While Education and Labor decisions are reached in a constantly charged partisan atmosphere, Ways and Means members generally bring in partisan issues only after the major technical decisions have been made in a more neutral manner. A Ways and Means staffer says of his group:

> I think you will find that Ways and Means is a partisan committee. There are usually minority reports. But partisanship is not that high when they discuss the bill and legislate. About 90 percent of the time, the members deliberate the bill in a nonpartisan way, discussing the facts calmly. Then toward the end (John) Byrnes (ranking Republican) and the Republicans may go partisan. But an awfully large part of it is nonpartisan.[35]

By following this pattern of restrained partisanship, Ways and Means members are able to satisfy party leader's demands for making decisions along partisan lines and their own desires to reduce intracommittee conflict in the interest of maintaining committee influence. Education and Labor members (more interested in policy than in committee influence) see no need to control partisanship in decision-making. Appropriations is the least partisan committee, and with good reason. Faced with the same demands as Ways and Means members to maintain committee influence, but without having to satisfy party leaders' requests to structure conflicts in partisan terms, Appropriations members can best maintain their committees' mystique of expertise by minimizing partisanship. "This is one committee where you will find no partisan politics. We carry on the hearings and we mark up the bill and we compromise our differences. We bring a bill to the floor of the House each year with the unanimous approval of the committee members." [36] By having every member's approval of the bill and by minimizing partisanship, the Appropriations Committee is able to get its bill accepted by House members impressed by its expert nonpartisan decision-making and by its unanimity.

In the Ninety-second Congress (1971–1973), Appropriations had fifty-five members and Ways and Means twenty-five. This was the size of the two committees during the period Fenno was doing his comparative study of House committees. In the Ninety-fourth Congress the size of Ways and Means increased to thirty-seven members and subcommittees were added. With these changes in Ways and Means and the already mentioned reform that required caucus approval of Appropriations, subcommittee chairpersons have restructured the system. The more institutionalized subcommittee autonomy on Appropriations and the slow developing nature of Ways and Means subcommittees as centers of power make the following discussion of committee expertise, based on Fenno's analysis, still relevant—if only for analytic rather than descriptive value.

This size difference greatly affects the way the two committees work. The expertise that characterizes Appropriations members is upheld by a subcommittee system emphasizing independent subcommittee decisions that are recognized as authoritative by other subcommittees, the full committee, and the House. Such a system permits a high level of participation by members but is limited to subcommittees and issues on which the member has developed some expertise. This specialization greatly facilitates the committee's strategy of cutting budgets. By focusing on a narrow area, members are better able to locate unnecessary expenditures. It is easier to make appropriations policy through a series of independent decisions than it is to make tax, trade, or social security decisions in the same manner. Because of its smaller size and because of the nature of its subject matter, Ways and Means is able to operate through full committee decisions. Committee influence is still dependent on members' knowledge of the subject, but this expertise is developed through participation in all decisions rather than through specialized subcommittees.

Testifying before the House Select Committee on Committees in 1973, Richard Fenno offered the observation that "the single most important thing to know about committee chairmen is whether or not a chairman agrees with the majority of the members of his committee on what the job of the committee is." [37] During the period in which Fenno and Manley studied the Ways and Means Committee, its chairman was Representative Wilbur Mills. For sixteen years prior to his downfall after a scandalous incident and his admission to being an alcoholic, Mills was the model of a successful House committee chairman. A 1968 feature story in the *New York Times* called him "the most important man on Capitol Hill today." A colleague said of his dealings with the chairman: "It's like being allowed to touch the hem of the Lord's gown." [38] Mills was able to exercise this leadership because he was in basic agreement with members' goals. He, too, wanted to maintain committee prestige by writing bills that would pass the House and by following a pattern of restrained partisanship. His style of leadership was one favoring compromise and consensus. An HEW official who often dealt with Ways and Means tells how the chairman sought this consensus:

> Mills wants more than anything not to have a minority report. He
> wants at least twenty votes and one way he does it is to drop out
> anything controversial. I don't mean just major policy questions that
> may be controversial but anything. If they come across a provision
> and some member raises an objection, he'll drop it.[39]

Mills's influence on the committee stemmed not only from his
seeking compromise and consensus, but also from his having superior information. Chairman since 1958, Mills's long service had
given him a technical expertise that was unchallenged: "He knows
the tax code inside and out and he knows what Ways and Means
has done for the last twenty years. He can cite and does cite section
after section of the code." [40] Another type of information possessed
by the chairman was the distribution of opinion within the committee and in the House. A colleague said of Mills: "He counts the
Heads in the Committee and he counts the heads in the House, he's
always counting." [41] Both sorts of information are keys to the great
influence Chairman Mills had in Ways and Means and in the
parent chamber.

Mills's successor as chairman of Ways and Means, Representative Al Ullman of Oregon, is a different sort of leader. Part of this,
no doubt, has to do with the fact that Ullman's committee has
twelve new middle-level or young Democrats on it and for the first
time in twenty years is subdivided into six subcommittees. Ullman
has also consciously rejected the conservative, consensus-based leadership style of Mills. Once, when a freshman member complained
about Ullman's alleged lack of leadership and suggested that Wilbur Mills was better able to push through legislation, Ullman an-
grily responded:

> If you follow the Mills philosophy you wouldn't do any of those
> things (health insurance, tax reform). You'd wait until after the con-
> troversy had run its course and then try to get something together.
> If that's the kind of leadership you want, we'll just sit back and wait.
> But I haven't done that. I don't worry about being defeated on the
> floor.[42]

Recent Appropriations chairmen, Mahon and Whitten, have
also sought compromise and consensus in their committees. Unlike
Mills, neither has dominated the committee decision-making. This
is so primarily because of the committee structure, with its emphasis on subcommittee autonomy, reciprocity, and specialization.

The Appropriations chairman has influence stemming from his power of appointment to subcommittees and his information about the activities of all subcommittees. But informal norms of the committee dictate minimal interference in subcommittee activity by the full committee chairperson. This greatly circumscribes the chairman's range of activities and precludes the type of coalition formation exercised by Wilbur Mills. The Appropriations chairperson can best meet members' goals of House influence by supporting the specialized subcommittee structure and expertise on which that influence rests.

Policy Committees

Committees such as Education and Labor, Foreign Affairs, Banking and Currency, and Government Operations are populated by members of Congress more interested in policy goals than in congressional influence or constituency projects. Fenno's study showed that no member of Education and Labor or Foreign Affairs used the word "influential" or "powerful" to describe his committee.[43] Being on either committee generally has little or no effect on the member's standing in his or her district. "Politically, it's not a good committee for me. My constituents are interested in bread and butter, and there's no bread and butter on Foreign Affairs." [44] An Education and Labor Democrat expresses a similar attitude:

> I'm the most issue-oriented guy you'd ever want to meet. I know there won't be a Wagner Act with my name on it during my first term. But if I can get a few of my ideas in I'll be satisfied. Legislating in Washington, for the district and in the public interest. That's what interests me the most. Serving your constituency—that's a noble effort, too. But, frankly, I consider any time spent with a constituent as time wasted that I could have spent doing more important things.[45]

Freshman legislators seeking policy goals will generally request an assignment to Education and Labor, Foreign Affairs, or Banking and Currency. They do so because such an assignment offers them an opportunity to deal with exciting and controversial issues.

The most important external groups for members of the policy committees are groups that dominate the policy coalitions for particular issues. Because they seek good policy rather than congressional influence, members of Foreign Affairs and Education and Labor are more sensitive to groups playing a major role in formulating policies than they are to fellow legislators. Legislators who are not on these committees permit this attention to outside policy coalitions because neither welfare policies nor foreign affairs matters are regarded as key issues determining the relative influence of the House in the larger political system.[46]

The Foreign Affairs Committee deals with an environment dominated by the executive branch. The president's influence on foreign policy and his or her near monopoly on information in this area make the executive branch the chief policy coalition with which Foreign Affairs must contend.[47] Education and Labor is confronted with a different environment. Instead of facing a homogeneous policy coalition dominated by one group, Education and Labor must deal with coalitions made up of executive officials, party leaders, clientele groups, and other House members. High priority presidential programs, such as welfare reform, bring a flood of executive proposals and proponents to the committee. The importance of partisan disagreements on Education and Labor is shown in Table 4–2. The degree of clientele interest in the committee is suggested by the remark of an AFL-CIO official:

> We watch the Education and Labor Committee very carefully; but it's the only one we're interested in. Otherwise, you would spread yourself too thin. We have to control the labor committee. It's our life blood.[48]

Other House members are brought into the policy debate on issues facing Education and Labor because of the electoral and partisan importance of the issues considered by this committee. In contrast to the stable, executive-dominated environment of Foreign Affairs, members of Education and Labor face a constantly changing array of highly partisan policy coalitions.

Foreign Affairs members generally feel that they can best satisfy their goal of good policy and the demands of their only important policy coalition by approving and building support for the administration's foreign aid program. Although the committee does provide a focus for opponents of foreign aid, most members see their role as one of making minor changes in the president's program and getting that bill passed. The nature of the subject matter, described by one committeeman as "all undefined and amorphous;

TABLE 4-2 Partisanship on Committees (1955–1965)

	Total Major Legislation	Percent Recorded Disagreements	Percent Party Disagreements	Party Disagreements as Percent of All Disagreements
Ways & Means	114	52% (59)	26% (30)	50%
Education & Labor	96	56 (54)	25 (27)	50
Interior	82	33 (27)	7 (6)	20
Post Office	42	38 (16)	7 (3)	19
Foreign Affairs	66	24 (16)	5 (3)	19
Appropriations	154 [a]	7 (11)	0 (0)	0

[a] Original appropriations bills only.

Source: Richard Fenno, *Congressmen in Committees* (Little, Brown, 1973), p. 84.

all up in the air," makes it difficult for members to get the information and expertise needed to play a more active role.[49] Some
Foreign Affairs members, because of their great interest in policy
goals, do not like this executive dominance:

> I have the feeling that we sit over here like a lot of little birds get-
> ting fed, and if you are for the Administration then you are sup-
> posed to like the food. But I don't like that. Sure I'm for foreign
> aid, but is that all I'm supposed to do? [50]

There is no easy solution to this problem of presidential initiative
and control over information. The subject matter and the policy
goals of the members do not permit Foreign Affairs to adopt a
strict budget-cutting norm like Appropriations. Expanding the
committee staff would perhaps provide more technical information
for members who wish to challenge the expertise of the administration. But even this staff must rely on information that comes primarily from executive sources.[51]

Education and Labor reflects the depolarized, volatile nature
of its environment. Highly charged issues are continually being
brought to the committee by numerous coalitions making demands
upon it. The committee responds by emphasizing partisan and individualistic norms of behavior. "You can't get a resolution praising
God through this Committee wihout having a three-day battle over
it." [52] Another committee member observes:

> Usually the Committee splits up in factions. They change from
> issue to issue, but on any one you know who they are. . . . Sometimes
> our side is so fragmented we have to pick up some votes on the other
> side. We go off in six directions at once.[53]

As Table 4–2 indicates, the issues split the committee generally
along party lines. Ideological positions and party labels do not always coincide, and members sometimes find themselves on a different side of the fence from their party leaders. Fenno suggests
that Education and Labor norms support members pursuing their
individual policy preferences in such situations. This can be justified because committee members have the experience and information to support their policy stands. Unlike Foreign Affairs, where
the committee faces an executive coalition with superior information and expertise, Education and Labor members can best pursue

policy goals by becoming embroiled in fragmented battles among many coalitions with relatively equal information resources.

The measures of internal structure—partisanship, participation/specialization, and leadership—show different ways these two policy committees react to different environments. Foreign Affairs, like Appropriations, is a nonpartisan committee. "There's a feeling on the Committee that you don't want to exacerbate partisan feelings if you don't have to. Doc (the chairman) will say many times, 'It makes no difference; under Eisenhower, Kennedy, or Johnson we did this.' " [54]

Members of both parties in the Senate are more liberal than their party colleagues in the House. They generally support the foreign aid program and they believe that good policy in this area can best be reached by minimizing partisan differences. On Education and Labor, as we have observed, party cues are relevant to the individual member's policy position. The issues considered by the committee touch on the basic differences between Republicans and Democrats and preclude members adopting a nonpartisan stance. "This is probably the most partisan committee in the House, because this is where the fundamental philosophical battles are fought." [55]

The subcommittee structures of the two policy committees are different: Education and Labor emphasizes subcommittee activity much like the Appropriations Committee, while Foreign Affairs tends to ignore them. Here is the comment of a Foreign Affairs committeeman:

> I've been on the European subcommittee for five months and I haven't even heard NATO mentioned, haven't even heard the word. I read my hometown newspaper to find out what's happening to NATO. The subcommittees have displayed absolute irrelevancy in foreign affairs, amazing irrelevancy.[56]

One of the reasons for Foreign Affairs' not working through a subcommittee system in terms of major legislative matters is because at one time it dealt with only one big bill a year, the foreign aid bill. "If you had subcommittees," suggests a member, "the full committee would take it apart all over again. It's the one bill of the year. It's not like Education and Labor where you have all those big bills." [57]

Subcommittees are used on the Foreign Affairs Committee, but they are primarily a research tool. They hold hearings to gather information that might be of use to the full committee; they do not legislate. The only important legislation the committee dealt with at the time of Fenno's study was the annual foreign aid bill, and this was handled by the full committee. All members participated in committee activity on this one bill. Because of the lack of subcommittee activity, there is no deference to experts who have spent a lot of time on one narrow aspect of the bill. All members are expected to participate in the full committee activity, but it is a closely limited participation designed to facilitate passage of the Administration's program. All members are given only five minutes each for questioning witnesses in hearings on the foreign aid bill.

Education and Labor represents a different extreme. Subcommittees are the important arenas for policy debate, and all members enjoy a completely unrestricted participation in their activities. A somewhat surprised newcomer observes:

> I never dreamed the older members would have allowed us freshmen to contribute so much and participate and get into the legislative process as much as we have. I thought we would have to break the seniority system. But on my subcommittees I participate, get amendments passed and open doors I never thought I could. I was amazed at how little restraint and restriction is placed on us. I think Education and Labor is unique in the use that is made of freshmen.[58]

The committee uses subcommittees because the issues that come to Education and Labor can best be handled by allocating them to smaller units that isolate the conflicts surrounding a particular education or human resources program. The high participation level of all members is a direct result of committee members' emphasis on policy goals. There is no impetus to maintain committee prestige within the chamber by parading expertise. There is no acceptance of the idea that one member's opinion is worth more than another's:

> Expertise? Hell, everyone thinks he's an expert on the questions before our Committee. On education, the problem is that everyone went to school. They all think that makes them experts on that. And labor matters are so polarized that everyone is committed. You take sides first and then you acquire expertise. So no one accepts anyone as impartial.[59]

Education and Labor subcommittees do not make decisions for the whole committee. There is no expertise mystique preventing other subcommittees and the full committee from questioning decisions made in Education and Labor subcommittees. "On some two bit, piddling little bill, the full committee will say, 'that's what the subcommittee recommends, we'll vote it through.' But on major bills, the subcommittee has no standing with the full committee." [60] Committee members' interest in good policy and the committee norm of maximizing pursuit of individual policy goals lead to high levels of individual participation not only within one's subcommittee, but also in considering the work of other subcommittees.

Leadership on the Foreign Affairs Committee fits in with members' goals of passing the president's foreign aid bill. The chairman during the time of Fenno's study, Thomas Morgan, was able to help members achieve this goal. Beyond that, his influence over the broader issues of foreign policy was limited. The Senate Foreign Relations Committee dominates congressional debate in this area, and there is little the House committee can do to challenge the upper chamber's constitutional prerogatives. Fenno's interviews with committee members seeking a more active committee role showed some dissatisfaction with Chairman Morgan. "He's a perfectly delightful man," observed one, "so I have nothing against him personally; but he's the State Department's man. As a result, this precludes any aggressive or imaginative activity on the part of the Committee." [61]

One impact of congressional objections to the war in Vietnam was a change in the nature of leadership on the Foreign Affairs Committee. Chairman Morgan, a supporter of the war, was ordered to report out an anti-war amendment by the Democratic caucus in 1972. Young anti-war members began to use subcommittees more and more to focus on anti-war sentiment, and by 1973, Chairman Morgan himself had turned around on the issue. Morgan's successor, Representative Clement Zablocki of Wisconsin, has been a more persistent critic of Administration foreign aid programs, and the House Foreign Affairs Committee is likely to undergo more changes under his leadership.

Education and Labor presents a different picture. From 1952 to 1967, the committee was run by two men who, although at opposite poles ideologically, exercised great influence over the committee. Graham Barden of North Carolina chaired the committee for eight years. A conservative, Barden was able to control his committee by operating through ad hoc subcommittees over which he kept a wary eye. Subcommittees were used as burial chambers for legislation opposed by the chairman.

In 1961, Adam Clayton Powell became chairman of Education and Labor. He expanded the number of subcommittees but maintained his control by keeping their jurisdictions vague. There were three subcommittees for education and three for labor. Two of these subcommittees were called "general," two "special," and two "select." By expanding the number of subcommittees, Powell was able to elevate liberal Democrats to the position of subcommittee chairpersons. By keeping subcommittee jurisdictions unclear, he was able to determine where a bill would be sent. Powell's success as chairman relied on his giving the important coalitions affecting Education and Labor what they wanted. Subcommittee members were able to have a hand in policy-making. The liberal Democratic coalition making demands on the committee was rewarded with volumes of legislation, and the chairman and his party received great publicity for their programs.

The importance of policy goals to members of Education and Labor is demonstrated by the fact that both chairmen were, in effect, deposed. Barden was ousted because his conservative views clashed with the policy-oriented Democratic majority. Powell's influence was diminished after he alienated members of the liberal Democratic coalition by delaying action on bills dealing with the repeal of state right-to-work laws in 1965, a pro-labor picketing bill in 1966, and the poverty program of 1966. As long as the Education and Labor chairperson's views coincide with the policy conscious majority on the committee, he or she has great influence over the fate of legislation coming to the committee. When the chairperson becomes separated from that majority, the individualistic policy norms of the committee require that he or she be outvoted and stripped of power.

Constituency Committees

Fenno's research showed that members of the Interior and the Post Office committees are more concerned with serving constituency interests than with influence in the House or with broad questions of public policy. Other studies of the Agriculture and Armed Services committees suggest that most members of these committees think of them primarily as constituency committees.[62] People on these committees obviously have an interest in making good public policy. But unlike Foreign Affairs or Education and Labor committee members, their policy interests are narrower and more tailored to the interests of constituents. A representative sums up this attitude in telling Fenno why he wanted to be on Interior:

> I was attracted to it, very frankly, because it's a bread and butter committee for my state. I guess about the only thing about it that is not of great interest to my state is insular affairs. I was able to get two or three bills of great importance to my state through last year. I had vested interests I wanted to protect, to be frank.[63]

This concern with constituency interests is also reflected in comments by members of the Agriculture and Post Office committees:

> I vote for what I think will be the best economic interests of my people. Throughout the years I have gained an idea of what those interests are. This is the way representative government should work.
>
> We have over 10,000 civil service and postal employees in my state. While we are here first and foremost to represent the national interest, and while I'm a firm believer in that, nevertheless you have to look out for the interests of your people. Politics is a great way to promote your ideals, but first you have to be elected and then re-elected and to do this you have to help your constituents.[64]

Lewis Anthony Dexter's study of the House Armed Services Committee found members and staff characterizing their committee as a "real estate committee." They meant, notes Dexter, that the location of installations and related transfer, purchase, and sale of properties is the main concern of the House Armed Services Committee." [65]

The geographic distribution of seats on Interior, Armed Services, and Agriculture illustrates House acceptance of the idea that these committees are primarily constituency committees. Fenno's analysis showed Interior to be the most unrepresentative of the six committees studied. Legislators from western states accounted for 50 percent of the membership on Interior, while their percentage of seats in the whole House was only 14.[66] Over half of the Democrats on Armed Services and Agriculture in the Ninety-second Congress came from southern or border states. Charles Jones's study of Agriculture demonstrates how party affiliations and subcommittee assignments reinforce representation of constituency interests. Democrats dominate the tobacco, cotton, peanuts, and rice subcommittees that deal with commodities of interest to their constituents. Republicans have a similar edge on the corn, dairy, livestock and feed grains, and wheat subcommittees.[67]

The important environment groups for these committees are their respective policy constituencies, i.e., the groups that have electoral pull and certain demands on the committee. For the Post Office Committee these groups are postal employee unions (the National Association of Letter Carriers being the most important) who want higher wages, and mail user organizations (such as the Associated Third Class Users) who want lower postal rates. Both groups are continually locked in combat, not with other interest groups, but rather with the executive branch that opposes increased postal salaries and favors higher rates. The environment of Post Office is a monolithic one similar to Foreign Affairs. Instead of dominance by the executive, it is faced with constant pressure from organized postal interests. Listen to one member's description of committee life:

> Nobody in the Congress or in the public gives a damn about what we do. Oh, once every few years, we have an orgy on junk mail, but other than that, nobody cares. We are wooed by the whole panoply of outside groups. There's always a dinner somewhere. They come in and fawn over your staff. There isn't a day that goes by that someone doesn't come in here wooing me. This is the dominant fact of life, the distinguishing characteristic of the Committee.[68]

Interior committee members face a much more pluralistic environment. In Interior, each issue incites many groups against one another. For instance, a debate over using public lands will involve such groups as the National Lumber Manufacturers Association, the American Mining Congress, and the American Cattlemen's Association on one side, and the Wilderness Society, the Sierra Club, and the National Wildlife Federation on the other. The visibility of this pressure is muted by the fact that members of Interior often act as spokespersons for these groups. The pluralist nature of the environment, the use of legislators as spokespersons and the predisposition of western legislators to favor most federal projects all contribute to the members' feeling that they are subject to little pressure. "Maybe I don't know pressure when I see it," said one member in describing his contacts with clientele groups, "but all I ever get from them is information." [69]

The Agriculture Committee shows a similar pattern of representation, one in which there is no need for overt pressure because the member recognizes and responds to the interests of his or her policy constituency:

> You are in the position to know, of course, on a lot of things. I live there—there are many things I just know. I don't have to ask anybody. There are very few bills where I have to guess. If I did, I wouldn't be here as the representative. I am a native of _____. I get letters—though I don't get very much mail. I have sent out questionnaires, but I don't know. It is just the fact that I know and I can judge their needs.[70]

The Interior Committee is faced with a pluralistic environment and an overwhelming flood of legislation. One out of every five bills introduced in the House goes to Interior. In order to satisfy the member's goal of constituency service and the demands of clientele groups, the committee has adopted the basic strategic premise of passing all legislation sponsored by relevant constituents and supported by committee members. Such reciprocity does not preclude close scrutiny of legislation by the committee. This reciprocity also maximizes committee norms favoring the reelection of individual members. One result of adopting this strategy is that committee decisions generally favor western commercial interests over the competing claims of eastern conservation groups.

The Post Office Committee, with three-quarters of its members serving on other committees, is run by what Fenno calls an "efficient minority." Although some members object to the close ties between their colleagues and postal groups ("He's a bought man"; "He's in the pocket of the unions"; "He's in bed with all the groups; they raise money for him and he does their bidding"), this active minority is able to set the major strategic premise of the committee—support pay and benefit increases for postal employees and oppose all mail rate increases.[71]

One of the effects of the monolithic environment on the Post Office Committee is that it becomes a relatively nonpartisan committee. Party disagreements on the committee represented only 19 percent of all disagreements. This lack of partisanship is probably more a result of the environment of the committee than it is of the constituency orientation of committee members. By minimizing partisan conflict, the clientele groups that dominate committee activity are better able to present a united front. Introducing partisan debate would only serve to weaken the present lobbying monopoly enjoyed by postal employee and mail user groups.

Interior is also free of most partisan conflict, but for different reasons. It is the nature of the issues the committee faces, rather than the character of the environment, that accounts for Interior's low partisanship. Its environment, like Education and Labor's, consists of many groups. Other than debate over public versus private power, the issues handled by Interior are not structured in ideological terms. Says one member:

> There's a kind of cohesiveness in the Committee that overrides partisan considerations. The key here is that there aren't any ideological issues. You don't hear the Republicans saying we can't afford this or that. And the reason is that everyone has a project in his district that he wants or will want.[72]

Reciprocity norms and the Interior members' desire to maintain House support for the committee in order to meet their goal of passing many bills also account for the relative lack of partisan conflict.

Until 1965, the Post Office Committee used only ad hoc subcommittees on legislative matters. The comments of one member suggest the ineffectiveness of this system: "Murray would appoint some fluffy subcommittee, a temporary sort of thing, with mostly newcomers. They'd issue some half-assed report which no one would read."[73]

A rules change in 1965 led to every member sitting on three subcommittees. Freshmen were given assignments designed to encourage participation in committee decision-making. But even with these changes, subcommittee activity on Post Office is not of great importance in affecting policy outcomes. This is the case because of the working alliance between outside groups and the efficient minority that runs the committee, and because most members of the committee take little interest in its work.

Subcommittees play an active part in Interior decision-making. The committee itself was formed in 1946 by combining six standing committees. These became the basis for subcommittees in the new Interior and Insular Affairs Committee. This emphasis on subcommittees is similar to that of Appropriations, but differs from the latter because it does not rely on the money committee's structure of subcommittee expertise and autonomy. There is specialization on Interior subcommittees, but it is more tailored to meeting members' constituency needs than to developing substantive expertise. As a result of this active subcommittee system and the lack of expertise norms, newcomers to Interior are able to participate actively in committee decision-making. Every member respects the right of others, including freshmen, to work vigorously for projects at home. Because of this pattern of heavy participation by all members, incoming legislators feel that Interior is "the best training ground for active participation and debate in the House." [74]

The Agriculture Committee's internal structure illustrates the importance constituency matters have to its members. There are two types of subcommittees. One deals with specific commodities and the other with general agricultural problems such as farm production. Legislators on the committee are much more interested in the commodity subcommittees; subcommittee assignments almost always match representatives with products of importance to their district. However, party ratios require that some members be assigned to subcommittees of no importance to their constituents (midwestern Republicans on the cotton subcommittee; southern Democrats on the wheat subcommittee). Participation norms reinforce the importance of constituency matters in such cases. As Professor Jones observes, "members who have little interest in the proceedings are expected either to remain silent during hearings or not to attend." [75]

Leadership on Post Office and Interior could not be more different. A member of both committees during the period studied by Fenno compared Interior Chairman Wayne Aspinall and former Post Office Chairman Tom Murray:

> Aspinall's a marvelous chairman. He knows more about that jurisdiction than any other person in the country, bar none. He's in at 8:00 a.m., works all day, no social life. He dominates those subcommittee chairman; they have no autonomy at all. He's with them every step of the way. And everything's by the numbers, according to good parliamentary procedure. When we wanted rules for Post Office, we followed Aspinall's rules. He lets everybody talk, he's fair. He'll say if a freshman has anything to say, let's hear it. Aspinall's the best chairman anyone could have. It's time consuming, time consuming as hell; but it's run perfectly.
>
> On the other hand I'd go over to Post Office and it was a miserable mess. Everyone yelling and shouting, "Who's got the

floor?" "I don't know." "Is there a quorum?" "Who cares." It was utter chaos—screaming, fighting, a miserable mess—and all old Murray would do is stare off into space. When we did want to do something, we'd meet in Morrison's office then leave by twos so no one would get suspicious. Then we'd come in, vote cloture and get a bill out. But even after we ran a steamroller over Murray in committee, we'd have to prod him to go before the Rules Committee for a God damn rule.[76]

Post Office members stripped Murray of almost all of his powers in 1965, not only because of the inertia caused by his aging but also because he tended to favor executive proposals and thus worked against the strategic premises of the majority.

Wayne Aspinall was often compared to Wilbur Mills in the extent to which he controlled Interior. He sat on all six subcommittees and actively participated. He made the basic scheduling decisions that determined when a bill moved from subcommittee to committee to the floor. He had an enormous reputation for success on the floor ("I don't think Aspinall has ever gone down on the floor, at least I can't remember a time." "When you come to the floor with the Interior Committee, you feel like a member of the varsity team.").[77]

The Postal Reorganization Act of 1970 took away from the Post Office and Civil Service Committee jurisdiction over the appointment of postmasters, postal employee salaries, and postal rates. This removal of the committee's bases of power changed the nature of the committee from a constituent-oriented one that could help important organized groups by positive action to a lower level constituent-oriented group. Now the focus is on aiding such groups as civil service workers by simply continuing legislative benefits granted earlier (such as the 1 percent cost-of-living *add-on* granted retired federal employees). Most members who serve on Post Office and Civil Service definitely consider it to be the least important of their two committee assignments.

The House Interior Committee has also undergone dramatic change since Fenno's study. Wayne Aspinall was defeated in a primary race in 1972, mostly because of the opposition of environmental groups. His successor as chairman, James Haley of Florida, has demonstrated a leadership (or nonleadership) style different from that of Aspinall. Instead of the consensus-based, centralized leadership of Aspinall, Chairman Haley has given free reign to Interior's subcommittees. "Today," concluded an analysis of the committee in late 1975, "the Interior Committee exists in name only. It has become balkanized with subcommittees taking on a life of their own." [78] Such decentralization is what we would expect from a committee whose chief goal is the satisfaction of constituency interests. It represents an example of the representational expectations accorded House committees that are supposed to be the centers of lawmaking activity in Congress.

A CONCLUDING NOTE ON COMMITTEES

Throughout this section it has been clear that committees are different from each other and that they change. Most of this section has been drawn from Richard Fenno's comprehensive study of committees as they operated from the Eighty-fourth through the Eighty-ninth Congresses (1955–1966). Fenno's book was published in 1973 and contained an epilogue that updated the book's description of committee behavior, with primary emphasis on the committees that had undergone the most change (Post Office, Interior, Foreign Affairs, and Education and Labor). My updating of Fenno's material, scattered throughout this section, indicates that congressional committees continue to experience change. By the time you read this, more updating will be required in order to provide any truly contemporary description of House committees.

The underlying framework of Fenno's analysis, in my opinion, is one that withstands changes in the actual configuration of congressional committees. By focusing on members' goals, on the environmental constraints that set the limits of committee members' behavior, and on the strategic decision-making behavior members adopt to meet those twin demands, Fenno tapped some fundamental determinants of committee behavior that apply regardless of change. In the past few years, a number of congressional scholars have employed the concepts put forward in Fenno's work, the concepts discussed in this chapter, in analyzing the many changes that have taken place in the Agriculture, Education and Labor, Foreign Affairs, Interstate and Foreign Commerce, Post Office and Civil Service, Public Works, Rules, and Ways and Means Committees.[79]

In a 1973 appearance before the House Select Committee on Committees, which proposed a major overhaul of the House committee system, Professor Fenno noted:

I have just published a book on congressional committees that contains one major conclusion. It is that committees differ from one another. My guess is that that will make people smile because they will say:

"That is just about what we expect from a political scientist. He spends years, hundreds of dollars, comes in interviewing us as to our committee work, and then what does he tell us? He tells us that committees differ. If there is anything we already know, it is that committees differ."

My rejoinder to that is simply while I think it is the thing that Congressmen best know, it is the thing they first forget when they set about to reform their committees. Therefore, the sum and substance of what I have to say here is simply keep in mind that House committees differ from one another. Don't automatically propose equal reforms in equal dosages for all committees.[80]

The select committee (known as the Bolling committee, after its chairman, Representative Richard Bolling of Missouri) proposed the most extensive overhaul of the House committee system since the Reorganization Act of 1946. The jurisdiction of every standing committee (except Veterans Affairs) would have been altered by the Bolling committee's proposed reforms. In 1974, the House rejected the Bolling committee's reform proposals. Instead it adopted a more moderate substitute that did not affect so many standing committees' jurisdictions. The defeat of the Bolling committee's reform proposals came about not as a result of legislators ignoring Fenno's advice and treating all committees as though they were alike, but rather because of the notion of politics as property and policy turfs. The Bolling committee's proposals would have destroyed the policy turfs of too many influential people.[81] Education and Labor was to be split into two separate committees, and this greatly upset liberals having a seat on the committee (such as Phillip Burton of California, John Brademas of Indiana, and Frank Thompson of New Jersey). This would also have had an effect on education and labor groups who were used to working with the established committee and its staff. Conservative Representative Richard Ichord did not like the proposal because it would have eliminated his Committee on Internal Security (something that was done in 1975). Congresswoman Leonor Sullivan opposed the committee proposal for the same reason—the Merchant Marine and Fisheries Committee she chaired would have been abolished. An Energy and Environment Committee was to replace the Interior and Insular Affairs Committee, and the Ways and Means Committee would have lost jurisdiction over both foreign trade and health insurance. It is easy to see why the Bolling committee's reforms, which would have greatly rationalized the House committee system and increased the committees' effectiveness as policy coordinators, was replaced by a more moderate committee reform proposal that left the existing committee structure pretty much intact.

Because of the many jurisdictional overlaps and conflicts in the basic committee structure that has been in effect since 1946, House leaders had to create ad hoc committees especially designed to deal with issues such as energy and development of the outer continental shelf in the Ninety-fifth Congress.[82] Recognizing that its committee structure had to be reorganized if the House were to be capable of dealing with the major issues of the 1980s, the House, on March 20, 1979, again created a Select Committee on Committees along the lines of the earlier Bolling Committee. The committee was directed to make recommendations for restructuring the committee system by February 1, 1980.

The Senate, as I have already mentioned, moved in the direction that many in the House sought to go when it passed a resolution on February 4, 1977, that reduced the number of standing committees and rationalized jurisdictions. Instead of having fourteen committees and more than forty subcommittees involved in establishing energy policy, for instance, the Senate created a new committee, Energy and Natural Resources, which has jurisdiction in this area. The committee reforms adopted by the Senate also eliminated the Aeronautical and Space Sciences, District of Columbia, and Nutrition Committees and transferred their jurisdictions to the Commerce, Science, and Transportation Committee, the Government Affairs Committee, and the Committee on Agriculture, Nutrition, and Forestry. In addition to these changes in the committee structure, the Senate also limited the number of committees and subcommittees on which senators could serve, a topic discussed earlier in this chapter.

The reform proposals considered in the House and the reforms adopted by the Senate seek to improve the lawmaking ability of Congress by providing a more coordinated and centralized committee structure. In the final section of this chapter, we will have a look at another congressional reform aimed at centralizing the congressional budget process and coordinating the authorization and appropriation of funds by committees and subcommittees. This reform, clearly aimed at improving the lawmaking process, is the Congressional Budget and Impoundment Control Act of 1974.

THE BUDGET PROCESS

In 1946 Congress adopted a major budgetary reform provision as part of the Legislative Reorganization Act. Members of both House and Senate tax committees and appropriations committees were required each February to determine the "maximum amount to be appropriated for expenditures" for the following fiscal year. In other words, they would set a spending ceiling for the coming fiscal year. It didn't work. "The first year, 1947, the two houses could not agree on a ceiling. The second year, having agreed on one, they failed to abide by it. The third year, without even bothering to amend the reorganization act, they gave up trying." [83]

Congress waited almost thirty years before another attempt was made. The Congressional Budget and Impoundment Control Act of 1974 was a response to many of the same forces that led to the abortive attempt at congressional budgetary reform in 1946. These forces included a galloping rate of inflation, a tremendous increase in the level of federal government spending, a resultant increase in the national debt, and a general feeling that control over spending levels and the national economy in general was slipping away from Congress and into the hands of the president.

Specific criticisms of congressional performance on the key budgetary matters of appropriations and taxing all focused on the fragmentation and decentralized nature of congressional decision-making and on the delay resulting from this process.

An expert on congressional and presidential spending and on budgetary processes, Louis Fisher, has pinpointed the major deficiencies of the old budgetary process that led to the reforms of 1974: [84]

1. *Late appropriations*–Under the old system a fiscal year ran from July to July. Congress was often unable to pass the necessary appropriations for federal agencies before the fiscal year had expired. This led to dependence on a disoriented, crisis-motivated, pattern of appropriations. Federal agencies had to look toward an unreliable system of funding based on congressional continuing resolutions, which covered only a part of the fiscal year.

2. *The size of the budget deficit*–In 1969, the federal deficit was $5.5 billion. In 1970 it was $13.1 billion. In 1971 and 1972 it was $29 billion, and in 1973 it was $34 billion. About one-fourth of the total national debt had accumulated during this short period of time. While there are sharp differences among economists about the relative value of a balanced budget and the countercyclical policies of the federal government pump-priming a national economy during private sector economic downturns, most economists agree that Congress should begin paying closer attention to the overall economic impact of its spending and taxing policies.

3. *Uncontrollable expenditures*–More than seventy-five cents of every dollar spent by the federal government comes under the heading of uncontrollable expenditures. These expenditures are not dependent on, or subject to, congressional action for their being paid. The bulk of expenditures is accounted for by entitlement programs (they establish a government expenditure or benefit for persons fitting a particular category—retired federal employees, those whose income is below the poverty level, and the unemployed), and by the fact that such program expenditures are generally "indexed" (i.e., the level of benefits is tied in to the rate of inflation as measured by the cost-of-living index). By passing such programs, Congress made a lot of people happy (and met their economic needs), but it also lost control over a large part of its power of the purse and also all of its ability to exercise some overall fiscal control by limiting expenditures.

4. *Backdoor spending*–This is a general term referring to any of the processes Congress uses to provide funds for agencies and programs without going through the normal channel of congressional appropriations. There are three different processes:

a. *contract authority*–This permits executive agencies to enter into contracts paying funds to private firms (consulting agencies) that promise the payment of certain fees for services received. Congressional approval of appropriations to pay such contract fees has generally been automatic.

b. *borrowing authority*–This is a process by which agencies spend funds by borrowing directly on agency debt receipts or by tapping more general Treasury Department debt receipts.

In both cases, an agency is able to rely on leftover funds rather than on congressional appropriations committees.

c. *entitlement programs*–The level of expenditures here is indirectly fixed by congressional action, which establishes who is entitled to benefits guaranteed by the particular program. Because the economic factors determining the level of benefits are beyond congressional control, the level of expenditures on such programs is also beyond congressional control.

Backdoor spending, in 1975, represented more than half of all federal government spending.[85]

5. *Impoundment of funds by the executive*–This is perhaps the most blatant form of executive control over national economic issues. The impoundment of funds appropriated by Congress meant simply that the president and the executive branch refused to spend funds allocated for certain programs by Congress. It was another way the executive branch had come to exercise greater budgetary control than the Congress. As of September 30, 1973, $7.4 billion had been impounded by the executive branch. By February, 1974, that total had leaped to $11.8 billion in federal funds appropriated by Congress that the executive branch selectively failed to spend.[86]

The Congressional Budget and Impoundment Control Act of 1974 was an attempt by Congress to deal with the problems listed above. This act gave Congress the machinery for providing overall coordination between spending and revenue programs and for determining budget priorities. There was another reason for passage of this act—a political reason. The Democratic-controlled Congress wanted to show that it was not the reckless, spendthrift institution that President Nixon had said was the cause of the nation's inflation. By passing this legislation, Congress showed that it too was concerned with growing budget deficits and the rate of inflation. Reaction to the 1974 act ranged from high optimism about the real impact on congressional behavior to the more cynical observation that "the more things change, the more they remain the same." The former is reflected in the words of a political columnist: "Congress is like the teen-ager about to inherit its own jalopy. Congress is fondling the keys, the registration, the insurance, and is wide-eyed with anticipation. Now if the old heap will really go. Congress is on the verge of fulfilling that adolescent dream of politics—setting one's own budget." [87] The more cynical view was expressed by a House staff member who sniffed: "There are a lot of guys who voted for this thing (budget reform) who don't really believe in it. They feel that the substantive programs that they are interested in—for instance on health programs, they act on the premise that the more dollars they put in, the quicker they'll find a cure for cancer—that that's more important than the orderly management of fiscal affairs." [88]

The 1974 Act is a comprehensive piece of legislation. Briefly, its ten titles do the following:

1. establish new Budget Committees in both chambers

2. establish a Congressional Budget Office to provide economic information and analysis

3. set up new congressional budget procedures and a detailed timetable for action on the budget

4. create a new fiscal year, beginning in October, that gives Congress more time to react to the president's budget (introduced in January) than did the old fiscal year

5. require the use of sixteen functional budget categories so that information and action are coordinated with the Office of Management and Budget and with the Treasury Department

6. prohibit presidential impoundment of funds through rescissions unless both houses of Congress approve the action within forty-five days of his impoundment proposal.

The two Budget Committees differ in size and composition. The House Budget Committee consists of twenty-five members: five from the Appropriations Committee; five from Ways and Means; thirteen from other standing committees in the House; and two members who represent the majority and minority party leadership. The party caucuses officially select all members of the House Budget Committee and its chairperson. Inclusion of Appropriations and Ways and Means members represents an attempt to insure some expertise on money matters and a way to gain some support from these two committees. The representation of a wide range of viewpoints is the reason for drawing thirteen members from other committees. It is also the reason for providing a rotating committee membership and leadership by prohibiting any member from serving on the committee for more than six years in five successive Congresses.[89]

The Senate Budget Committee consists of twenty members (twelve Democrats and eight Republicans) who are chosen the same way all other committee members are chosen (by the Senate Democratic Steering Committee and the Republican Committee on Committees). The Senate party caucuses voted to select Senate committee members without regard to seniority in the chamber, a move that opened the way for naming one of the principal authors of the budget legislation, Senator Edmund Muskie of Maine, as committee chairman.

Despite these differences in size and composition, the two Budget Committees have the same function in both chambers. As Figure 4–1 shows, the Budget Committees are responsible for hearings and other information-gathering procedures and for producing the two concurrent resolutions that serve to guide all congressional spending and revenue activities.

The Congressional Budget Office is the professional research and information agency created by the 1974 Act. It is headed by a director who is appointed, for a term of four years, by the presiding officers of the House and the Senate. Either house may remove the director. In the fall of 1975, after being in existence for only eight months, the Congressional Budget Office had a staff of 193 people. At that time, its director was asking Congress to increase the staff by sixty-six and to approve a budget of over $10 million. Such requests led some legislators to accuse CBO Director Alice Rivlin of empire building—a common Washington phenomenon both on and off Capitol Hill.[90] During its first year of existence, the Congressional Budget Office was also criticized for having too many liberal economists, for being too aggressive in pushing alternatives to the Republican Administration's budget, and for proposing lower spending in some areas than that sought by labor groups.[91] According to the first director of the Congressional Budget Office, the House and the Senate had two different notions of what the CBO's chief functions should be. The House wanted basically a "numbers shop"—a central place where legislators could get details on federal spending. The Senate saw the Congressional Budget Office as a major source of economic policy alternatives.[92] The 1974 legislation gave the Congressional Budget Office three major functions: (1) to assist the House and the Senate (especially their Budget

FIGURE 4–1 The Congressional Budget Process

October 1	Previous fiscal year begins.
November 10	President submits Current Services Budget (an estimate of the budget outlays needed to carry on existing programs for the next fiscal year, given certain economic assumptions).
December 31	The Joint Economic Committee reports its analysis of the Current Services Budget to the Budget Committees.
January (last week)	President submits budget (fifteen days after Congress convenes).
February	House and Senate Budget Committees hold hearings and begin work on the First Budget Resolution.
March 15	All House and Senate committees and joint committees submit budget estimates and views regarding spending in their policy areas to the House and Senate Budget Committees.
April 1	The Congressional Budget Office submits its report on fiscal policy and national priorities (including programming at alternative budget levels) to the House and Senate Budget Committees.
April 15	Budget Committees report First Budget Resolution (on or before April 15).
May 15	Deadline for all committees to report legislation authorizing new budget authority.
May 15	Deadline for Congress to complete action on First Budget Resolution (prior to this date, neither chamber may consider any revenue, spending, entitlement, or debt legislation for the coming fiscal year).
June, July, and August	Congress enacts appropriations and spendings bills; the Congressional Budget Office issues periodic scorekeeping reports that compare congressional spending with the First Budget Resolution; Committee reports on new budget authority and expenditures must contain comparisons with the First Budget Resolution and five-year projections submitted by the president and by the Congressional Budget Office.
August	House and Senate Budget Committees prepare Second Budget Resolution and report it to their respective chambers.

FIGURE 4–1 Continued

September (7th day after Labor Day)	Deadline for Congress to complete action on all regular budget authority and entitlement bills (entitlement bills, it should be noted again, are those that set up benefits to certain categories of people [retired civil servants, the unemployed, those whose incomes are below the poverty level] whose membership in that class or category automatically entitles them to receive those benefits).
September 15	Congress completes action on Second Budget Resolution. The second resolution confirms or revises the target levels of spending, income, and debt limit contained in the first resolution; it is based on new information, changed economic circumstances, and congressional actions since adoption of the first resolution. After this date, Congress is precluded from considering any bill, amendment, or conference report that would result in an increase in spending ceilings contained in the Second Budget Resolution or a reduction in revenues contained in that resolution.
September 25	Congress completes action on reconciliation bills or resolutions that implement the Second Budget Resolution. These reconciliation bills or resolutions are an offshoot of the Second Budget Resolution's demanding a report and reconciliation for any changes made in spending or revenue levels by any committee. Congress may not adjourn until it completes action on the Second Budget Resolution and all reconciliation matters.
October 1	Fiscal year begins.

Source: Adapted from George Gross (executive director of the House Committee on the Budget), *The Congressional Budget and Impoundment Control Act of 1974: A General Explanation*, U.S. House of Representatives, Committee on the Budget (October, 1975), pp. 7–14, 20–21.

Committees) by providing them with information on the federal budget and on the economic impact of spending and tax legislation; (2) to provide periodic scorekeeping reports that track all congressional spending decisions to date and relate them to the budgetary targets and levels established by the concurrent resolutions on the budget; and (3) in April of each year, to furnish the two Budget Committees with a report on fiscal policy alternatives and national budget priorities.

In Figure 4–1, I have outlined the budgetary timetable established by the Congressional Budget and Impoundment Control Act of 1974. This figure shows the parameters set by the new fiscal year and the key dates for specific actions to be taken within the timetable. Some of these dates are absolute deadlines (May 15), while others are more correctly regarded as the approximate timing of certain actions (September dates for action), which Congress can adapt to its own pace of legislative activity. The two budget resolutions lie at the heart of the new budget process. Both are concurrent resolutions and do not require the president's signature in order to become effective. The First Budget Resolution sets targets designed to guide the actions of all committees. It includes spending levels for the coming fiscal year, both in the aggregate and broken down into the major functional categories of the budget; [93] the level of the budget deficit (or surplus) for the coming fiscal year; the level of federal revenues or income; the recommended level of the national debt; and any other issues or information of use to the congressional budget process. As Figure 4–1 indicates, the Second Budget Resolution updates the first, in light of congressional actions and economic changes, and formally binds all committee actions to conform to these budget levels.

Five years after Congress had established the new congressional budget process, the director of the Congressional Budget Office, Alice Rivlin, pointed out that whether or not members thought that it was working depended on what their expectations for the process had been. "Conservatives wanted the budget process to put a ceiling on expenditures. They saw the purpose as being to hold down expenditures. Liberals, on the other hand, saw it as a way of weighing priorities. They wanted a priorities debate." [94] Neither group has seen its expectations met. Conservatives continue to complain that the Budget Committees have been the allies of the "big spenders," while liberals have not seen their hopes of a consideration of priorities leading to a more equitable tax policy become a reality. Complicating any assessment about the effectiveness of Congress in making fiscal policy is wide disagreement about what the effects of any fiscal policy will be. While some would argue that a tax cut, for instance, would create greater consumer demand

and thus serve as fuel for inflation, others would argue that a tax cut would lead to greater investment, greater production, and a reduction in prices. It is difficult, therefore, to measure the effectiveness of the new budget process in terms of policy results.

Another way to evaluate the new budget process is to look at the process itself, rather than policy outputs, and to determine whether the committees and members of Congress are now behaving in the ways intended by passage of the budget reform. In this respect, the 1974 reform has surpassed the record of the 1946 reform simply by surviving. Early questions about whether the standing committees of Congress would comply with the budget timetable outlined in Figure 4–1 have been answered. They do. Questions about whether Congress as a whole could be forced to consider not just the separate parts of the total budget as it had been doing for decades but rather the federal budget as a whole have been answered positively every time Congress debates the budget resolutions. The Senate budget successes in 1978 in particular, in winning a floor battle with the Agriculture Committee over an emergency farm bill and forcing the Finance Committee to rewrite legislation dealing with tuition tax credits, indicate that the budget process has successfully passed its early survival stage.

In measuring the impact of the congressional budget process, one member of the House committee suggests that the 1974 Act has had the following procedural effects: [95] (1) authorizing committees now plan ahead in a more comprehensive and coordinated way; (2) Congress, under the new system, has been enacting appropriations bills before the end of the fiscal year, thus making planning for the future easier for state and local governments; (3) Congress is paying attention to spending programs that it previously overlooked because of the nature of the appropriations process; and (4) creation of the Congressional Budget Office has greatly increased the amount of information available to members about the economic impact of legislation that they are considering. In addition to these changes, the new budget process, by providing long-term cost estimates (as well as short-term estimates), makes members of Congress more aware of the uncontrollable aspects of the federal budget, such as spending provided by entitlement programs, and makes them think in a longer time frame than simply annual authorizations. The President's Budget for Fiscal 1980, for example, contained spending projections for a three-year period, and some members of Congress have proposed that the legislature act on two-year budgets rather than the current annual schedule.

While the debate over the policy effects of the new congressional budget process are bound to continue, it does seem clear that the Congressional Budget and Impoundment Control Act of 1974 has already had an effect on the procedures of Congress. That effect is a coordinating and centralizing one that improves the ability of Congress to function as a lawmaking institution.

NOTES

1. All of the quotes used in this account are from: William Delaney, "Cast Came to Senate Sitcom But Audience Stayed Away," *Washington Star,* April 13, 1976, p. C1; and "This Senate Issue is Not So Burning," *New York Times,* April 13, 1976, p. 5.

2. Two sources were used to determine these conflicts. Foreign Relations Committee members' other assignments were taken from Hugh A. Travis, Printing Clerk, *Subcommittees and Select and Special Committees Together With Certain Joint Committees of the United States Congress,* Ninety-fourth Congress, (U.S. Government Printing Office, December 19, 1975). The schedule of other committee and subcommittee hearings during the same time is in the *Congressional Record,* April 9, 1976, pp. D506–D507.

   For a study of committee and subcommittee scheduling conflicts in the House, see U.S. Congress, House, *Administrative Reorganization and Legislative Management,* Commission on Administrative Review, Ninety-fifth Congress, first session, September 28, 1977, pp. 27ff. For the Senate, prior to the 1977 reforms, see *The Senate Committee System, First Staff Report to the Temporary Select Committee to Study the Senate Committee System,* U.S. Senate, Ninety-fourth Congress, second session, July, 1976.

3. Harold M. Schmeck, "A Senate Panel's Fictitious Meeting," *Washington Star,* October 4, 1976, p. A6.

4. George B. Galloway, *History of the House of Representatives,* (Crowell, 1968), p. 58.

5. George Goodwin, Jr., *The Little Legislatures: Committees of Congress* (University of Massachusetts, 1970), p. 46.

6. Ward Sinclair, "Administration's Bill Loses Out As Rules on Hill Have Changed," *Washington Post,* November 14, 1978, p. A1.

7. For an excellent discussion of this aspect of congressional leaders' behavior see Louis P. Westefield, "Majority Party Leadership and the Committee System in the House of Representatives," *American Political Science Review* vol. 68, no. 4 (December, 1974), pp. 1593–1604.

8. David R. Mayhew, *Congress: The Electoral Connection* (Yale University Press, 1974), p. 95.

9. U.S. Congress, House, *Administrative Reorganization and Legislative Management, Hearings and Meetings Before the Commission on Administrative Review,* Ninety-fifth Congress, first session, September 8, 1977, p. 247.

10. Representative Butler Derrick (D-S.C.), quoted in Elizabeth Drew, "A Reporter At Large (Washington, D.C.)," *The New Yorker,* April 9, 1979, p. 104.

11. This summary is taken from Bruce F. Freed, "House Reforms Enhance Subcommittees' Power," *Congressional Quarterly Weekly Report,* November 8, 1975, pp. 2407–2412. For more on these reforms and their effects, see Leroy N. Rieselbach, *Congressional Reform in the Seventies* (General Learning Press, 1977); Leroy N. Rieselbach, ed., *Legislative Reform: The Policy Impact* (D. C. Heath, 1978); and Susan Welch and John G. Peters, eds., *Legislative Reform and Public Policy* (Praeger, 1977).

12. Norman J. Ornstein, "Causes and Consequences of Congressional Change: Subcommittee Reforms in the House of Representatives, 1970–1973," in Norman J. Ornstein, ed., *Congress in Change: Evolution and Reform* (Praeger, 1975), p. 102.

13. For a discussion of the impact of this oversight subcommittee requirement see the remarks of Representative Lee Hamilton in the *Congressional Record,* January 22, 1976, pp. E137–E138.

14. Quoted in Freed, "House Reforms Enhance Subcommittees' Power," p. 2410.

15. Ornstein, "Causes and Consequences of Congressional Change: Subcommittee Reforms in the House of Representatives," p. 103; and Freed, "House Reforms Enhance Subcommittees' Power," p. 2410.

16. U.S. Congress, House, *Administrative Reorganization and Legislative Management, Hearings and Meetings Before the Commission on Administrative Review,* Ninety-fifth Congress, first session, September 28, 1977, vol. 2, pp. 21, 32.

17. Richard L. Lyons, "Retirements From Hill Reach A Record High," *Washington Post,* April 16, 1976, p. 1.

18. Quoted in Ornstein, "Causes and Consequences of Congressional Change: Subcommittee Reforms in the House of Representatives," p. 108.

19. Lauros G. McConachie, *Congressional Committees* (Crowell, 1898), p. 136 cited in Thomas R. Wolanin, "Committee Seniority and the Choice of House Subcommittee Chairmen: 80th–91st Congresses," *The Journal of Politics* vol. 36, no. 3 (August, 1974), p. 687.

20. *Committee Organization in the House: Hearings Before the Select*

Committee on Committees, House of Representatives, Ninety-third Congress (U.S. Government Printing Office, 1973), vol. 2, p. 813, and vol. 3, p. 197.

21. Quoted in Freed, "House Reforms Enhance Subcommittees' Power," p. 2407.

22. B. Drummond Ayres, Jr., "House Democrats Slow Reform; O'Neill Gains Power," *New York Times,* December 8, 1978, p. A17. Also see B. Drummond Ayres, Jr., "Democrats in House Relax Reform Plan," *New York Times,* December 7, 1978, p. A19, and Mary Russell, "House Democrats Limit Subcommittee Service: Back Curbs on Roll Calls," *Washington Post,* December 6, 1978, p. A2.

23. Woodrow Wilson, *Congressional Government* (Meridian, 1967), p. 66.

24. Clem Miller, quoted in John Baker, ed., *Member of the House: Letters by Congressman Clem Miller* (Charles Scribner's Sons, 1962), p. 110.

25. For a hierarchy of committee preferences, 1949–1968, see William L. Morrow, *Congressional Committees* (Charles Scribner's Sons, 1969), pp. 42–43.

26. Quoted in David S. Broder, "Budget Becomes Popular," *Boston Globe,* January 14, 1979, p. C7. The committee preferences in 1979 were derived from this article and from a staff interview, Majority Whip's Office, U.S. House of Representatives, Washington, D.C., January 11, 1979.

27. Donald R. Matthews, *U.S. Senators and Their World* (Vintage, 1960), pp. 154–155.

28. Goodwin, *The Little Legislatures: Committees of Congress,* pp. 102ff.

29. Richard F. Fenno, Jr., *Congressmen in Committees* (Little, Brown, 1973), p. 58.

30. Ibid.

31. Ibid., p. 3.

32. Ibid., pp. 20ff. For a more thorough discussion of this criterion see Nicholas Masters, "Committee Assignments," in Robert Peabody and Nelson Polsby, eds., *New Perspectives on the House of Representatives* (Rand McNally, 1969), pp. 240ff.

33. Richard F. Fenno, Jr., "The Appropriations Committee as a Political System," in Peabody and Polsby, eds., *New Perspectives on the House of Representatives,* p. 129.

34. John Manley, *The Politics of Finance* (Little, Brown, 1970), p. 218.

35. Ibid., p. 67.

36. Quoted in Richard F. Fenno, Jr., *The Power of the Purse: Appropriations Politics in Congress* (Little, Brown, 1966), p. 200.

37. *Committee Organization in the House: Hearings Before the Select Committee on Committees, House of Representatives, Ninety-third Congress* (U.S. Government Printing Office, 1973), vol. 2, p. 7.

38. Julius Duscha, "The Most Important Man on Capitol Hill Today," *New York Times Magazine*, February 25, 1968; and Manley, *The Politics of Finance*, p. 137.

39. Quoted in Manley, *The Politics of Finance*, p. 113.

40. Ibid., p. 125.

41. Ibid., p. 107.

42. Quoted in Mary Russell, "Aged Aid Rise Approval Seen," *Washington Post*, January 18, 1976, p. A2. For an analysis of Ullman's leadership and the postreform Ways and Means Committee, see Catherine Rudder, "The Policy Impact of Reform of the Committee on Ways and Means," in Rieselbach, ed., *Legislative Reform: The Policy Impact*, pp. 73–89.

43. Fenno, *Congressmen in Committees*, p. 9.

44. Ibid., p. 12.

45. Ibid., p. 10.

46. This is in contrast to the Senate Foreign Relations Committee, which is charged with maintaining the Senate's constitutional powers in this area similar to the House money committees' function of preserving the House fiscal powers outlined in the Constitution. See Fenno, *Congressmen in Committees*, pp. 151ff.

47. For documentation and analysis of this presidential dominance see Holbert N. Carroll, *The House of Representatives and Foreign Affairs* (Little, Brown, 1966); Michael K. O'Leary, *The Politics of American Foreign Aid* (Atherton, 1967); and Randall B. Ripley and Grace A. Franklin, *Congress, the Bureaucracy, and Public Policy* (Dorsey, 1976), Chapter Seven.

48. Fenno, *Congressmen in Committees*, p. 31.

49. Ibid., p. 73. The post-Vietnam House Foreign Affairs Committee has begun to play a broader role in foreign policy-making. Issues now regularly considered, and occasionally made the subject of legislation, include: a country-by-country evaluation of the impact of U.S. economic and military assistance; U.S. arms sales to other countries; international economic policy as determined by such institutions as the World Bank, the International Monetary Fund, and OPIC (Overseas Protective Investment Corporation); general trade policies and commodity agreements; and human rights considerations involved in foreign policy. The level of congressional expertise has been increased by the committee's developing a highly professional committee staff. But the committee's big bill (or bills, since economic and military aid are now con-

sidered in two separate pieces of legislation) is still foreign aid, and the committee's dependence on the executive branch for initiation and setting the parameters of debate on that issue remains.

50. Ibid., p. 72.

51. The interaction among Foreign Affairs members, the full committee staff members, subcommittee staff members, and staff members from the personal offices of committee members provides an interesting insight into the roles of congressional staffs, the importance of control over information for gaining institutional power, and the continued dominance of the executive branch in this area. The most precious type of information relevant to the committee's decisions is information that is classified secret, top secret, etc. by the Administration. The committee staff closely guards all such classified information in the committee offices in the Rayburn building. Only members and committee and subcommittee staff with a security clearance have access to this information. Other classified information is divulged in closed sessions to which only members and cleared committee/subcommittee staffers have access. While the substantive value of such classified information is often questionable (one member of the committee who previously had a job with the State Department poring over classified cables and documents said that he learned more from reading the *New York Times* and the *Washington Post* than he did from classified materials), the close control over such classified information is one of the ways that the committee staff is able to maintain control over members' personal staffs and—indirectly—members themselves. The fact that it is the State Department and other executive agencies which originally classify such information and control its dissemination gives the executive branch an edge over the legislative branch in this policy area.

52. Fenno, *Congressmen in Committees*, p. 86.

53. Quoted in Richard F. Fenno, Jr., "Congressional Committees: A Comparative View," paper delivered at the annual meeting of the American Political Science Association, Los Angeles, 1970, p. 50.

54. Fenno, *Congressmen in Committees*, p. 90.

55. Fenno, "Congressional Committees: A Comparative View," pp. 48–49.

56. Fenno, *Congressmen in Committees*, p. 108.

57. Ibid., p. 107.

58. Ibid., p. 101.

59. Ibid., p. 103.

60. Ibid., p. 102.

61. Ibid., p. 135.

62. Charles O. Jones, "The Agriculture Committee and the Problem of Representation," pp. 155–174, and Lewis Anthony Dexter, "Congress-

men and the Making of Military Policy," pp. 175–196 in Peabody and Polsby, eds., *New Perspectives on the House of Representatives*. For a thorough analysis of the relationship between defense spending and Senate voting patterns, see Bruce M. Russett, *What Price Vigilance?* (Yale University Press, 1970); and James Phillips, "The Military Industrial Complex," *Congressional Quarterly Special Report*, May 24, 1968, pp. 1155–1178.

63. Fenno, *Congressmen in Committees*, p. 6.

64. Jones, "The Agriculture Committee and the Problem of Representation," p. 169, and Fenno, *Congressmen in Committees*, p. 6.

65. Dexter, "Congressmen and the Making of Military Policy," p. 182.

66. Fenno, *Congressmen in Committees*, p. 62.

67. Jones, "The Agriculture Committee and the Problem of Representation," pp. 158ff.

68. Fenno, *Congressmen in Committees*, p. 65.

69. Ibid., p. 63.

70. Jones, "The Agriculture Committee and the Problem of Representation," pp. 170–171.

71. Fenno, "Congressional Committees: A Comparative View," pp. 41–42.

72. Fenno, *Congressmen in Committees*, p. 92.

73. Ibid., p. 110.

74. Ibid., p. 100.

75. Jones, "The Agriculture Committee and the Problem of Representation," p. 160.

76. Fenno, *Congressmen in Committees*, p. 136.

77. Ibid., p. 123.

78. Freed, "House Reforms Enhance Subcommittees' Power," p. 2408.

79. See, for example, David E. Price, "Policy Making in Congressional Committees: The Impact of 'Environmental' Factors," *American Political Science Review*, vol. 72, no. 2 (June, 1978), pp. 548–574; Glenn R. Parker and Suzanne L. Parker, "Factions in Committees: The U.S. House of Representatives," *American Political Science Review*, vol. 73, no. 1 (March, 1979), pp. 85–102; and the collection of articles on committees in Rieselbach, ed., *Legislative Reform: The Policy Impact*.

80. U.S. Congress, House, *Committee Organization in the House, Hearings Before the Select Committee on Committees*, Ninety-fourth Congress, first session, vol. 2, June 13, 1973, p. 5.

81. For an excellent discussion and analysis of the Bolling Committee proceedings, see Roger H. Davidson and Walter J. Oleszek, *Congress Against Itself* (Indiana University Press, 1977).

82. For more on the topic of ad hoc committees, see David J. Vogler, "The

Rise of Ad Hoc Committees in the House of Representatives: An Application of New Research Perspectives," a paper prepared for delivery at the annual meeting of the American Political Science Association, New York, N.Y., August 31 to September 3, 1978; and Bruce I. Oppenheimer, "Policy Effects of House Reform: Energy Legislation, 1975–1977," a paper prepared for delivery at the annual meeting of the American Political Science Association, New York, N.Y., August 31 to September 3, 1978.

83. Peter Milius, "Minding Money on the Hill: Is Change Real?" *Washington Post*, January 18, 1976, p. Fl.

84. Louis Fisher, "Budget Reform and Impoundment Control" (The Library of Congress, Congressional Research Service, Issue Brief Number IB 74079, updated February 23, 1976), pp. 1–3.

85. George Gross, *The Congressional Budget and Impoundment Control Act of 1974: A General Explanation*, U.S. House of Representatives, Committee on the Budget, October, 1975, p. 2.

86. *Congressional Quarterly Weekly Report*, March 2, 1974, pp. 569–570. For a thorough discussion of the process of impounding funds see Louis Fisher, *Presidential Spending Power* (Princeton University, 1975), Chapters Seven and Eight.

87. Martin F. Nolan, "Growing Up With a Budget," *Boston Globe*, May 11, 1975, p. B7.

88. Quoted in *Congressional Quarterly Weekly Report*, September 7, 1974, p. 2418.

89. This four-year limit has the effect, according to at least one member of the committee, of making the committee a secondary one. Budget committee members, especially those who also serve on Appropriations and Ways and Means, are more likely to give more of their time to the latter committees, where they can put in years and develop great committee influence, than they are to a committee on which they will be serving only four years. Representative Barber Conable (R-N.Y.), talk before the American Political Science Association Congressional Fellows, November 13, 1975.

90. See the comments in Walter Taylor, "Now the Budget Office Boss Wants Her Own Limousine," *Washington Star*, October 30, 1975, p. 1.

91. See the interview with Rivlin in Donald Smith, "CBO Director Alice Rivlin: No 'Hidden Agenda' for Congressional Action on Economic Recovery," *Congressional Quarterly Weekly Report* vol. 33, no. 36 (September 6, 1975), pp. 1924–1925.

92. Alice M. Rivlin, Congressional Budget Office Director, talk before the American Political Science Association Congressional Fellows, November 21, 1975.

93. The sixteen functional budget categories are: national defense; international affairs; general science, space, and technology; natural resources, environment, and energy; agriculture; commerce and transportation; community and regional development; education, manpower, and social services; health; income security; veterans benefits and services; law enforcement and justice; general government; revenue sharing and general purpose fiscal assistance; interest; and undistributed offsetting receipts.

94. *Congressional Quarterly Weekly Report,* January 6, 1979, p. 11.

95. Ibid., pp. 12ff. Assessments of the congressional budget process may be found in John W. Ellwood, "The New Congressional Budget Process: Its Causes, Consequences, and Possible Success," in Susan Welch and John G. Peters, *Legislative Reform and Public Policy* (Praeger, 1977); Louis Fisher, "Congressional Budget Reform: The First Two Years," *Harvard Journal on Legislation,* vol. 14, no. 3 (April, 1977), pp. 413–457; Joel Haveman, *Congress and the Budget* (Indiana University Press, 1978); and James A. Thurber, "New Powers of the Purse: An Assessment of Congressional Budget Reform," in Rieselbach, ed., *Legislative Reform: The Policy Impact.*

5

RULES AND NORMS

At 7:30 in the morning on Sunday, October 15, 1978, a weary
House of Representatives cast a final vote and sent to the president
the National Energy Act of 1978. The legislation was a five-part
energy package which contained only some of the energy measures
proposed by President Jimmy Carter almost a year and a half earlier
in April, 1977. The five major sections of the bill provided for decon-
trolling the price of natural gas by 1985, conversion from oil or gas
to coal by industry, utility rate reforms, conservation measures for
homes and public buildings, and tax incentives for greater conservation of energy in residential and business use.

Final passage of the energy legislation represented an end to a
number of events: a lengthy and complex process that had seen
House leaders go outside the standing committee structure to create
a special ad hoc committee on energy and orchestrate House passage of the comprehensive energy bill in three months, long dead-
locks in the Senate when senators on the conference committee
could not agree on a formula for pricing of natural gas, and a series
of last minute attempts by a coalition of senators and representatives opposed to sections of the energy program to use the rules of
both chambers to block final passage of the energy bill.

A few days before final passage of the bill, on Thursday,
October 12, 1978, the Senate began consideration of the conference
report on the energy tax bill—one of the five energy bills in the
Senate that together constituted the omnibus energy program.

When a motion was made for unanimous consent to dispense with the actual reading of the bill, Senator James Abourezk of South Dakota objected to this routine measure for facilitating legislative consideration, and the Senate clerk had to spend seventy-five minutes reading aloud the complete text of the bill. Senate majority leader Robert Byrd responded to this delaying tactic by pulling the bill from the floor and scheduling for that Saturday a cloture vote to limit debate on the energy tax proposal.

At the same time that this was going on in the Senate, the House Rules Committee was meeting to decide in what form the energy bill would be considered on the floor of that chamber. House leaders wanted a rule that permitted only one vote on the entire energy package, while opponents of the energy bill wanted separate floor votes on the different sections of the energy program because they felt this would increase their chances of defeating the natural gas provisions in the program. A Rules Committee tie (eight to eight) on motions both to have the bill considered as one package and to consider it in sections kept the Rules Committee deadlocked all day Thursday. By the next morning, one of the three Democrats who voted against a single floor vote in the Rules Committee had changed his mind, and the Committee sent to the House floor a rule calling for one vote on all five sections of the energy bill. That proposal squeaked by on Friday afternoon when the House, by a 207–206 vote, supported a motion to order the previous question (i.e., to end debate) on adoption of the Rules Committee resolution to waive points of order so that the House could consider all of the energy conference reports in one motion. That House vote, technically convoluted as it might seem, represented a victory for House leaders seeking passage of the energy bill. Opponents of the energy bill, however, had not given up the fight.

A coalition of representatives and senators started a new attack. On Saturday morning, October 14, the Senate voted seventy-one to thirteen to invoke cloture and end debate on the energy tax bill. Each senator is permitted one hour of debate time after a cloture vote, and Senator Abourezk and his allies took advantage of Senate rules by appealing parliamentary rulings, issuing quorum calls, and moving to recommit the conference report. This post-cloture filibuster tied up the Senate for fifteen hours throughout Saturday night and early Sunday morning. Until the Senate passed the energy tax bill, the House could not act on the five-part energy bill it had agreed to treat as one package because the energy tax bill was part of that package. The Senate filibuster was thus delaying House action as well as Senate action.

As the Senate filibuster dragged on, a number of House members went over to the Senate floor to watch, and a few representatives began shuttling between the two sides of the Capitol in hopes of striking a deal. A group of northeastern Democrats told Speaker Tip O'Neill that Senator Abourezk would end his filibuster if O'Neill would agree to let the House take up an alternative energy tax credit bill, which had already passed the Senate and provided larger tax credits for homeowners and none for businesses. O'Neill refused. Representative Richard Ottinger of New York hoped that continuation of the Senate filibuster past midnight would give him the opportunity to move to adjourn the House and to begin a new legislative day. The alternative energy tax bill could then be brought forward as new business in the new legislative day. But the leaders of both chambers refused to give in to what they considered legislative blackmail; House leaders promised Senate majority leader Byrd that under no circumstances would they permit the House to consider the alternative energy tax bill. "That bill is down the drain, dead, d-e-a-d," Senator Byrd informed his fellow legislators.[1]

Early Sunday morning, October 15, 1978, Senator Abourezk finally admitted defeat and ended his filibuster. The Senate immediately passed the conference report on the energy tax bill by a vote of sixty to seventeen. At 2:45 A.M., the House began debate on final passage of the omnibus energy bill. Most members were off somewhere sleeping during most of the debate, but at 7:30 that morning they reassembled to pass the five-part energy bill by a vote of 231–168.

The events of the last four days of congressional action on the National Energy Act of 1978 are instructive not only because they highlight different approaches to dealing with a national crisis but also because they suggest that there are some fundamental differences between the two chambers of our national legislature. That the House produced an omnibus energy bill three months after the president's call for action while the Senate spent about a year and a half formulating legislation does not mean simply that the House is more responsive to pressing social needs or that the Senate is always the more conservative body. Rather, the structure of each chamber and the rules of behavior related to that structure reflect two different conceptions of the legislative function. The structure and rules of the Senate emphasize the deliberative, or representational, role, as seen in the long debate on energy, while House rules emphasize a lawmaking role that requires less talking and speedier dispatch of legislative business.

The Senate is expected to be a great forum for debate and the representation of all interests and viewpoints in the nation as a whole; the House is regarded as a legislative mill that must process an overwhelming amount of technical legislation. These basic functional differences produce different rules and norms in the two bodies. I will discuss some of the more important of these rules, but first let us look at some of the basic differences between the two sides of Capitol Hill.

HOUSE-SENATE DIFFERENCES

"If the Senate has been the nation's great forum," a representative has written, "the House has been its workshop." [2] Most of us tend to think of Congress as a whole and discuss it in terms of its shared characteristics (decentralization, seniority, the existence of two co-equal chambers). Yet there are important differences between the House and the Senate—differences that exist despite many changes in the House (the facilitation of floor voting, the increasing importance of subcommittees, and the expanded staff allowances), that have tended to make the House more like the Senate as a representational body rather than a lawmaking body. These differences are reinforced by the rules and norms governing legislative behavior in the two houses. Some of the more important differences are discussed below.[3]

Size

Most of the dissimilarity between the two chambers stems from the fact that the House is made up of 435 members elected for two-year terms while the Senate consists of one hundred members elected for six-year terms. The impact of this fundamental difference is enormous. Senators, even newly elected ones, are much more visible than representatives. They can more readily obtain media coverage when they want to discuss some issue; they rank higher in Washington's social protocol; and they have a larger allowance for staff and office expenditures. Most important, the upper chamber is regarded as a prime source of candidates for the presidency.

Because the House is more than four times the size of the Senate, it cannot operate in the informal relaxed manner characteristic of the upper chamber. The House is more formal, more impersonal, more hierarchically organized. There is a sharper division of labor in the House. It is a decentralized system that maximizes the technical consideration of complex legislation by committee and subcommittee experts.

Committees

Committee work is generally more important to a representative than to a senator. The House, with 435 members, has twenty-two standing committees; the Senate, with 100 members, has fifteen. Most senators serve on three standing committees, while most representatives serve on two. Because the Senate has one hundred subcommittees while the House has 147, senators serve on many more subcommittees than do representatives. The average senator's total committee and subcommittee assignments are about twice that of the average House member. In the Ninety-fifth Congress (1977–1978), for example, the average senator served on eleven committees and subcommittees, while the average representative served on six committees and subcommittees.[4] The Senate's overlapping membership on many committees and subcommittees greatly reduces the mystique of committee and subcommittee expertise that is so important in the House. Committee and subcommittee membership in the Senate gives members a wider range of issues over which they can have some influence.

This greater dispersion of power in the Senate can be seen even more clearly when we look at the distribution of committee and subcommittee chairmanships rather than just membership. Senators of the majority party are more likely to be committee or subcommittee chairpersons than are House members of the majority party. In the Ninety-sixth Congress (1979–1980), 98 percent of the Senate Democrats held committee or subcommittee chairmanships, whereas only 53 percent of House Democrats held these positions.[5]

Because fewer people are competing for committee and subcommittee leadership positions in the Senate, the amount of time it takes to assume these positions is shorter for a senator than for a representative. All of these factors, when put together, suggest the different impact committees have on legislative behavior in the two chambers and on the careers of senators and representatives. In the House, committees are primarily a place for legislative work, a place for senior members with great expertise to deal with complex matters of lawmaking. To have any real influence on policy, an individual legislator must be on the committee that handles legislation in that area. While Senate committees must necessarily perform lawmaking functions, there is greater opportunity for senators to play a representational role in committee, and there is a better chance for a senator to have some influence over a wider range of policy areas.

Leadership Control

Its greater size forces the House to be organized in a more formal, hierarchical way than the Senate. This, in turn, requires that the leadership in the House be given more direct control over members. Both the formal rules and the unwritten norms of the two chambers support this difference.

A leading student of the Senate once described it as a place where "no one finally can make anyone else do anything." [6] This scholarly description fits with a lighter definition of the Senate, sometimes put forward by senators themselves, as a place where a person makes a speech that says nothing, nobody listens, and then everybody disagrees. Leadership in the Senate reflects this pattern of concern for the individual senator. For instance, in scheduling floor debate on a bill, majority party leaders will generally canvass the membership and arrange the timing of the debate to suit all members' schedules. Such a practice would be impossible in the House, where leaders schedule floor action after consultation only with the principal party and committee leaders. This leads to individual House members being subject to leadership control over their actions to a much greater degree than are Senate members.

House and Senate rules reflect this difference in control over the behavior of individual members. House rules are more complex and more specific than Senate rules. In the Ninety-fifth Congress (1977–1978), it took more than 300 pages to outline the rules of the House and eleven volumes to spell out precedents of interpretation and procedure; the Senate rules, on the other hand, filled about a third as many pages, and its precedents were contained in one volume. The loose structure of the Senate encourages the full representation of all views, whereas the rules of the House, in the words of an expert on the subject, "show a constant subordination of the individual to the necessities of the whole House as the voice of the national will." [7] While both chambers are charged with fulfilling both lawmaking and representation functions, the House emphasis on lawmaking and the Senate emphasis on representation is a difference that is reinforced by the rules of both chambers, particularly by the stricter control over the actions of members that the House rules provide.

Policy Roles

The House-Senate structural differences we have been discussing are closely tied to the roles each chamber plays in the policy process. The two chambers are best suited for two different sorts of policy-producing activities.

The House, with its well-ordered division of labor, is best able to play a policy role of drafting legislation in conjunction with subject matter experts in executive agencies and bureaus. Committees are the policy workshops of the House. Career patterns based on seniority and subject matter expertise put highly placed House members on an equal footing with executive technicians in drafting legislation. When an executive spokesperson goes before a House committee such as Ways and Means, a former Treasury official has observed, "he is confronted with an independent panel of specialized experts who usually possess vastly more experience than he." [8] The House role in policy-making is primarily one of lawmaking. This function is carried on in committee by subject matter experts well versed in the technical details of complex legislation.

The Senate's policy role is different. As Nelson Polsby has written, " 'passing bills,' which is central to the life of the House, is peripheral to the Senate. In the Senate the three central activities are (1) cultivating national constituencies; (2) formulating questions for debate and discussion on a national scale (especially in opposition to the president); and (3) incubating new policy proposals that may at some future time find their way into legislation." [9] Policy incubation is the process of keeping a new proposal alive. It involves continuing to introduce a proposal until it gains enough supporters to assure passage or until the political climate has changed enough so that a proposal that at first seemed "radical" becomes accepted as a possibly rational solution to some problem. To accomplish these policy goals, the Senate must emphasize the representational values of extensive debate, of mutual deference to individual legislators rather than to committees, and of an unstructured informal legislative chamber that gives as much time to discussing ideas as it does to passing legislation.

To become a law, policy proposals must pass both chambers and emerge from Congress in one form. If the Senate gives one nickel more than the House does in a bill to finance a housing program, the program does not come into being until the two chambers agree on an identical bill. After running the gamut of these two chambers with their different policy orientations, most important bills wind up in a joint House-Senate conference committee that must reconcile the differences between the bills and produce a compromise bill that can win acceptance on both sides of Capitol Hill.

A growing body of literature on conferences suggests that the Senate generally wins most conference battles with the House.[10] These studies do not really mean that the upper chamber always has the upper hand in conflicts over policy. Rather, the Senate victories in conference are directly related to the different policy roles of the House and the Senate. Senate conferees follow a role of supporting broadly based proposals that have the backing of the whole chamber, while House conferees defend proposals advanced by committee experts that do not necessarily have widespread support among that chamber's membership. The policy role differences between the two chambers are carried on into the final interchamber bargaining sessions for producing bills.

Table 5-1 provides a summary of the major differences between the House and the Senate. Because these many differences make the two chambers distinct legislative bodies, the next two sections will discuss separately some of the more important rules that help to shape each chamber.

HOUSE RULES

Senate rules tend to support representational values, while House rules are directed more toward decision-making. In both chambers there are many opportunities for delaying or defeating a measure. In the Senate, procedures favoring such tactics as the filibuster are defended in terms of their providing for personal and minority representation. House rules that have the same delaying effect more often stem from procedures intended to facilitate the decision-making function. The House Rules Committee, which on occasion

TABLE 5–1 Differences between the House and Senate

House	Senate
435 members	100 members
2-year term	6-year term
Constituency: about 500,000 in district	Constituency: entire state, ranges from 300,000 to 20 million
Low visibility in press and media	High visibility in press and media
Rules strictly limit participation	Rules maximize full participation by all members
Committee and subcommittee work very important	Committees and subcommittees not as important
Distribution of power is hierarchical	Distribution of power is more diffuse
Strict leadership control of floor proceedings	Less leadership control of floor proceedings
Less reliance on staff	More reliance on staff
Policy specialists	Policy generalists
Lawmaking emphasis	Emphasis on representation

Source: Adapted from Walter J. Oleszek, *Congressional Procedures and the Policy Process* (Congressional Quarterly Press, 1978), p. 24. Some items added.

has served to delay or defeat legislation, is designed to perform the important decision-making functions of controlling the flow of legislation to the floor and the conditions under which that legislation is considered. By performing this function, the Rules Committee plays a key role in moving bills along the legislative treadmill. Because it is another point at which a decision must be made, the Rules Committee can be used to slow down or stop legislation. Even when it agrees to hold hearings on a bill, the Rules Committee can block legislation by refusing to grant a rule permitting floor consideration. Between 1965 and 1974, for instance, the Rules Committee refused to grant a rule on thirty-eight bills, thus blocking any floor consideration.[11] Bills that have fallen by the wayside at this juncture include some major legislative proposals: a strip mining bill in 1974, income tax credits for social security taxes in 1978, and a balanced budget amendment in 1979. Although a series of reforms and, as of 1979, a new committee chairman sympathetic with the House leadership have made the Rules Committee quite unlike the graveyard of liberal legislation that it has been in earlier times, the committee represents a stage in the lawmaking process in which decisions must be made and delays can occur.

Two aspects of House rules are most important here: calendars and the Rules Committee. When a bill has been cleared by committee and awaits floor action, it is placed on one of many lists of bills called calendars. The Union Calendar lists bills raising revenue, general appropriation bills, and other public bills that directly or indirectly appropriate money or property. The House Calendar lists public bills that do not raise revenue or directly or indirectly appropriate money or property. The Private Calendar lists bills that affect only those named in the bill. Bills that have appeared on the Union or House Calendars but are likely to be unopposed because of their minor character may be placed on the Consent Calendar.

Most bills that pass the House do so on the Private Calendar. Lewis Froman suggests that 300 to 500 private bills are reported by committee each session and placed on the Private Calendar. He found that over a third of the bills passed by the Eighty-eighth Congress were private bills.[12] There are two basic types of private bills: (1) those that pay an individual who has suffered personal injury, property damage, or nonpayment of benefits as a result of government action and (2) immigration bills that allow certain people to enter the country as exceptions to immigration quotas. Bills on the Private Calendar are called up on the first Tuesday of each month; they may also be called up on the third Tuesday of each month at the discretion of the Speaker. No other business may be considered on these days except by a two-thirds vote of the House. Each side is given five minutes to debate a bill. If two members object to consideration of a bill on the Private Calendar, it is returned to committee. Committees seldom report such a bill a second time. Bills on the Private Calendar must be approved by unanimous consent. Because most members do not want to waste time on the floor during consideration of private bills, both parties designate official objectors to be present during the call of the Private Calendar. These objectors, acting for the party or for individual legislators, are able to prevent passage of any unwanted private legislation.

Another calendar used to improve House efficiency in producing legislation is the Consent Calendar. Bills passed on the Consent

Calendar are generally noncontroversial bills that provide minor benefits to specific constituencies. Naming a VA hospital, making a minor administrative change in existing law, disposing of public lands are all actions that might be handled in this way. The Consent Calendar is called on the first and third Monday of each month. If one member objects to a bill called on the Consent Calendar, the bill is passed over to the next call of the calendar. Three members objecting at that time is enough to have the bill stricken from the calendar. Bills defeated on the Consent Calendar may be returned to the House or Union calendars and brought to the House floor in another way. Few members are on the House floor during consideration of Consent Calendar bills. As in the case of the Private Calendar, both parties have official objectors. In spite of these procedures allowing a small minority to reject a bill, the Consent Calendar accounts for the second largest number of bills passed by the House.

The Private Calendar and the Consent Calendar are both devices for expediting the flow of legislation through the House. They permit minor and noncontroversial legislation to move through without taking up much of the members' time or clogging up channels needed for consideration of important legislation. Other procedures also exist for the purpose of bringing bills quickly to the floor. On the second and fourth Monday of each month, bills reported by the District of Columbia Committee are privileged business. This permits the whole House to deal expeditiously with the fifteen or so bills reported in each Congress by the District of Columbia Committee, bills which have to do with raising revenue and managing the District of Columbia. Another procedure designed to permit the House to maximize its lawmaking function is known as suspension of the rules. Since the Ninety-fifth Congress (1977–1978), the House may consider bills under suspension of the rules on Monday and Tuesday of every week at the discretion of the Speaker. Earlier, suspensions could take place only on every other Monday. Under the suspension process, debate on a bill is limited to forty minutes, and no amendments may be offered to the bill unless they are permitted by the floor manager of the bill. A two-thirds vote is required to pass legislation under suspension of the rules. While the suspension of the rules procedure is designed to save time in passing noncontroversial or minor bills, the House leadership in the Ninety-fifth Congress (1977–1978) used the suspension process with increasing frequency for passing some more important legislation, including large authorization bills. This increase in the use of suspension of the rules is reflected in the fact that the Ninetieth Congress (1967–1968) considered 167 bills under suspension, whereas the Ninety-fifth Congress (1977–1978) considered more than 400 under the suspension process.[13] A number of Democrats joined Republican members in protesting that the suspension process was being used by House leaders to avoid full debate and amendments on major pieces of legislation. Suspension bills, in the words of one member, "are like greased pigs. You turn them loose and you can't get hold of them." [14] Because of these complaints, House Democrats changed the rules governing suspensions at the beginning of the Ninety-sixth Congress (1979–1980) and limited the use of suspension of the rules to bills authorizing less than $100 million.

Another way bills may be brought quickly to the floor is through a discharge petition. Any public bill that has been before a standing committee for thirty days or any committee-approved bill that has been before the Rules Committee for seven days without receiving a rule may be brought to the floor through a discharge petition signed by a majority of the House (218 members). A petition gaining the necessary signatures is placed on the Discharge Calendar, which is in order on the second and fourth Monday of each month. A majority vote on these days will bring the bill to the floor for immediate consideration. From 1910, when the rule was adopted, until 1975, 860 discharge petitions were filed, but only 25 of them were successful.[15]

House rules also provide that certain committees may bring special types of legislation directly to the House floor at any time without having to get a rule from the Rules Committee. The six committees and the privileged legislation that may be brought directly to the floor are: Appropriations (general appropriations bills), Budget (budget resolutions), House Administration (resolutions for printing materials and spending money from the House contingent fund), Rules (rules and the order of business), Standards of Official Conduct (resolutions recommending censure, reprimand, or other actions for misbehavior), and Ways and Means (revenue-raising bills).

All of the procedures we have discussed so far provide for ways to bring legislation to the floor without going to the Rules Committee. They are designed to help the House perform its legislative function by providing quick consideration of low-conflict legislation. Most important legislation, however, does not follow this path. Instead, a rule from the Rules Committee is required to bring the bill from the House or Union calendar to the floor. The form of such a rule will vary, but the following example gives some indication of what a typical rule looks like:

> *Resolved,* That upon the adoption of this resolution, it shall be in order to move that the House resolve itself into the Committee of the Whole House on the State of the Union for the consideration of the bill (H.R._____), entitled, etc. After general debate, which shall be confined to the bill, and continue not to exceed _____ hours, to be equally divided and controlled by the chairman and the ranking minority member of the Committee on _____, the bill shall be read for amendment under the five-minute rule. At the conclusion of the consideration of the bill to the House with such amendments as may have been adopted and the previous question shall be considered as ordered on the bill, and amendments thereto to final passage without intervening motion except one motion to recommit with or without instructions.[16]

Four types of rules are granted by the Rules Committee. Most legislation comes to the floor under an open rule that permits the House to amend the committee bill. An open rule helps organized minorities who are not satisfied with the committee bill and wish to add or delete certain provisions.

A second type of rule granted by the committee is a closed rule that prohibits certain types of amendments. James Robinson's study of the Rules Committee showed that closed rules are seldom used. Between 1939 and 1960, there were 1,128 open rules and eighty-seven closed rules granted by the committee.[17] A closed rule is most often used in conjunction with bills coming from the Ways and Means Committee. Tax bills or social security legislation are both highly vulnerable to special interest demands and represent a delicate balance worked out by experts on Ways and Means. Floor amendments, it is argued, would upset that balance. As one member of the committee said: "It'd be suicide if you ever tried to write a tax or social security bill on the floor. We sit in there surrounded by experts to keep us from going off on a tangent so you can imagine what would happen on the floor." [18] In 1973, the Democratic caucus changed the rules governing issuance of a closed rule from the Rules Committee. The new procedure requires that a committee chairperson give four days notice of a request for a close rule. During that period, fifty members of the Democratic caucus may call for a meeting of that body, and a majority of the caucus may instruct the Rules Committee to permit certain floor amendments when the bill comes up. This new procedure was used soon after it went into effect, when the Democratic caucus instructed the Ways and Means Committee to permit amendments dealing with the oil depletion allowance in floor consideration of a tax bill in 1974, and when the caucus instructed the Rules Committee to permit amendments to the Committee Reform Amendments considered the same year. A variation on this second type of rule is the modified closed rule, or complex rule, which permits amendments to only certain parts of the bill during floor consideration. In recent years the Rules Committee has increasingly relied on complex rules for important legislation. When the National Energy Act of 1977 came to the House floor, for example, the rule limited the permitted number of amendments to twenty from the Ad Hoc Committee on energy and twelve from individual representatives.[19]

The third type of rule granted by the committee is one that waives points of order against a particular bill. This rule is used most often by the Appropriations Committee when it has a bill that contains legislative provisions as well as appropriations. House rules permit any member to raise a point of order against legislative provisions in general appropriations bills. A single objection is enough to have the measure stricken from the bill. In order to avoid this the Appropriations Committee asks for a rule waiving points of order against the bill. Because the inclusion of such provisions in an appropriations bill can produce serious conflict with the legislative committees, this procedure of waiving points of order for appropriations bills is used sparingly. During the period 1939–1954, the Appropriations Committee received an average of two waiver rules per year.[20]

The fourth type of rule is one that sends a bill to conference when it has passed the House and Senate in different form. Prior to 1965, any member could object to sending a bill to conference, thus requiring that the Rules Committee grant a rule for sending the bill to conference. A rules change in that year provided that a majority of the House be able to send a House-passed bill with Senate amendments to a conference with the Senate, thus avoiding the Rules Committee.

In the Ninety-fourth Congress (1975–1976), a total of 300 rules were granted by the Rules Committee. The committee declined to hold hearings on twenty bills, and it denied or deferred a rule on five bills. This high rate of approval of candidate bills was not always the case with the Rules Committee. From 1955 to 1966, while chaired by Representative Howard Smith of Virginia, the Rules Committee consistently defeated major legislation in the areas of civil rights, aid to education, and economic policy. Under the direction of Chairman Smith the Rules Committee was able to effectively veto all legislation opposed by the conservative coalition then dominating the committee. But House reforms and changes in the makeup of the Rules Committee have changed the role of the Rules Committee from what it was during the Smith era. In 1961, the size of the Rules Committee was increased from twelve to fifteen, giving the Democratic House leadership an effective one-vote margin on the committee. In 1965, the House adopted the twenty-one–day rule, which permitted House leaders to call for consideration bills that had been sitting before the Rules Committee with no action taken on them for twenty-one days. In 1966, a number of rules changes were adopted that eliminated the ability of the chairperson to run the Committee in an arbitrary way. Finally, in 1975, the Speaker of the House was given the power to appoint all Democratic members of the Rules Committee. These reforms, coupled with membership changes that saw liberal and moderate Democrats replace retiring or defeated conservatives, have made the Rules Committee today a strong ally of the House Democratic leadership. Studies that measure the Democratic party unity scores for members of the Rules Committee and that look at committee decisions show that the Rules Committee has moved from being an independent source of conservative power at odds with the Democratic leadership to being an arm of that leadership itself.[21] Representative Richard Bolling's emergence as Rules Committee chairman in 1979, the first chairman under seventy years old in twenty-four years and a strong ally of Speaker O'Neill, was symbolic of the active, pro-leadership role now being played in the House by the Rules Committee.

The House calendars and the Rules Committee are designed to increase the efficiency of House decision-making. By reducing the amount of floor time spent on minor legislation, these devices seek to increase the rationality of legislating. Any organization of this size must provide institutionalized procedures for decision-making. Most House rules seek to achieve this rationality by providing automatic procedures for handling legislation. Instead of each representative being asked to make a political judgment on every bill, the structure of House rules provides a hierarchy of experts who make rational decisions after careful consideration of all factors. Specialization is reinforced by House rules that greatly limit the participation of unqualified members in legislative decisions.

While procedural reforms and structural changes have had a profound impact on the workings of the House, and have made it more like the Senate, all of these changes have not totally altered the fundamental structure of the House. Leadership use of House calendars and the Rules Committee still determines which matters will come to the floor for a vote, when they will come, and the conditions under which they will be considered by the whole chamber. Leadership control over the conditions of floor debates and floor voting is still formidable. House leaders tend to accept the notion that the lower chamber is the place for making laws and that the luxury of extensive debate on issues can only be afforded in the Senate.

SENATE RULES

In the Senate, bills are brought to the floor in a simpler, more direct way than in the House. The Senate has no Private Calendar, Consent Calendar, District of Columbia Calendar, Discharge Calendar, or Rules Committee. There are only two Senate calendars: the Calendar of Business, which lists all legislation, and the Executive Calendar for nominations and treaties. When a bill has been reported by committee it goes on the appropriate calendar to await action by the majority party leadership. When the Democrats control the Senate, floor scheduling is handled by the Democratic Policy Committee, a nine-member committee chaired by the majority leader. In practice, the scheduling is done by the majority leader after consultation with the minority leadership and other interested individual senators. When a bill is stalled between the committee report and floor action, it is not the result of a Rules Committee impeding action, but rather of the majority leadership's respect for minority wishes or the schedule of an individual senator. In the Senate there might be as many as five bills on the floor at the same time, while the House always limits itself to consideration of only one bill at a time.

Once a bill comes to the Senate floor, the differences between the two chambers become even more apparent. Two important rules governing Senate floor proceedings help to explain most of these differences. They are procedures relating to the germaneness of debate and to concluding debate.

The Senate adopted a germaneness rule in 1964, but it is more often violated than followed. Because the Senate floor is viewed as an excellent forum for speeches, members want to be able to come to the floor and deliver a prepared speech at any time. If all such speeches had to be related to the topic under consideration, senators would have great difficulty meeting their other commitments and still being on the floor when that particular topic came up. All senators know that they will be in this position at some time, therefore they support any member's right to speak on any subject at any time by not objecting to unanimous consent to waive the germaneness rule. Although this practice often makes the Senate proceedings seem chaotic compared to the House, it does permit consideration of many measures at once and allows the Senate to function as the chamber of comprehensive debate.

Congress would be brought to a standstill, however, if the Senate only debated measures without taking any legislative action. Within this framework of unfettered debate, the Senate rules must also provide a way for the Senate to meet its lawmaking responsibilities by passing legislation. There must, in other words, be a way for Senate leaders to control the floor just as the many calendars and the Rules Committee of the House permit House leaders to control the floor. In the Senate this structure is provided by unanimous consent agreements. These are agreements, accepted by all senators, to set aside the formal rules of the Senate in order to expedite legislative consideration. There are two types of unanimous consent agreements: simple and complex. Simple unanimous consent agreements are those made orally on the floor of the Senate by individual senators and deal with routine business. They include requests to have certain staff members on the floor during debate, for insertion of material into the *Congressional Record,* for extensions of time for roll-call votes, and for permission for committees to meet while the Senate is in session. Visitors to the Senate gallery will hear endless repetitions of the phrase, "Mr. President, I ask unanimous consent," followed by a wide variety of requests.

Complex unanimous consent agreements, on the other hand, serve much the same function as rules granted by the Rules Committee do in the House. They set the guidelines under which the Senate will consider major legislation. These unanimous consent agreements are developed by Senate party leaders and key senators involved in the issue. They are written agreements that indicate the order in which particular measures will be considered, which senators will control floor time during consideration of these measures, and the guidelines for debate, often including a statement about what types of amendments will be considered germane and thus given a hearing. In 1977, Senate majority leader Robert Byrd began the practice of providing senators with a list of bills to be considered by unanimous consent agreement a day before floor action was scheduled. Table 5-2 compares the Senate unanimous consent agreement procedure with its House counterpart, the House rule procedure.

There are three ways to conclude debate in the Senate: un-

TABLE 5-2 House Rules and Senate Unanimous Consent Agreements

House Rule	Senate Unanimous Consent Agreement
Specifies time for general debate	Specifies time for debating amendments and on final passage
Permits or prohibits amendments	Usually restricts only the offering of nongermane amendments
Formulated by Rules Committee in public session	Formulated by party leaders in private sessions or sometimes on the floor
Approved by majority vote of the House	Approved by unanimous approval of senators present on the floor
Adoption generally results in immediate floor action on bills	Adoption geared more toward prospective action
Covers more aspects of floor procedure	Limited primarily to debate restrictions on amendments and final passage
Does not specify date and exact time for vote on final passage	May set date and exact time for vote on final passage
Effect is to waive House rules	Effect is to waive Senate rules

Source: Walter J. Oleszek, *Congressional Procedures and the Policy Process* (Congressional Quarterly Press, 1978), p. 142.

animous consent, cloture, or everyone simply stops talking. Although unanimous consent is the most common means for bringing a matter to a vote, the cloture rule is important because of the profound impact it has on all Senate behavior.

On March 7, 1975, after two weeks of debate, the Senate adopted the first major change in Rule 22 (which determines the procedure for invoking cloture and ending a filibuster) since any limit on floor debate had first been introduced in 1917. Prior to this change, Rule 22 specified the following procedure for invoking cloture: sixteen senators must sign a cloture petition; on the second calendar day after the petition is filed, the Senate votes on the motion to end debate; if two-thirds of those present and voting support the cloture motion, then senators may speak for one hour each on the bill under consideration, no additional amendments may be offered, and only germane amendments may be voted on. The 1975 change in Rule 22 changed the required number needed to end debate from two-thirds of those present and voting to a constitutional three-fifths of the entire Senate membership—regardless of how many members are present and voting. Under the old rule, if all members were present and voting, sixty-seven senators were required to support cloture in order to end a filibuster. Under the new rule, sixty members can limit debate by invoking cloture, regardless of how many members are present and voting.

This rules change in the Ninety-fourth Congress came about after the Ninety-third Congress had seen a record number of cloture votes taken by the Senate in any one Congress. The new procedure was intended to make it easier for the Senate to control filibusters by invoking cloture. It was clearly a reaction to the increased use of the filibuster and the resulting increase in cloture attempts that took place in the 1970s. Between 1919 (when the first cloture vote was taken on the Versailles Treaty) and 1970, there were forty-nine cloture votes taken in the Senate. Between 1971 and February 1975 (the month before the change in Rule 22), there were fifty-two such votes.[22] That represents a jump from less than one cloture vote a year to thirteen votes a year. It also represents the increased willingness of liberal senators to employ the filibuster (once considered the primary tool by which conservative southerners successfully defeated progressive legislation supported by a majority of the Senate).

What happened after the 1975 rules change provides an interesting example of how congressional reforms sometimes have unintended effects. The purpose of changing Rule 22 in 1975 was obviously to reduce the power of obstructionist senators to threaten filibusters and to increase the likelihood of Senate leaders' being able to win on cloture votes by reducing the number of supporters needed to invoke cloture. At first glance, it might seem that the rules change did weaken the filibuster as an obstructionist tool. In 1975, the year of the change, there were twenty-three cloture votes, eleven of which were successful. In 1976, there were only four, and in 1977, there were only five. But this drastic reduction in cloture votes did not, by any means, indicate the demise of the Senate filibuster. As you might recall from the discussion in Chapter 1, it was in 1976 that Senator James Allen first violated the unwritten rule that a cloture vote ended a filibuster and used the Senate rules to conduct a post-cloture filibuster. By taking advantage of the fact that each senator still had one hour of debating time after a cloture vote and that Senate rules did not count time spent on parliamentary tactics, such as quorum calls and the introduction of amendments, against that allotted hour, Senator Allen was able to tie up the Senate for hours after cloture had been invoked. The post-cloture filibuster device was used in 1977 by two liberal Democrats to delay Senate action on a natural gas deregulation bill for two weeks after cloture had been voted. That filibuster was broken only by an extraordinary procedure in which the Senate majority leader and its presiding officer, Vice President Walter Mondale, were able to rule out of order the long string of dilatory amendments being offered by the filibusterers. Use of the post-cloture filibuster threat to delay action on bills in the Ninety-fifth Congress (1977–1978) led majority leader Robert Byrd to call for a second reform in Rule 22, since the 1975 reform had not had its intended effect. On February 22, 1979, the Senate changed its rules to include in the post-cloture one-hour time limit given each senator all time spent on quorum calls, roll-call votes, and other parliamentary devices for stalling action on legislation. Because it takes sixty senators to end a filibuster, Rule 22 still permits a minority to block action by a majority in the Senate. But the 1979 rules change means that a minority of fewer than forty can no longer use the post-cloture filibuster to block a majority of sixty or more senators and hamstring the Senate.

In concluding this section on Senate rules, it is perhaps worth mentioning again the basic difference between House and Senate rules. House rules are designed to allow a majority to work its will; they seek to facilitate decision-making. In the Senate, Rule 22 illustrates that chamber's emphasis on representation to the extent that a minority can prevent a decision from being made.

It should also be clear that the net effect of the rules in both chambers is not neutral. Those who seek to change the status quo must first seek to change the rules that work against them. This is hard to do for two reasons. First, a majority that can change the rules can generally exercise its will within the existing framework anyway. As the authors of a book on congressional reform put it:

> When majorities are able to work their will in Congress, they see little need for procedural change. When majorities are slender or unstable, the need for attaining high priority legislative goals diverts attention from reform efforts. Thus reform-minded Congressmen often find themselves in the dilemma of the old man with the leaky roof: when the sun was shining, there was no need for repair; when it was raining, it was too difficult to repair.[23]

A second reason for the difficulty of changing rules is found in the fact that one rule or procedure may have multiple purposes. A quorum call can be an effective tool for party leaders seeking to make sure the necessary supporters are present and also a useful instrument of delay for those opposing the measure. When a rule has different purposes for different groups of members, it is difficult to reach consensus as to the implications of changing that rule.[24] As a result, it is hard to put together a majority coalition supporting the rule change.

HOUSE AND SENATE FOLKWAYS

On September 8, 1970, the Senate began debate on an amendment to replace the electoral college with direct popular election of the president. Consideration of the measure was done in the common "two-shift" schedule of the Senate—the electoral reform measure would be debated for a portion of the day, the Senate would move to other matters by unanimous consent, and the reform measure would be picked up again on the next day. A coalition of southern and small state senators opposed to the measure were successful in blocking a vote on the amendment by insisting that there had not been enough debate. A cloture vote to end this tacit filibuster failed by six votes on September 17, and the two-shift consideration continued. One week later, Senator Birch Bayh, floor manager for the bill, undertook a strategy designed to force a Senate decision. By objecting to unanimous consent requests that the Senate move to other business and by objecting to allowing committees to meet while the Senate was in session, Bayh was able to bring Senate business to a halt. From September 24 to 29, the senator from Indiana was able to force the Senate to debate his amendment exclusively. After a second cloture vote failed on September 29, Bayh admitted defeat by agreeing to unanimous consent that the amendment be put aside and the Senate move to other business.[25]

Individual actions of this kind are not confined to the Senate. After the House passed the Civil Rights Act of 1964, Representative John Bell Williams of Mississippi showed his disfavor by tying up the House for an hour with similar objections to unanimous consent motions. The rules of both chambers make it possible for a single member to greatly hamstring his or her colleagues. Such measures are seldom used, however, and the reasons for this reflect the influence of unwritten norms, or folkways, on the behavior of members of Congress.

Any organization must develop norms of behavior that contribute to its achieving organizational goals. Such norms provide the stability and predictability necessary for the institution's maintenance and goal achievement. Donald Matthews's study of the post–World War II Senate is the primary source of any discussion about legislative folkways.[26] A major study of Senate norms in the 1970s found that of the six folkways discovered by Matthews in the Senate in the 1950s, five remained in effect within the modern Senate (although the interpretation of who benefitted from at least one of those five had changed from the earlier period).[27] Other studies of the House of Representatives and state legislatures have uncovered similar patterns of expected behavior in these bodies.[28]

Legislative norms may be classified by the primary functions they perform. Some contribute to the chamber's goal achievement in terms of decision-making or representation; others contribute to maintaining the existing system by regulating the level of conflict. Folkways that help Congress perform its decision-making function are those of specialization, apprenticeship, and legislative work. The norm of reciprocity aids decision-making in the House but seems to be more geared to achieving representational goals in the Senate. Folkways helping to maintain the existing system by controlling conflict are those of courtesy and institutional patriotism.

Specialization

Norms that contribute to the function of decision-making are more important in the House than in the Senate. The House must have thorough rules governing the handling of legislation. It also must have informal norms supporting a more structured decision-making process. By encouraging representatives to specialize in one or two subjects, House norms prevent the chaos that would result from every member attempting to speak on each subject, and at the same time insure that there will be a number of experts on each subject coming before the House. The results of specialization were noted by one congressman when he observed: "There is always someone around here who's an expert on something you need to know. I dare say there is not one subject you could think of that doesn't have at least one member of the House particularly qualified to give you advice about it." [29] Matthews's study of the Senate found general agreement that: "The really effective senators are those who speak only on the subjects they have been dealing with at close quarters, not those who are on their feet on almost every subject all the time." [30]

Even though we find a norm of specialization in both houses, specialization means different things in the House than it does in the Senate. In the House, specialization is tied to the importance of committee work, the development of subject matter expertise, and the division of labor necessary for accomplishing that chamber's lawmaking function. In the Senate, specialization is much less committee-oriented and is conceived mainly as expertise to enhance the senator's standing with a national constituency associated with that subject.[31] Specialization helps the Senate to play a policy incubation role by insuring that there will be at least one senator to keep debate alive on an issue that does not yet command the majority necessary to become law. In short, the specialization norm in the House helps to fulfill the lawmaking responsibilities of that chamber, while the specialization norm in the Senate helps that chamber to provide for the representation of many diverse interests throughout the country.

Apprenticeship-Seniority

The apprenticeship norm aids decision-making by giving the greatest impact on decisions to members who have been in Congress (or on the committee) the longest. It is another part of the process, described earlier, of maximizing the influence of those "best qualified" to make each type of decision. Freshmen are limited in their participation by norms that suggest that the prudent first-termers are those who talk little, tend to their committee work, cooperate with their leaders, and spend their time learning how to be good legislators. "Like children," one said, "we should be seen and not heard." [32]

At the other end of the hierarchy, apprenticeship norms are reflected in a seniority system that grants influence over policy chiefly on the basis of length of service. Those who support the idea of seniority and like to quote scripture can find a rationalization for seniority in *The Federalist Papers* of Alexander Hamilton, John Jay, and James Madison. The author of Federalist Number 53, writing in 1788, observed: "No man can be a competent legislator who does not add to an upright intention and a sound judgment a certain degree of knowledge of the subjects on which he is to legislate. A part of this knowledge may be acquired by means of information which lie within the compass of men in private as well as public stations. Another part can only be attained, or at least thoroughly attained, by actual experience in the station which requires the use of it." [33] Defenders of the apprenticeship-seniority system suggest that Congress is no different from any other organization in this regard. As a former Speaker noted:

> No sane man would for one moment think of making a graduate from West Point a full general, or one from Annapolis an admiral, or one from any university or college chief of a great newspaper, magazine or business house. A priest or preacher who has just taken orders is not immediately made a bishop, archbishop or cardinal. In every walk of life, "men must tarry at Jericho till their beards are grown." [34]

Nelson Polsby, a leading scholar of Congress, has noted that "the great advantage of the seniority system is that it decentralizes power in the House of Representatives by creating multiple centers of policy influence and increasing the number of good Congressional jobs. This adds to the incentives of the Congressional career." [35] Defense of the seniority system generally follows a pattern of focusing mainly on the House goal of lawmaking and on individual House-career patterns to achieve that goal.

Among those who attack the seniority systems are, not surprisingly, young members of Congress who seek to play a representative role and want to influence policy rather than follow a safe House-career pattern. Others are journalists, citizen groups, and academicians who emphasize the unrepresentativeness of the seniority system because of its benefits to southern, rural, or one-party districts. Senator Don Riegle of Michigan is a former "young" congressman. In his book, *O Congress*, Riegle laments the fact that his five years as a congressman give him little influence over policy. He places much of the blame for this on a congressional seniority system in which:

> A man can come to Congress when he's thirty-five, serve here twenty years and emerge, at fifty-five, as the ablest man on his committee. But because he has to wait for all the members ahead of him to retire or die, he may have to wait another twenty years—until he's seventy-five—before he becomes a chairman. The practical and psychological implications of this are obvious.[36]

Those involved in Ralph Nader's Congress Project represent the second group of critics of the seniority system. In *Who Runs Congress?* the authors point out that the average committee chairperson in 1870 was in his forties, in 1910, he was fifty, and in 1972, he was sixty-seven; that 87 percent of the committee chairpersons from 1950 to 1970 came from one-party districts; that in 1970, thirteen of twenty-one House committee chairpersons came from rural districts; and that southerners held more than one-half of the committee chairmanships from 1921 to 1966.[37] In 1979, the average age of House chairpersons was sixty-two, with twenty-five years of service in the House, compared with the average House member's age of forty-nine and nine years of service. In the Senate, the average age of chairpersons was sixty-five, with twenty-three years of service, compared with the average membership age of fifty-three and ten years of service.[38]

Although apprenticeship norms in the House continue to support a system of decision-making by experienced committee experts, the impact of a strict seniority system has been diminished. Studies of committee assignments, the distribution of power within committees, conference committees, and party leadership selection have suggested that the seniority system is a flexible one that permits consideration of factors other than just tenure.[39]

Of the six norms discussed in Matthews's earlier study apprenticeship is the only one that no longer existed in the Senate of the 1970s.[40] In the House, there is a great deal of evidence to show that apprenticeship and strict adherence to seniority have become a thing of the past. Freshmen representatives of 1974 were successful in toppling three senior chairmen from positions of power (in early 1975) and also in gaining acceptance for freshmen to play a more active role in lawmaking. By 1979, the same junior members who were responsible for the earlier overthrow of three senior chairmen engineered another upset by passing over three senior members for subcommittee chairmanships on the Commerce and Government Operations Committees and electing more junior members to these positions. Indeed, one of those elected, Representative Henry A. Waxman of California, had been one of the 1974 freshmen involved in the earlier anti-seniority move. The 1979 seniority upset is even more striking because it did not remove autocratic committee leaders as the 1975 action did, but reflected the fact that many members passed over the senior contenders on ideological grounds. The new attitude toward the seniority system among younger representatives was summed up by Congressman Waxman when he noted: "We don't feel bound by it." [41]

The apprenticeship-seniority norm has always been most evident in the House, especially on committees. Representative Tom Foley, who became chairman of the House Agriculture Committee as one of those three chairmen replacing more senior members in 1975, talks about how the old system worked. When he first came to the House in 1964, Foley and the other freshmen on the Agriculture committee were given a lecture by the committee chairman that went something like this. "I hate and detest to hear a new member interrupt a senior member asking a question," said chairman Harold Cooley. "You new members will come to realize that, if you remain silent, the senior members will ask all the relevant questions needed to illuminate every point." [42] The idea of Foley or any modern committee chairperson giving such a speech to freshmen members is unthinkable today. This alone suggests the magnitude of change the apprenticeship-seniority norm has undergone in one decade.

In assessing factors that led to the elimination of the apprenticeship norm in the Senate, the 1970s study concluded that the nature of election and the character of the class of 1958 had a great deal of impact. The Senate apprenticeship norm provided limited benefits most directly to the southern clique that controlled that chamber. All of the fifteen new senators elected in 1958 came from outside the South, and most of them were liberals. The economic recession of 1958 helped to sweep in most of these new Democratic senators, and they were determined to play an active role in doing something to correct this recession. The activist nature of the freshmen of that year and their impact on the apprenticeship norm is captured in the observation of a senior senator: "It [apprenticeship] was absolutely true when I first came. . . . But then when the class of '58 came in, they landed talking and they never quit, and those that are still there are still talking." [48] The House Democratic freshman class of 1974 has often been described in remarkably similar terms. This would suggest that one of the reasons for the decline of apprenticeship as a legislative norm is the nature of these incoming classes who immediately seek to play an active policy role rather than waiting the expected time to achieve some position of influence.

A second reason why apprenticeship-seniority is no longer so important in either chamber is the institutional change embodied in reforms adopted by both parties. These reforms, which pre-dated the arrival of the House class of '74, have been used by them to gain influence and have been expanded upon since then to consolidate that influence. A brief summary of important House reforms instituted in 1971, and ratified and expanded upon by succeeding congresses, should illustrate this.

In 1971 both parties in the House adopted reforms in the seniority system for determining committee positions. The Democrats agreed that:

1. The Democratic Committee on Committees would recommend to the caucus nominees for the chairmanship and membership of each committee, and such recommendations need not necessarily follow seniority.

2. The Committee on Committees would make recommendations to the caucus, one committee at a time; upon the demand of ten or more members, nominations could be debated and voted on.

3. If a nomination is rejected, the Committee on Committees would submit another nomination.

4. No member could be chairperson of more than one legislative subcommittee.

Republicans in the Ninety-second Congress also adopted seniority reforms affecting the selection of ranking members. These reforms included the following guidelines:

1. The nomination for ranking Republican member of each committee would be put to an automatic vote of the entire Republican membership in the House.

2. The Republican membership would vote in secret on these nominations.

3. The member nominated need not be the member with the longest consecutive service on that committee.

4. If the nomination was rejected, the Republican Committee on Committees would submit another nomination.

Additional reforms by House Democrats in 1973 and 1975 consolidated the check on the seniority system given to all members by providing for a secret ballot vote on all nominations for committee and Appropriations subcommittee chairpersons and by giving the Democratic Steering and Policy Committee the power to make all committee assignments.

Senate reforms followed the same pattern as those of the House. In 1973, Senate Republicans provided that the ranking minority member of each committee would not be automatically elevated to that position because of seniority but would be elected by Republican members of the committee, subject to approval by all Senate Republicans. In 1975, Senate Democrats agreed that a secret ballot would be held on Steering Committee nominations for committee chairpersons whenever one-fifth of all Democratic Senators requested such a ballot.[44]

The changes in the seniority system serve to institutionalize the flexibility in the seniority norm that earlier studies had discovered. The changes also indicate the extent to which the old apprenticeship-seniority norm has been greatly diminished as a controlling factor of legislative behavior. But they do not completely eliminate seniority as a norm that helps to determine who will have the most influence over certain policy areas. And again, the different structures of the two chambers lead to a different impact of the same norm in the House and the Senate.

Seniority is a norm essential to lawmaking and to providing incentives for long-term careers. For this reason, seniority has a more immediate effect on the individual representative than it does on the individual senator. The representational function of the Senate, its structure of overlapping committee membership, and its more diversified career patterns (based on higher visibility, the opportunity to cultivate national policy constituencies, and the possibility of using a Senate career as a launching pad for national office candidacies), produce a higher tolerance for young "upstarts" in that chamber and a more flexible application of the seniority norm in terms of controlling the behavior of members.

Legislative Work

A third norm crucial to decision-making is that of legislative work. Because most of the legislator's work is "highly detailed, dull, and politically unrewarding," it is important to the functioning of both chambers that the system reward those who put in the long hours needed to fashion sensible legislation.[45] Matthews's study of the Senate showed the importance of this norm to that body:

> The words used to describe those senators who seem to slight their legislative duties are harsh—"grandstanders," "demagogues," "headline hunters," "publicity seekers," "messiahs." They are said to do nothing but "play to the galleries," and not to be "team players." It is even occasionally hinted that they are mentally or emotionally deranged.[46]

The importance of legislative work in the modern Senate is clearly visible in the office and the activities of the majority whip. When the Senate is in session, the majority whip must be available to all members in order to consummate bargains, see that amendments are submitted and acted on in the proper fashion, and schedule all floor activities for that day and the next. Senator Robert Byrd of West Virginia defeated Senator Edward Kennedy of Massachusetts for the whip post in 1971. Byrd was able to hold on to the post partially because he was willing to perform conscientiously the day-to-day tasks of scheduling, which many senators shun not only because of the drudgery but also because these tasks require the constant presence of the majority whip in Washington. It is clear that this requires sacrifices in terms of cultivating national constituencies or running for president, but the rewards for performing this routine legislative work include the position of formal party leadership and a great deal of influence over policy outcomes.

In the House, the norm of legislative work is most clearly demonstrated in the case of such high prestige committees as Ways and Means and Appropriations. Richard Fenno's study of the latter led him to conclude:

> By adopting the style of hard work, the Committee discourages highly individualized forms of legislative behavior, which could be disruptive within the Committee. It rewards its members with power, but it is power based rather on work inside the Committee than on the political glamour of activities carried on in the limelight of the mass media.[47]

This norm helps to account for the fact that some of the most influential members of the House are virtually unknown outside Congress. Most of the important committee work is done backstage. The member who increases his or her influence by diligence in committee work is unlikely to have much time left over to develop a media image. Indeed, as one legislator commented, "the very ingredients which make you a powerful House leader are the ones which keep you from being a public leader." [48]

Reciprocity

A reciprocity norm operates in both chambers, but with quite different effects. In the House, reciprocity is manifested in the respect committee members have for the expertise of other committee members. The norm functions to support decision-making in the House. An example of this type of reciprocity is the relationship between a substantive committee and its counterpart appropriations subcommittee. According to Fenno, "there normally exists a mutual recognition that the Appropriations Committee should not define programs, i.e., legislate, in an appropriation bill and that the authorizing committee must accept the dollar figure set by the appropriating committee." [49]

Reciprocity in the Senate focuses more on the interaction between individuals than between committees. Because senators serve on many committees, the membership of any one committee will represent a broad spectrum of the other Senate committees. Unlike the House, where reciprocity operates through a specialized committee structure, Senate reciprocity works through a "relatively undifferentiated, interlocking decision-making structure." [50] The result is that senators will go out of their way to insure that every member's views are given a hearing, that there is "the maximum participation of a maximum number of its members" on every decision.[51] Senate reciprocity, rather than contributing to a smooth decision-making process, primarily serves the goal of representation.

Courtesy and Institutional Patriotism

Decision-making arises from and also produces conflict. The structure of Congress and such norms as specialization and legislative work provide a focus for conflict as part of the decision-making process. The wide dispersion of power in both chambers creates a great potential for conflict among individuals and among committees, and between leaders and followers. In order to maintain itself as an institution capable of achieving decisional goals, Congress must keep this conflict within manageable bounds. Two folkways are most important here: courtesy and institutional patriotism.

The norm of courtesy prescribes that even the most intense conflict over issues should not lead to personal conflict. One way to accomplish this is to maintain an impersonality in debate—to address an opponent as "the Senator from Maine," rather than "Mr. Muskie" or "Ed." At times this formality shades into the comic:

> Mr. JOHNSON of Texas. The Senator from Texas does not have any objection and the Senator from Texas wishes the Senator from California to know that the Senator from Texas knew the Senator from California did not criticize him . . .[52]

The norm of courtesy creates an aura of good feeling as shown in the following observation by Clem Miller of California:

> One's overwhelming first impression as a Member of Congress is the aura of friendliness that surrounds the life of a congressman. No wonder that 'few die and none resign.' Almost everyone is unfailingly polite and courteous. Window washers, clerks, senators—it cuts all ways. We live in a cocoon of good feelings.[53]

Another congressman captures this mood of good feeling in describing the scene in January of 1972 when the House reconvened for its second session:

> The chamber buzzed with loud hellos, story-swapping and laughter and I was reminded once again how physical a place this is. Congressmen don't just speak to one another. They punch each other on the arm, slap each other on the knee, grab at each other's jackets and occasionally give each other a goose.[54]

This air is maintained by a courtesy norm that not only proscribes any sort of personal attack but also actively supports members' going out of their way to keep matters on a friendly plane:

> Mr. Chairman, at the appropriate time, I intend very humbly and very prayerfully to offer an amendment. I hope the gentleman from Texas, my distinguished intellectual leader and my athletic leader, will help me a little bit with it, and if he would I would bestow upon him the highest accolade of all and call him my spiritual leader, if he will help me to correct an injustice that I know he does not want to be meted out upon the gentleman from Florida.[55]

Senator Edward Brooke of Massachusetts, after sitting through a long floor discussion filled with verbal manifestations of the courtesy norm, suggested that if the word *distinguished* were taken out of floor speeches, legislators could save 10 percent of their time. Senate majority leader Mike Mansfield's response to Brooke's suggestion: "I appreciate the remarks of the distinguished senator from Massachusetts for his views." [56]

Although this courtesy norm often strikes the outside observer as a bit silly, the norm does greatly affect both the style and the content of congressional debate. Just as the conversational style of the British House of Commons discourages demagogic speeches, so too does the courtesy folkway in Congress provide a limit to conflict. It is difficult to accuse a colleague of being either a Marxist or a Fascist after referring to him as "the distinguished senator from New York." Senators cited in the Matthews study were quite aware of the importance of this courtesy norm to the smooth functioning of the Senate and were quite supportive of it. As one senator commented about the norm and the behavioral patterns it generates:

> These are little things that at times look highly exaggerated in the Senatorial context and they are; but very frankly, I don't think, if we didn't practice these, that we would have any semblance of order in the Senate. I think that it's the catalyst that maintains a semblance of order. If we didn't stand up and go through a lot of this "my dis-

tinguished colleague" and on and on, we'd end up probably in trouble at times.[57]

Courtesy demands that members of Congress avoid any sort of personal charges even if the charge is common knowledge. Even though many senators considered the 1970 debate on providing $290 million for developing a supersonic transport airplane to be a question of helping out the influential Senators Jackson and Magnuson of Washington (home of Boeing Aircraft), they shuddered when Senator Proxmire of Wisconsin brought this fact into the open by remarking:

> There are just two very good reasons for the Federal financing of an SST. One is the senior senator from Washington and the other is the junior senator from Washington.[58]

Exchanges on the House floor have also indicated breaches in the courtesy norm. After being sharply and personally criticized by Representative Wayne Hays of Ohio in a 1974 debate over school busing, Representative Morris Udall of Arizona retorted:

> Mr. Chairman, I have rarely done anything around here that the gentleman from Ohio approved of. However, I was reminded of a story I heard about the Quaker funeral. They were trying to think of something good to say about this fellow. Finally, somebody shuffled his feet and said, "He wasn't much, but I will say this about him: He wasn't as mean sometimes as he was usually." [59]

A similar exchange took place on April 29, 1976, in the floor debate over budget priorities. After a black congressman from California criticized the priorities in the budget resolution, a conservative Republican stated that such comments were in "particular bad grace" coming from a member of the black race. This statement prompted a liberal from New York to suggest that the conservative's comments were racist. This remark provoked the conservative Republican to leap up and shout, "I am not going to stand here and let this pipsqueak lecture me." [60] It is clear from this encounter that the courtesy norm does not always prevent such outbursts in heated debate over hotly contested issues.

Institutional patriotism is also a norm that helps to limit the level of conflict in Congress. It is more obvious in the Senate because of the higher status of that body and because in the House members are more likely to aspire to the Senate or to a governorship back home. Few things can so quickly unite the Senate as an attack on its integrity. A House chairman tried to force a settlement on the 1964 Appropriations Bill then in conference by noting: "Nobody on earth can find out names of everyone who is on a Senator's payroll. I personally know of a Senator who keeps two call girls on his office payroll. I know because I've been at parties where they've been." [61] The Senate reacted to this attack by defeating the conference report, eighty-eight to two. When Senator Joseph McCarthy was censured in 1954 after browbeating witnesses and making unsubstantiated accusations of persons being Communists and traitors, the primary charge in the Senate's censure resolution was that McCarthy "acted contrary to Senatorial ethics and tended to bring the Senate into dishonor and disrepute." [62] The norm of institutional patriotism helps to reduce conflict within Congress by providing a shared sense of values that even the most hostile opponents can agree on. When institutional patriotism comes into play in congressional conflicts, it provides a basis for unity in each chamber. Proponents of a measure can sometimes increase the size of their coalition by making it a matter of the House versus the Senate, or Congress versus the president.

One rather perverse form that institutional patriotism seems to take is the congressional practice of "protecting its own." As the Joseph McCarthy case illustrates, Congress is most reluctant to provide any self-regulation of its own members. This norm of mutual self-protection was highlighted in the spring of 1976, when the House Committee on Standards of Official Conduct (more popularly known as the House Ethics Committee) reluctantly began the first inquiry into the alleged misdeeds of a member. This happened only after forty-five House members agreed to allow the charges against the member brought by the public interest group, Common Cause. This marked the first time in the committee's eight years of existence that a formal inquiry into the ethical behavior of a member had been undertaken. During those eight years, several members of Congress had been charged with violations of the law, some had been indicted, and some had even gone to jail. This lack of self-regulation of legislators' behavior could be justified in terms of some of the folkways we have been discussing—reciprocity, courtesy, and institutional patriotism—but it does seem to be a distortion of the norm of institutional patriotism. A behavioral pattern could develop that would seriously undermine the legitimacy of the institution and continue to provide support for the low opinion of Congress.

The Functions of Legislative Folkways

All of the legislative folkways we have discussed serve more than just one function. For instance, the seniority system that is part of the apprenticeship norm is defended not only in decision-making terms but also for contributing to conflict reduction. By making the selection of committee chairpersons a relatively automatic process, the seniority system allows Congress to avoid this potentially high conflict area. The norm of reciprocity also plays an important role in maintaining a low conflict situation. The folkways of Congress are generally evaluated as being functional for the legislative system; that is to say, they help Congress achieve its decision-making and representational goals and they help maintain the existing legislative system. In an institution where the individual has power to block actions by the group, informal norms that keep individuals from exercising that power are crucial. Without such norms to constrain individualistic behavior, it is unlikely that Congress could achieve its decision-making tasks.

But what is functional for the legislative system is not necessarily functional for the larger society. Some critics argue that the high premium that legislators place on cooperation and bargaining leads to their avoiding conflict by postponing or passing difficult or sensitive decisions on to others.[63]

It is not necessary to adopt a conspiratorial view to see that one effect of both the formal rules and the informal norms of Congress is to strengthen the hand of those who wish to maintain the status quo. By the time a member of Congress is in a position to exert major influence over important issues, he or she will have acquired a heavy stake in the existing system. Both in terms of legislation in the areas of the member's expertise and in the existing distribution of influence within the chamber, the status quo is a means of evaluating that legislator as a member of Congress.

CONFERENCE COMMITTEES

Most books about Congress discuss conference committees in the "committees" section of the book. This makes sense because the members of these ad hoc committees responsible for settling House-

Senate differences are drawn from the standing committees of the two chambers. Such treatment often overlooks some of the points raised earlier in this book: that the House and Senate play different roles in the policy process, that committees in the House have a more direct impact on representatives' policy influence and general legislative action, and that conference committee members are called upon to play different roles in settling interchamber disputes than they are in dealing with legislation in their respective standing committee bailiwicks. These differences are not completely a product of chamber rules governing conference committees, for the formal procedures of conference are generally similar in both the House and the Senate.

Conference Rules

When one chamber produces a bill that differs from the measure already passed by the other chamber, two things can happen: either the chamber that first passed the legislation concurs in the changes made in the second house and the bill goes to the White House for signing into law; or, both houses agree to set up a joint conference committee to compromise the differences and to produce one bill that both chambers can approve. About 15 percent of the laws passed by Congress go through the conference committee route; this 15 percent often includes the major legislation handled in that session.[64] Because of the importance of this third house of Congress, about thirty pages of the House and Senate *Rules and Manuals* deal with the questions of who selects the conference delegates, who sits on conference, how the conference goes about drafting a compromise bill, and the procedures for voting on the finished product of conference negotiations.

Conference rules in both chambers say that the presiding officer (i.e., the Speaker of the House and the president pro tem of the Senate) is given the power to appoint conferees. The actual appointment power belongs to the chairpersons of the House and Senate committees that handled the legislation in their chamber. The committee leaders make up a list of conferees and give it to the presiding officers; the latter officers then "appoint" those people listed.

The Legislative Reorganization Act of 1946 provides that members of conference committees must have supported the legislation under consideration when it passed their respective chambers. This is not always the case and has been the object of some concern. "If one wanted to stretch the point a little," remarks a student of Congress, "one might whimsically claim that any similarity between the views of the House or the Senate and those of the conferees is purely coincidental." [65] The reason for this is the seniority system. When committee chairpersons appoint conferees, they normally select the most senior members from the committee or subcommittee responsible for that chamber's legislation. Because senior members are sometimes out of step with the party majorities in their chamber, following seniority in appointing conferees could mean that a majority of the conference delegation sent to uphold their chamber's version of the bill actually opposed that version in their own house.

The important question is how often does this happen. Former Senator Joseph Clark thought it happened often enough to justify a strict interpretation of the 1946 provision. He cited a 1959 conference on an unemployment compensation bill in which four of the five Senate conferees opposed the Senate's adoption of the liberalizing McCarthy amendment to the bill. The stated position of the Senate was overturned in twenty minutes of conference deliberation. [66] A 1967 conference on the congressional redistricting bill produced a strange situation in which the leader of the Senate delegation, Sam Ervin, was arguing for the House version of the bill, while the leader of the House delegation, Emanuel Celler, supported the Senate version. To no one's surprise, the bill died in conference.

In spite of these instances, recent research suggests that following seniority in appointing conferees does not always lead to conference delegations consisting of members who opposed the bill in their chamber. A survey by the *Congressional Quarterly* in 1959 found only four instances in which conference delegations included members who had opposed major provisions of the bill passed by their chamber. [67] In *The Third House,* I looked at the conference delegations in five Congresses covering a twenty-year period. I found that committee chairmen, by following subcommittee rather than committee seniority or by skipping over some senior committee members in appointing conferees, were able to increase the number of bill supporters on the conference delegation. The mean percentage of bill supporters on these delegations if strict committee seniority had been followed was 70 percent, while the actual mean percentage brought about by the chairmen's screening of conferees was 82 percent. [68]

It seems clear, from the evidence we have today, that the membership of conference delegations is best characterized as being a collection of senior committee and subcommittee people who generally support their chamber's position in the interchamber dispute.

At the beginning of the Ninety-fourth Congress in 1975, both chambers adopted reforms that required conference committees to hold open sessions unless a majority of the delegates from each chamber voted otherwise. Prior to that time, conference committees were the most secretive of formal congressional gatherings. No minutes or written records of conference proceedings were kept, and the only printed accounts associated with a conference committee were the conference report (the compromise bill) and a statement by House conferees as to the effects of the compromise on the House-passed bill. The actual conference deliberations, the votes of members, the arguments advanced for striking or retaining certain measures, and the evidence for supporting certain changes were not part of the public record. It is no wonder that when Albert Gore of Tennessee left the Senate in 1970, he berated conference committees for being "secret meetings often not even announced until the last minute [where] a few men can sit down and undo in one hour the most painstaking work of months of effort by several standing committees and the full membership of both houses." [69]

Throughout the Ninety-third Congress open conferences were held on only twelve bills. In the Ninety-fourth Congress, after the passage of these reforms, almost every conference session was open to the public. (The important ones were heavily attended by both press and special interest lobbyists.) The chief rationale for previously having closed conference committees was to facilitate bargaining or decision-making. The idea was that members would be more willing to compromise on their own public statements or on the positions adopted by their parent chambers if the machinations of such compromises (including the who and why of compromising exactly what and when) would not be known beyond the conference doors. This is the same rationale for invoking secrecy used by the Philadelphia convention of 1787 to fashion the Constitution—to facilitate bargaining in order to achieve a final solution to a complex political problem. Critics of the closed conference, such as former Senator Albert Gore, generally based their criticism on representational grounds. They objected to the fact that a small group of people could, in secret, change and even overturn decisions previously arrived at by elected officials operating in a public forum. It is clear that open conferences do serve the representational function of Congress better than closed conferences. What also seems clear is that such representation is sometimes gained at the loss of efficiency in decision-making. "A first impression," writes a close observer of the month-long conference committee on the energy conservation bill held in the fall of 1975, "is that a congressional conference is even more inefficient and disorganized than a committee meeting." [70] Another commentator at that conference traces inefficiency directly to the reforms that opened up conference committees to the general public:

> Traditionally, conference committees in Congress met in closed sessions, but the energy conference has been held in public. One result is that several Senators and Representatives tend to give long-winded speeches, and members from both sides find the need to meet regularly in private to plot strategy for the public sessions.[71]

Having made the move to open up conference proceedings, Congress is unlikely to go back to the old system of closed door sessions. Such a retrogression would run counter to the *sunshine* bills and opening-up measures adopted in the last few years. But it does seem clear that while the old system of the closed door conference could legitimately be criticized for violating basic representational expectations, the new open door conference system may be criticized on grounds of inefficiency in the making of decisions.[72]

What happens to conference reports when they come to the floor of their respective chambers? Most of them pass. In the Ninetieth Congress (1967–1968) 640 laws were enacted by Congress; 129 of these were the product of successful conferences. Only six unsuccessful conferences were held.[73] Part of the explanation for the success of conference bills in Congress lies in the timing (when these reports are brought to the floor), and part is related to the formal rules governing floor voting on conference bills.

About half of all conference reports are voted on during the last two months of each session. Debate, while formally unlimited, is often subject to a unanimous consent measure that sets a time limitation. But the rule that has the most dramatic effect on floor consideration of conference bills is that which specifies that each chamber must accept or reject the compromise bill *in toto*. Members cannot support certain parts of a conference bill while objecting to other parts. The choice presented to legislators is simple: they must vote yea or nay on the whole compromise bill. No amendments from the floor are accepted. While some members might feel that their representatives could have done a better job of defending their chamber's version of the bill, they are faced basically with a choice of accepting the conference bill or having no bill at all that session. The only alternative open to legislators who are not happy with the conference compromise is to pass a resolution instructing their chamber's delegation to retain or drop certain provisions or to raise a point of order against new material inserted in the conference bill.

Studies of conferences by Richard Fenno, David Paletz, and myself indicate that both chambers are reluctant to instruct their conference delegations.[74] Such instructions run counter to the basic norm of compromise that dominates conference activity. Also, motions to instruct a chamber delegation are regarded as a sign of little confidence in the bargaining ability of one's conference representatives. Section 135 of the Legislative Reorganization Act of 1946 provides that conference committees may not insert material that was not included in the bills passed by the two chambers into the compromise bill. This rule is often violated by conference committees' writing substitute bills that are quite different from chamber bills. If this happens, members may raise a point of order when the conference report is brought to the chamber floor. Like motions to instruct, though, points of order are seldom made. "The subjects are complex, debate time is limited, and most legislators are willing to believe their representatives on the conference committee have done as well as could be expected." [75]

We may summarize this section by noting that conference committees are made up of senior committee or subcommittee members chosen by the respective chairpersons in each house; that conferees generally are supporters of the legislation as passed by their chamber; and that the rules governing floor consideration of conference bills lead to their high acceptance rate in both chambers. What we have yet to consider is how the rules governing conference committees affect the content of conference legislation, and how the House-Senate differences discussed earlier in this chapter are reflected in the nature of conference settlements.

Conference Settlements and House-Senate Policy Differences

One way of looking at conference committee outcomes is to ask the question: Are conference bills generally closer to the original bill of the House or of the Senate? Gilbert Steiner's study of conference committee outcomes in the period 1928–1948 found that the House won 57 percent of the conference battles, the Senate position prevailed in 27 percent, and 16 percent of the conference settlements represented an even split between the two chamber positions.[76] Richard Fenno's study of appropriations conferences held between 1947 and 1962 came up with these findings: the Senate won 65 percent of the conference battles, while the House won 35 percent.[77] I discovered a similar pattern to Fenno's in my research of all conferences held from 1945 to 1966. For the 297 conferences in which it was possible to compare conference outcomes with each chamber's bill, 59 percent were Senate victories, 32 percent were House victories, and 9 percent evenly split the difference between the chamber positions.[78] John Manley's *The Politics of Finance* also considered conference outcomes in the fields of tax, social security, and trade legislation. He found that conference bills dealing with taxes were generally closer to the Senate than to the House bill; that House conferees tended to prevail over their Senate counterparts on social security legislation; and that there was a mixed pattern of chamber dominance in conferences dealing with trade bills.[79] Finally, a study of congressional action on defense budgets from 1960 to 1970 discovered overall Senate dominance of the conference process. The House accepted the Senate's position on budget levels 57 percent of the time, while the Senate accepted House figures only 23 percent of the time.[80]

A word of warning about interpreting these findings is in order here. Fenno, Manley, and Kanter were quite explicit about the problem of measuring conference outcomes in terms of chamber influence and about the danger of assuming that a chamber's winning conferences in particular policy areas meant that one chamber was more influential in overall policy-making in that area. While Senate conferees might more often win defense appropriation conferences, as measured by the number of Senate changes accepted in the final bill, it is often the case that these Senate changes dealt with the least important, most noncontroversial parts of the bill. In such cases, the House has a greater impact on the overall defense budget policy process in spite of the Senate's winning more points in the conference struggle.

The studies that show the Senate conference delegations' mastery in retaining Senate bill provisions in the final conference bill can be partially explained in terms of the differences between the two chambers discussed earlier. Senate rules and norms support members' fulfilling their representational role by adding a wide variety of amendments to bills on the floor. For instance, tax bills are brought to the House floor under a closed rule that precludes amendments to the committee-approved bill. In the Senate, as many as a hundred amendments favoring interests in senators' home states are tacked on to the Finance Committee bill. A conference compromise that accepts only half of these Senate amendments, then, will appear to be a Senate victory in conference.

When the House delegation prevails in conference, most observers attribute this to the superior expertise of the House managers:

> House conferees have usually spent more time studying the legislation and probably know the details better than the Senators, who after all, have more demands on their time than House members.[81]

> By general agreement, the House conferees are better prepared, better organized, better informed, more single-minded in their interest, and employ a more belligerent bargaining style.[82]

This expertise of House conferees is directly related to the greater specialization in the House illustrated in Table 5-1. Conference representation reflects the same pattern. Conference assignments are distributed more widely among the membership in the Senate than in the House. David Paletz found that in the Eighty-sixth through the Ninetieth Congresses, half of the members in the Senate had participated in six or more conferences, whereas the comparable figure for the House ranged from a low of 4.6 percent to a high of 14.25 percent.[83] House managers in conference, then, are generally subject matter experts who are there to protect policy decisions made in House committees.

The behavior of Senate conferees is different from that of House conferees. Instead of representing a committee's decision made in the parent chamber, most Senate conferees emphasize that body's reciprocity norm and push for retaining all amendments accepted on the Senate floor. The comments of a House Appropriations Committee member and a Ways and Means Committee member are similar in describing how senators behave in conference:

> We go over there and I say, "This item is not authorized. The Corps of Engineers hasn't agreed. It's ridiculous and I'm not going to vote for it." And they say, "Oh, that's Senator so and so's project;

oh, that's Senator such and such's project. We can't touch that."
They have a system over there where any Senator can get anything
in a bill he wants—a gentleman's agreement.

Someone on the other side will say, "Senator so and so wants
this project or Senator so and so is interested in this item." That
Senator isn't even on the Committee and hasn't attended the hearings, but he wants something and the rest look out for him. He
isn't physically in the conference room but he's in there just the
same.

All the Senators are interested in getting their amendments into
these tax bills, when we come to conference. They make no bones
about it. They're very open. They'll sit down for God's sake and
say, "Now let's see, whose amendment was this? Oh yes, it's _____
and I told him I would support it. We are going to stand firm on
that." [84]

One explanation of Senate victories in this least visible arena
of congressional activity can be found in the representational nature
of Senate conferees' roles. Fenno suggests that:

The Senate is stronger in conference because the Senate Committee
and its conferees draw more directly and more completely upon the
support of their parent chamber than do the House Committee and
its conferees. . . . When the Senate conferees go to the conference
room, they not only represent the Senate—they are the Senate. The
position they defend will have been worked out with a maximum of
participation by Senate members and will enjoy a maximum of support in that body.[85]

John Manley's study of tax legislation also points to the
Senate's emphasis on the representational function in explaining
Senate dominance in these conferences.

The reason the Senate does better in cases of conflict with the Ways
and Means Committee is because politically Senate decisions are
more in line with the demands of interest groups, lobbyists, and constituents than House decisions. Ways and Means decisions, made
under the closed rule, tend to be less popular with relevant publics
than Senate decisions.[86]

While Fenno suggests that Senate conferees are more successful because they represent the entire chamber and not just the committee position in conference, Manley broadens the concept of repre-

sentation as it applies to tax conferences: Senate conferees are more successful because they represent a wider range of interests in the general public, while House conferees represent fiscal decisions arrived at in closed door Ways and Means Committee sessions.

The most recent study of conference outcomes suggests that the reasons generally given for the Senate's winning most conferences have little to do with the influence of outside forces or the permeability (i.e., openness to noncommittee sources of influence) of Senate committees as compared with House committees. These researchers suggest that the phenomenon of the Senate seeming to win more conferences than the House stems from the fact that generally the House acts first on legislation and the Senate makes marginal changes in the original bill generated by the House. Seventy-two percent of the bills that went to conference during the time of this study (Ninety-second Congress, 1971–1972) originated in the House. On the whole, the Senate added a range of amendments to the House bill, and most of these amendments, which were marginal changes in the original bill, were retained in conference. Studies of conference outcomes generally show that the Senate won most of these conferences because of the retention of these many Senate amendments in the final bill. But, according to the authors of this study, this notion of the Senate winning in conference really reflects a strategic advantage stemming from its being the second chamber to act. It by no means indicates that the Senate has a greater legislative impact on the final conference outcome than does the House. By creating the original bill and setting the agenda for debate on the issue, the House is judged to have a greater real impact on the final shape of legislation as it passes through conference than does the Senate.[87] While this recent study of conference outcomes raises legitimate questions about the explanations offered for Senate victories in earlier studies and, indeed, about the very existence of such victories, it does emphasize the fact that the House and Senate perform essentially different policy roles. By framing legislation and acting first on final passage of most legislation, the House plays a dominant lawmaking role in the political system. By offering many marginal changes in this original legislation, the Senate plays a key representational role.

This consideration of joint House-Senate interaction in conference committees brings us back to the observations made at the beginning of this chapter. The rules and norms governing the behavior of representatives and senators are different because the two chambers play different roles in the policy process. Congress must pass laws and at the same time serve as a forum for the representation of a wide range of interests. The structure of the House of Representatives and the rules and norms governing the behavior of its members serve to emphasize that body's concern with lawmaking. The Senate, on the other hand, is more suited to acting as a forum where the interests and the ideas of a heterogeneous public are introduced into the political process. When these two chambers come together in conference to determine the final form of legislation, these differences are not eliminated, but maintained. House conferees come to the bargaining table to uphold bills fashioned in committee workshops; Senate conferees come to make sure that individual senators' provisions to help certain segments of the public are not dropped from the final bill.

The important question about the final outcome is not just whether the Senate or House position is closest to the bill that emerges from conference. Rather, we are concerned with who gets helped and who gets hurt by the congressional policy decision. To attempt to answer that we must look at some of the policy outcomes of the congressional process, and we must consider the influence of noncongressional actors, such as lobbyists and the president, in helping to shape policy.

NOTES

1. Quoted in Ann Pelham, "Energy Bill: The End of an Odyssey," *Congressional Quarterly Weekly Report,* October 21, 1978, p. 3042. The account given here of legislative action is taken from that report and from Mary Russell and Robert G. Kaiser, "The Marathon: Nonstop 34 Hours of Waltzing, Stumbling, Struggling," *Washington Post,* October 16, 1978, pp. A1 and A6.

2. Charles L. Clapp, *The Congressman: His Work as He Sees It* (Brookings Institution, 1963), p. 39.

3. Lewis Froman and Nelson Polsby discuss these differences in Froman's *The Congressional Process* (Little, Brown, 1967), pp. 5–151, and Polsby's *Congressional Behavior* (Random House, 1971), pp. 6–9. David Mayhew touches on this basic underlying difference between the House and Senate in his discussion in *Congress: The Electoral Connection* (Yale, 1974), pp. 73ff. The essential representational role of the Senate is captured in the following observation of a senator in David W. Rohde, Norman J. Ornstein, and Robert Peabody, "Political Change and Legislative Norms in the United States Senate," paper

delivered at the annual meeting of the American Political Science Association, 1974, p. 40:

> Now, the necessity to know something about everything probably comes from the difference in the kind of world we live in today compared to just a quarter of a century ago. You can't go into a major community of your constituency without some television commentator asking you anything he wants to, and most people are reluctant to say "I don't know." I learned to do it. It's pretty hard to learn to do, but I don't know how the public accepts that. I would like to think they're impressed with an honest answer from someone, but the tendency in human nature is that you expound whether you know anything or not; you feel compelled to say something. And so this may, in self defense, compel many Senators to know a very little bit about a great many things.

4. Walter J. Oleszek, *Congressional Procedures and the Policy Process* (Congressional Quarterly Press, 1978), p. 26.
5. Compiled from data in *Congressional Quarterly Weekly Report*, April 14, 1979. In the Senate, fifty-eight of the fifty-nine Democrats were committee or subcommittee chairpersons; in the House, 147 of the 276 Democrats were committee or subcommittee chairpersons.
6. Ralph K. Huitt, "The Internal Distribution of Influence: The Senate," in David Truman, ed., *The Congress and America's Future* (Prentice-Hall, 1965), p. 80.
7. Asher C. Hinds, quoted in Oleszek, *Congressional Procedures and the Policy Process*, p. 24. Information on the length of House and Senate rules also comes from this source.
8. Quoted in John Manley, *The Politics of Finance* (Little, Brown, 1970), p. 378.
9. Polsby, *Congressional Behavior*, p. 7.
10. Richard Fenno, *The Power of the Purse* (Little, Brown, 1966); Manley, *The Politics of Finance;* David Vogler, *The Third House* (Northwestern University Press, 1971); Arnold Kanter, "Congress and the Defense Budget," *American Political Science Review*, vol. 66, no. 1 (March 1972), pp. 129–143.
11. Oleszek, *Congressional Procedures and the Policy Process*, p. 90.
12. Froman, *The Congressional Process*, pp. 44–45.
13. Ann Cooper, "House Use of Suspensions Grows Drastically," *Congressional Quarterly Weekly Report*, September 30, 1978, p. 2693.
14. Representative James Collins (R-Texas), quoted in Cooper, "House Use of Suspensions Grows Drastically."
15. Oleszek, *Congressional Procedures and the Policy Process*, p. 97.

16. Froman, *The Congressional Process*, p. 67.

17. James Robinson, *The House Rules Committee* (Bobbs-Merrill, 1963), p. 44.

18. Quoted in Manley, *The Politics of Finance*, p. 72.

19. Bruce I. Oppenheimer, "Policy Implications of Rules Committee Reforms," in Leroy N. Rieselbach, ed., *Legislative Reform: The Policy Impact* (D. C. Heath, 1978), p. 101.

20. Fenno, *The Power of the Purse*, p. 422.

21. Oppenheimer, "Policy Implications of Rules Committee Reforms," in Rieselbach, ed., *Legislative Reform: The Policy Impact*, pp. 91–104; Bruce I. Oppenheimer, "The Rules Committee: New Arm of Leadership in a Decentralized House," in Lawrence C. Dodd and Bruce I. Oppenheimer, eds., *Congress Reconsidered* (Praeger, 1977), pp. 96–116; Spark M. Matsunaga and Ping Chen, *Rulemakers of the House* (University of Illinois Press, 1978); and Ted Siff and Alan Weil, *Ruling Congress: How the House and Senate Rules Govern the Legislative Process* (Penguin, 1977).

22. *Congressional Quarterly Weekly Report*, vol. 33, no. 9 (March 1, 1975), p. 452. This and the two following issues of *Congressional Quarterly Weekly Report* (March 8 and March 15) contain excellent and instructive accounts of the cloture rule change and the nature of Senate rules and floor proceedings in general.

23. Roger Davidson, David Kovenock, and Michael O'Leary, *Congress in Crisis: Politics and Congressional Reform* (Wadsworth, 1966), p. 110.

24. Froman, *The Congressional Process*, p. 65.

25. *Congressional Quarterly Weekly Reports* September 18, 1970, pp. 2239–2240; September 25, p. 2320; and October 2, p. 2396.

26. Donald Matthews, *U.S. Senators and Their World* (Vintage, 1960), pp. 92–117.

27. Rohde, Ornstein, and Peabody, "Political Change and Legislative Norms in the United States Senate," paper delivered at the 1974 annual meeting of the American Political Science Association, August 29–September 2, 1974. The authors found that only two of the forty senators questioned at that point in the study said that a period of apprenticeship was still expected of members. Of the six folkways uncovered by Matthews, then, it is clear that apprenticeship, at least in its old strict form, is no longer present in the Senate. This research also showed that specialization as a norm still existed, but that it no longer was directed at maintaining the conservative southern bloc it served in the 1950s. I have organized this discussion of legislative norms in terms of the representational and lawmaking framework followed throughout the book. Rohde, Ornstein, and Peabody provide another framework for evaluating these norms, and it is one worth considering as you read

this section. They talk about Senate folkways that provided limited benefits in the 1950s to the relatively small inner club of southern senators who dominated that body for years and folkways that provided general benefits for any member of the Senate, regardless of region or ideology. Senate norms providing general benefits include courtesy, reciprocity, institutional patriotism, legislative work, and specialization. Those providing limited benefits (i.e., helping to maintain the dominance of the southern conservative club) were apprenticeship and specialization. The demise of the old specialization norm (designed to keep people in their place and support the institutional system of committees dominated by the southern conservatives) has been replaced by a system of specialization that reinforces the representational role of the Senate by providing a legitimate platform from which all one hundred members can make statements about substantive policy issues within their corral of recognized policy turf.

28. For House norms, see Richard Fenno, "The Appropriations Committee as a Political System," in Peabody and Polsby, eds., *New Perspectives on the House of Representatives,* pp. 124–154; *The Power of the Purse;* and "The Internal Distribution of Influence: The House," in Truman, ed., *The Congress and America's Future,* pp. 52–76.

   A comparative study of four state legislatures found forty-two rules of the game mentioned by members. See John Wahlke, Heinz Eulau, William Buchanan, and Leroy Ferguson, *The Legislative System* (John Wiley and Sons, 1962), pp. 141–169. Although this list at times resembles the Scout Law, most of the rules of the game are similar to the broader categories delineated by Matthews.

29. Quoted in Clapp, *The Congressman: His Work as He Sees It,* p. 18.

30. Matthews, *U.S. Senators and Their World,* p. 96.

31. See Nelson Polsby's discussion in *Congressional Behavior,* p. 7.

32. Matthews, *U.S. Senators and Their World,* p. 93.

33. Alexander Hamilton, John Jay, and James Madison, *The Federalist* (Modern Library, n.d.), p. 349.

34. Champ Clark, *My Quarter Century of American Politics* (Harpers, 1920), vol. I, p. 209. Quoted in George Goodwin, Jr., *The Little Legislatures* (University of Massachusetts Press, 1970), p. 118.

35. Polsby, *Congressional Behavior,* p. 13.

36. Donald W. Riegle, Jr. and Trevor Armbrister, *O Congress* (Doubleday, 1972), p. 141. Copyright © 1972 by Donald W. Riegle, Jr. and Trevor Armbrister. Reprinted by permission of Doubleday and Co.

37. Mark J. Green, James M. Fallows, and David R. Zwick, *Who Runs Congress?* (Bantam, 1972), pp. 58–62.

38. Foundation for the Study of Presidential and Congressional Terms, "The Seniority Gap," Research Report no. 7 (July, 1979).

39. For the relevant areas, see Nicholas Masters, "Committee Assignments in the House of Representatives," *American Political Science Review* (June 1961), pp. 345–357; Richard Fenno, "The House of Representatives and Federal Aid to Education," in Peabody and Polsby, eds., *New Perspectives on the House of Representatives*, pp. 195–235; David Vogler, "Flexibility in the Congressional Seniority System: Conference Representation," *Polity* (Summer 1970), pp. 494–507. More general discussions of seniority are George Goodwin, Jr., "The Seniority System in Congress," *American Political Science Review*, 1959, pp. 412–436; Michael Abram and Joseph Cooper, "The Rise of Seniority in the House of Representatives," *Polity* (Fall 1968), pp. 52–85; and Nelson Polsby, Miriam Gallaher, and Barry Rundquist, "The Growth of the Seniority System in the U.S. House of Representatives," *American Political Science Review* (September 1969), pp. 787–807.

40. Rohde, Ornstein, and Peabody, "Political Change and Legislative Norms in the United States Senate," p. 35.

41. Quoted in Ann Cooper, "New Setbacks for House Seniority System," *Congressional Quarterly Weekly Report,* February 3, 1979, p. 183.

42. Quoted in Paul R. Wieck, "Making Out on the Hill," *Washington Post,* May 2, 1976, p. C5. For an excellent description of the most effective moderate role adopted by some freshmen, see David Nyhan, "Freshman Tsongas Stars in Confrontation with House Chiefs," *Boston Globe,* June 23, 1975, p. 52. Lyndon Johnson's calculated and elaborate courting of Senator Richard Russell, who was the undisputed leader of the Senate's inner club in the late 1940s and 1950s, provides one of the best examples of how the old apprenticeship norm (and its providing limited benefits to the southerners in control) worked during this earlier period. An intriguing account of this courtship may be found in Doris Kearns, *Lyndon Johnson & the American Dream* (Harper & Row, 1976), Chapter Four.

43. Rohde, Ornstein, and Peabody, "Political Change and Legislative Norms in the United States Senate," p. 36.

44. Randall B. Ripley, *Congress: Process and Policy* (W. W. Norton, 1978, second edition), p. 126.

45. Matthews, *U.S. Senators and Their World,* p. 94.

46. Ibid., p. 95.

47. Fenno, "The Appropriations Committee as a Political System," p. 133.

48. Clapp, *The Congressman: His Work as He Sees It,* p. 23. Copyright © 1963 by the Brookings Institution.

49. Fenno, "The Internal Distribution of Influence," p. 73.

50. The description is Fenno's in *The Power of the Purse,* p. 511.

51. Ibid., p. 509.

52. *Congressional Record,* April 24, 1956, p. 6148. Quoted in Matthews, *U.S. Senators and Their World,* pp. 97–98.

53. Clem Miller, *Member of the House* (Charles Scribner's Sons, 1962), p. 93.

54. Riegle and Armbrister, *O Congress,* p. 252. Copyright © 1972 by Donald W. Riegle, Jr. and Trevor Armbrister. Reprinted by permission of Doubleday and Co.

55. Miller, *Member of the House,* p. 40.

56. Quoted in Green et al., *Who Runs Congress?* p. 167.

57. Rhode, Ornstein, and Peabody, "Political Change and Legislative Norms in the United States Senate," p. 32. See the anecdote related in footnote 59 of this paper for an amusing comment on the limits of this norm.

58. Quoted in *Boston Globe,* December 6, 1970, p. 23.

59. *Congressional Record,* March 26, 1974, p. H2174.

60. *Congressional Quarterly Weekly Report* vol. 34, no. 18 (May 1, 1976), p. 1013. Members have until 9:00 P.M. to remove or change their remarks on the floor as they will appear in that day's *Congressional Record.* In this instance, both the "racist" and the "pipsqueak" remarks were removed before the *Record* came out the following day.

61. Quoted in *Congressional Quarterly Almanac,* 1963, p. 177.

62. Richard Rovere, *Senator Joe McCarthy* (Vintage, 1960), p. 230.

63. Theodore Lowi, *The End of Liberalism* (W. W. Norton, 1969).

64. Goodwin, *The Little Legislatures,* p. 242. My earlier study reported a lower percentage but agreed with Goodwin's evaluation of the importance of legislation passing through conference. See Vogler, *The Third House,* p. 4.

65. Bertram Gross, *The Legislative Struggle* (McGraw-Hill, 1953), p. 321.

66. Joseph Clark, *Congress: The Sapless Branch* (Harper & Row, 1964), p. 11.

67. *Congressional Quarterly Weekly Report,* vol. 17, no. 18, May 1, 1959, pp. 597–598.

68. Vogler, *The Third House,* pp. 45–48.

69. Quoted in Green et al., *Who Runs Congress?* p. 63.

70. Richard L. Lyons, "The Making of a Compromise," *Washington Post,* November 9, 1975, p. A3.

71. David E. Rosenbaum, "Senate and House Conferees Approve Separate Bills on Energy," *New York Times,* November 6, 1975, p. 16.

72. A good criticism of the old closed conference system is embedded in the account of the 1975 tax cut bill reported in Aaron Latham, "Behind Closed Doors: How Russell Long Won the Battle of the Tax

Bill," *New York Magazine*, vol. 8, no. 18 (May, 1975), pp. 61–68. The delays associated with the conference committee reconstituting the Federal Elections Commission in the spring of 1976 are often cited as examples of the drawbacks of the new, open, representational conference system. See, for instance, Warren Weaver, Jr., "Congressmen at Work, or How the F.E.C. Was Modified," *New York Times*, April 18, 1976, section 4, p. 4.

73. Goodwin, *The Little Legislatures*, p. 243.

74. Fenno, *The Power of the Purse*, pp. 657ff; David Paletz, "Influence in Congress: An Analysis of the Nature and Effects of Conference Committees," paper delivered at the 66th annual meeting of the American Political Science Association, Los Angeles, September 1970, pp. 9 and 11; Vogler, *The Third House*, pp. 94ff.

75. Clapp, *The Congressman: His Work as He Sees It*, p. 279. Copyright © 1963 by the Brookings Institution. See also Malcolm Jewell and Samuel Patterson, *The Legislative Process in the United States* (Random House, 1966), p. 481.

76. Gilbert Steiner, *The Congressional Conference Committee. Seventieth to Eightieth Congresses* (University of Illinois Press, 1950), pp. 170–172.

77. Fenno, *The Power of the Purse*, p. 662.

78. Vogler, *The Third House*, p. 55.

79. Manley, *The Politics of Finance*, pp. 269–294.

80. Arnold Kanter, "Congress and the Defense Budget: 1960–1970," *American Political Science Review*, vol. 66, no. 1 (March 1972), pp. 129–143.

81. Manley, *The Politics of Finance*, p. 293.

82. Fenno, *The Power of the Purse*, p. 668.

83. Paletz, "Influence in Congress," p. 3. See also Goodwin, *The Little Legislatures*, p. 245.

84. Fenno, *The Power of the Purse*, pp. 627–628 and Manley, *The Politics of Finance*, p. 269.

85. Fenno, *The Power of the Purse*, pp. 668–669.

86. Manley, *The Politics of Finance*, p. 279.

87. Gerald S. Strom and Barry S. Rundquist, "A Revised Theory of Winning in House-Senate Conferences," *American Political Science Review*, vol. LXXI, no. 2 (June, 1977). To test their theory that Senate victories in conference stemmed from the Senate's being the second acting chamber, the authors looked at the twenty-eight (out of 103) cases in the Ninety-second Congress where the Senate was the first acting chamber. Of those cases, the House was found to win 71 percent of the conferences. In other words, when the House acted first, the Senate won 72 percent of the conference outcomes; when the Senate acted first,

the House won 71 percent of the conference outcomes. While all of these aggregate studies do clearly indicate important differences between the House and Senate policy roles, it is often more useful to look at extensive analyses of individual conferences in order to capture the essence of conference committees in the legislative process. For the divisions in conference that turn out to be important often reflect differences within the House or the Senate that are more important in determining final conference solutions than are House-Senate differences. A good starting point for this latter type of conference interaction is provided in the excellent description and analysis of the Education Amendments of 1972 to be found in Lawrence E. Gladieux and Thomas R. Wolanin, *Congress and Colleges: The National Politics of Higher Education* (D. C. Heath, 1976), Chapter Eight.

POLICIES, PRESSURE GROUPS, AND PRESIDENTS

IN THE FIRST CHAPTER OF THIS BOOK, we had a look at evidence from public opinion polls, which showed that people base their evaluations of Congress as a whole on its legislative record, whereas they judge their individual representatives and senators in representative terms. The implications of this finding, in terms of helping to explain why such a high proportion of incumbents are reelected while the public approval ratings of the institution of Congress are so low, were also discussed. But there is an important characteristic of the public's evaluation of institutional lawmaking that was not touched on in this earlier discussion. It would be natural for us to conclude that because the public judges Congress in lawmaking terms, this public judgment is based on an assessment of public bills acted on by Congress. For if we are to evaluate the lawmaking record of Congress, what better place is there to look than the congressional performance in specific policy areas. Before we make the jump from recognizing the lawmaking basis of public evaluations of Congress to assuming that such evaluations have a policy content, however, we should consider another point that was discussed earlier in the book. And that is the consistent finding, discussed in Chapter 2, that the awareness of and information about issues and policies among even the voting public is very low. If most people are unaware of congressional actions, or inaction, in specific policy areas, it is difficult to argue that their judgments about Congress are based on evaluations of congressional performance in certain policy areas.

When we look at the reasons given in public opinion surveys for both positive and negative evaluations of Congress, we find that most public judgments about the lawmaking of Congress are expressed in procedural rather than policy terms. The national poll on public attitudes toward Congress conducted under the auspices of the House Commission on Administrative Review in 1977 demonstrates this emphasis on procedures rather than policies in the public's evaluation of congressional lawmaking. The most common reasons given for a negative evaluation of Congress illustrate this: "can't see that anything has changed, no signs of improvement, they haven't done anything"; "Congress opposed the president, wouldn't cooperate, stood in the way"; "they bicker, haggle, waste time, are too slow, too big, inefficient"; and "they care only about themselves, don't work hard, don't do their job." More than half of the reasons given for a negative opinion of Congress followed this pattern. They focused more on the procedures and behavioral patterns of Congress than on policies. Perceived congressional failures in specific policy areas ("haven't done anything about inflation, prices, the economy"; "unemployment is rising, no action about jobs"; and "lots of problems they didn't deal with, e.g., energy, crime, etc.") were mentioned only half as often as were procedural failures.[1]

When political scientists look at Congress they have a similar tendency to focus more on structure and procedures than on policies. Introductory textbooks on American politics almost always include a chart on "how a bill becomes a law" and an intricate description of the legislative maze through which a bill must pass. These books reflect the emphasis that research on Congress places on describing the legislative process rather than the content of the laws that come out of that process.[2] When scholars do look at congressional policies, it is generally as part of an attempt to explain the congressional policy-making process.

The same may be said about most discussions of the role of the lobbyist and the president in helping to form legislative policies. Some observers decry the great influence of lobbyists over the content of bills; yet, a number of studies find the power of lobbyists to be limited. While many scholars contend that the president has achieved such a dominant position in the legislative process as to render Congress an ineffective, second-rate partner in policy-making, others find the reports of Congress's death greatly exaggerated.

One reason for the confusing and contradictory evaluations of the influence of Congress, lobbyists, and the president on policy is the tendency to treat policy as a dependent variable. Policy is the thing to be explained by reference to the legislative process. If we reverse this formulation and consider policies as independent variables, we uncover new ground for understanding the politics of Congress. Certain types of policies produce certain types of congressional politics. For instance, river and harbor bills create a legislative process in which the roles and relative influence of lobbyists and the president are quite different from the configurations arising from a civil rights bill or from strategic defense policies.

There are a number of ways to classify policies. One of the most useful classification schemes, is that suggested by Theodore Lowi in a review essay of a book on trade policy. Lowi classified policies as distributive, regulatory, or redistributive, depending on their relative impact on society. Distributive policies directly affect few people in society, whereas redistributive policies have a broad impact on the whole society. An essential point of the Lowi formulation is that "these areas of policy or government activity constitute real arenas of power. Each arena tends to develop its own characteristic political structure, political process, elites, and group relations." [3] In Table 6–1, I have provided a summary of the major characteristics of each policy type and of the nature of political activity associated with each type.

TABLE 6–1 Policies and Their Politics

DISTRIBUTIVE

Examples: Rivers and harbors legislation, tax loopholes, government services such as agricultural subsidies, area redevelopment, defense procurement, water pollution policies.

Nature of Policy:

1. Short-run decisions are made without regard to limited resources.
2. It is easy to separate overall policy into component parts and to distribute them unit by unit.
3. There is no general rule to determine distribution.
4. Decisions are highly individualized.
5. There is no direct confrontation between those who gain something from the policy and those who lose something.
6. It is difficult to locate the deprived groups because they can be accommodated by a further separation of policy into component parts and further distribution of benefits.

TABLE 6-1   Continued

Nature of political activity:

1. There are a large number of small, intensely organized interests, a politics of "every man for himself." The single person or single group is the major political actor.
2. The politics is one of "mutual noninterference," i.e., each actor seeks his or her own rewards but does not oppose other's seeking theirs. It is a low-conflict political process.
3. Coalitions are made up of unlike interests; *logrolling* is the most common form of political interaction.
4. The congressional committee or subcommittee is the most important official decision-maker.
5. The individualized nature of the political conflict provides a basis for very stable coalitions that are not affected by the larger policy outcomes.

REGULATORY

Examples: Trade policies, federal aid to education, campaign finance regulations, medicare, general environmental regulations.

Nature of policy:

1. They are specific and individual in their impact, but they are not capable of being separated into component parts to the same degree as distributive policies.
2. Laws are stated in general terms, but their impact is to raise costs and/or reduce or expand alternatives of private individuals directly.
3. In the short run, the policy involves a direct choice as to who will receive benefits and who will pay costs.
4. Decision-making involves the application of a general rule to specific cases.
5. Policy is cumulative and is made up of a series of individual decisions involving similar groups.

Nature of Political Activity:

1. There are a number of groups organized on the basis of shared attitudes rather than just narrow economic interests.
2. Coalitions are formed on the basis of conflict and compromise among groups that share some common attitudes; *bargaining* is the most common form of political interaction.
3. Policy tends to be the residue of the interplay of group conflict.
4. The power structure is not as stable as that dealing with distributive policies; there are shifting coalitions that must compromise to build majorities on each particular issue.
5. Congress, as a whole, is the chief decision-maker.

REDISTRIBUTIVE

Examples: Employment Act of 1946, civil rights legislation, strategic defense policies, 1964 poverty program, school busing.

TABLE 6–1 Continued

Nature of Policy:
1. This is similar to regulatory in the sense that individual decisions are interrelated.
2. The policy affects broad groups of society (haves and have nots, big business and small business, whites and nonwhites, bourgeoisie and proletariat).
3. The policy involves not just the use of property, but the possession or transfer of property.
4. The nature of a redistributive issue is not determined by how redistributive it actually is but rather how redistributive it could become in the future.

Nature of Political Activity:
1. The group conflict involves *peak associations* (those who speak for very broad sectors of society such as the National Association of Manufacturers, the Chamber of Commerce, the AFL-CIO); there is a high degree of cohesion within these groups on *redistributive* issues and their demands are generally expressed in ideological terms.
2. There are never more than two sides of the conflict over redistributive issues.
3. Negotiation is possible only in terms of softening or strengthening the impact on society; neither logrolling nor bargaining characterize political interaction.
4. The power structure is very stable and is made up of basically institutionalized factors.
5. Differences among related but competing groups are likely to be settled outside the realm of government.
6. Because of the centralization of conflict and the need for overall balancing and decision-making, Congress plays only a minor role. Decisions are more likely to be made in the executive branch or in the private sector. Congressional policies may provide some exceptions to the general principles established by redistributive policies, but does not decide on the basic principles themselves.

Table 6–1 is a rough outline of Lowi's classification of policies. You should keep in mind that these different policy types are not distinct and mutually exclusive, but rather points on a continuum reflecting the impact of policies on society. It is not easy to fit all laws passed by Congress into one or another of these categories. Some exhibit characteristics of distributive and regulatory policies, or regulatory and redistributive policies. Tax legislation, for instance, is distributive in its granting loopholes and exemptions to some groups, regulatory in its providing general rules to be applied to individual decisions, and redistributive in its underlying principle of a graduated federal income tax. You must also remember that policies change over time. Lowi suggests that trade policies, which were distributive in an earlier part of this century, began to be handled as regulatory policies after World War II and had become completely regulatory by the time of the Trade Expansion Act of 1962.

Lowi's scheme is certainly not the last word on policy classifications. It raises a number of questions about how policies move from one arena to another, about the distribution of power throughout society that determines how policies are defined, and about the exact dimensions of policies that are being measured in this scheme. A number of political scientists have considered these matters in evaluating and refining Lowi's basic framework.[4]

You should keep in mind that this classification scheme is not intended to be deterministic. That is, it is not suggesting that there is something in the inanimate nature of a tax bill or rivers and harbors legislation that causes legislators to behave certain ways. Rather, Lowi suggests that it is the perceptions of legislators about the potential impact of legislation on society that will determine their behavior. Legislators' perceptions about societal impact will vary over time for different policy areas, and different legislators might have quite different perceptions about the potential impact of a single piece of legislation.[5] The framework of Lowi rests on the notion that underlying this variety in perceptions is a tendency for most legislators to share perceptions about the potential impact of certain types of legislation. And it is this pattern of shared perceptions that forms the basis of the policy classifications.

In the Ninety-fifth Congress (1977–1978), over 22,000 public bills and resolutions were introduced in the House and the Senate. From this total, 227 were passed by Congress and became public laws. To deal with this flood of proposed legislation, legislators must have some way of classifying and categorizing bills. Some will be considered routine legislation, and others major policy proposals. Some will be perceived as having no direct effect on a particular legislator's constituents, whereas others will be seen as having a profound impact on the lifestyle or economic situation of every person in the state or district. All legislators, in short, develop some scheme for classifying policies and allocating their time and efforts in terms of that classification. As students of the congressional process, we must do the same thing. There is no way we could possibly consider all 22,000 of the proposed bills introduced in each Congress and make any sense out of the legislative process. By classifying these bills according to policy types, however, we can hope to compare different patterns of congressional behavior and better understand the politics of Congress. That is the purpose of any classification scheme, and it is why the Lowi framework is deemed useful in this chapter.

I have introduced Lowi's classification of policies here because I think it provides a useful organizational focus for looking at the role of lobbyists and the president in the congressional policy-making process. Confronted with some studies that assert that lobbyists have a great deal of influence over legislative policies and other studies that suggest that lobbyists play only a minimal role, we can try to answer the question of who is right. The answer might indeed be that they all are; that some types of policies are dealt with in a process that gives special interest groups a lot of influence in determining the eventual outcome, while others are decided in a manner that minimizes the lobbyists' impact. Similarly, we might find that the executive has a great deal of influence in some areas of congressional policy-making, while in others the executive plays a minor role.

PRESSURE GROUPS AND CONGRESS

In 1906, David Graham Phillips wrote a book about senators and special interests entitled *Treason of the Senate*. He accused twenty-one senators of serving big economic concerns in return for favors or money. One senator from Texas was said to have received over $225,000 from oil interests in just a matter of months. Seven years later, the *New York World* ran a series of articles claiming that the National Association of Manufacturers had given "financial reward for services rendered for political purposes" to nine congressmen and former congressmen and to their chief pages in the House.[6]

In 1977, three years after a president of the United States had resigned because of his involvement in the illegal activities collectively known as Watergate, the House of Representatives was hit with its own scandal, called Koreagate. An agent for the government of South Korea admitted he had spent almost $1 million, distributed among thirty representatives, trying to buy support for foreign aid programs favorable to South Korea. Two representatives pleaded guilty to receiving over $200,000 from the South Koreans, and another was acquitted of charges that he had received about the same amount. At about the same time that the Koreagate story was unfolding, a former representative from Pennsylvania admitted to receiving about $35,000 for helping a hospital in his district to obtain a $14.5 million federal grant, and another representative from the same state was indicted on charges of receiving about $60,000 in bribes over a period of years.

Sensational press coverage of these incidents involving members of the House, coupled with stories about a senator who allegedly kept up to $45,000 from donations in the pocket of an old coat in his closet, helps give support to a belief that congressional policies are greatly determined by money given by special interests. Studies done by such watchdog groups as the Ralph Nader Congress Project and Common Cause reinforce that belief. The authors of the Nader project book, *Who Runs Congress?*, report: "With the lobbies' pressure bearing in from all sides, Congress ends up, for the most part, responding to the heaviest push." [7] A study published in 1979 by Common Cause, with the equally ominous title of *How Money Talks in Congress,* begins this way: "The message is clear: special interest money pouring into political campaigns is contributing to legislative paralysis and interest group domination of Congress." [8] Given this context, it is not surprising to hear one professional lobbyist confess: "When I say I'm a lobbyist, it's about the same as saying I'm a pimp." [9]

Congressional reaction to these various charges of influence by special interests and their lobbyists have remained fairly consistent. Senator William Borah's reaction to the 1913 *World* articles is typical:

> I suppose in popular parlance we mean by "lobbyist" a man who is employed, paid professionally, to influence legislation concerning a matter not because he is interested in the matter, not necessarily because he thinks it is right, but because he desires to earn his salary, and is paid like a lawyer sometimes to argue a bad case, to do the best he can in the situation. That is my idea of a lobbyist, and I have not seen any around here this year, although they may be here. [10]

Half a century later, political scientists still found most legislators denying the importance of lobbyists. In an interview with Donald Matthews one senator stated:

You know, that's an amazing thing. I hardly ever see a lobbyist. I don't know—maybe they think I'm a poor target but I seldom see them. During this entire natural gas battle (in which he was a prominent figure) I was not approached by either side.[11]

The 1946 Federal Regulation of Lobbying Act (Title III of the Legislative Reorganization Act) requires that lobbyists register with the Secretary of the Senate and the Clerk of the House and file quarterly financial reports showing how much money was spent in lobbying activities. Critics of the law have described it either as a souffle (there is less there than meets the eye) or swiss cheese (it is riddled with loopholes). In 1949, lobbyists registered under the act reported spending $10.3 million; in 1967, they spent $4 million; and in 1973, they spent $9.4 million. During the time when spending by lobbyists (as reported) declined, congressional activity skyrocketed. As one observer notes,

> Congress is intimately involved in Medicare, energy development, aid to education, welfare, railroad resurrections, and dozens of other money-laden issues that were only a glimmer in 1949. Perhaps a hundred posh new office buildings have risen uptown along the "lobby belt," the Connecticut Avenue corridor where companies and trade associations prefer to quarter their men in Washington.[12]

The highly regarded Washington journal *Congressional Quarterly* had kept tabs on spending levels reported by lobbyists. In 1974 the journal decided to discontinue that practice because the reported figures were so misleading. The great increase in the number of individuals and organizations who registered as lobbyists in the 1960s and the 1970s belies spending figures and reinforces the notion that lobbying is a booming business. In 1967, 439 individuals and firms registered as congressional lobbyists; in 1975, 1,524 individuals and organizations were registered.[13] The lax registration requirements of the 1946 law are reflected in the fact that the actual number of lobbyists in Washington, as distinguished from the number registered, was estimated at 15,000 in 1978, almost twice as many as there were five years earlier.[14]

The 1946 Federal Regulation of Lobbying Act requires that an individual register as a lobbyist only if he or she is paid by someone else to lobby. Registration and a financial report are required from an organization only if that organization's "principal purpose" is to influence legislation in Congress. In addition, only direct contact with a member of Congress is considered to be lobbying, so that spending thousands of dollars to generate a grass-roots lobbying effort in the members' district or state is not covered by the 1946 law. The "principal purpose" loophole meant that organizations such as the U.S. Chamber of Commerce and Mobil Oil did not have to register, since their principal purpose was not lobbying. Perhaps the biggest loophole in the 1946 law is its exempting grass-roots lobbying from coverage. Money spent to get constituents to send letters, postcards, or coupons to their senators and representatives need not be reported under the law. In the first half of 1977, industry and trade groups spent more than a million dollars on newspaper ads urging readers to send their legislators a coupon advocating a particular position on major energy legislation then under consideration. Because of the grass-roots exemption, however, none of this spending had to be reported as lobbying.[15]

Because of the obvious weaknesses of the Federal Regulation of Lobbying Act, there have been only four cases of prosecution brought for violating the act and only one conviction. In 1978, the House of Representatives passed the Public Disclosure of Lobbying Act, which was to replace the earlier toothless legislation. Two key provisions in the law passed by the House were a requirement that organizations disclose the names of major contributors and the inclusion of grass-roots lobbying activity in a group's list of lobbying expenditures. The first provision was aimed at letting the public know that the Calorie Control Council, for example, received almost all of its funds from the major soft drink companies, that the Electric Consumers Resource Council was financed by the major electric companies, and that the Natural Gas Supply Committee received its money from the major oil companies.[16] The grass-roots lobbying coverage of the House bill, requiring that organizations keep records of and report letter-writing campaigns and all efforts to get constituents to write their representatives, was perhaps the most controversial section of the lobbying reform legislation. Opponents said that such a requirement was a clear infringement of First Amendment free speech guarantees. Because of the controversy over these two aspects of the House bill, the 1978 reform bill died in the Senate. In the Ninety-sixth Congress (1979–1980), supporters of lobby reform legislation continued to try to work out a compromise that would produce accurate reporting of lobbying activities without violating the Constitution. This legislative search for a compromise lobbying reform act, not surprisingly, was accompanied by some of the most intense lobbying ever seen on Capitol Hill by groups such as the American Civil Liberties Union, the AFL-CIO, Common Cause, the Consumer Federation of America, Ralph Nader's Congress Watch, the Sierra Club, the U.S. Chamber of Commerce, and the United Church of Christ, to name just some of the one hundred or so groups arrayed on both sides.

When legislators downplay the importance of interest groups in the face of documented expenditures by lobbyists, it is not because they are lying, but rather that they do not think of most of this activity as lobbying. A union lobbyist tells this tale:

> One time during the minimum wage battle, Senator _____ began to weaken on the $1.00 minimum. Someone had touched his sympathy with a picture of what the bill would do to the sawmills of the South. He told me that he was contemplating making an exception in their case. I said, "_____ (first name), if you even hint that you might back down from your previous position, this place will be swarming with lobbyists!" "Lobbyists," he said, looking around him, "I don't see any lobbyists around here." Then he realized that I was one and laughed. Hell, we don't think of ourselves as lobbyists! [17]

Recent political science research on the role of interest groups in Congress gives some support to legislators' own descriptions of the lobbying process. In contrast to the muckraking descriptions of payoffs and the popular notion of legislators giving in to pressure, these studies suggest a network of accommodation and mutual assistance between lobbyists and legislators.[18] A congressman describes that network this way:

> A professional lobbyist becomes part of the woodwork here. He becomes a source of information. A lot of people talk about "the invidious special interests," but we shouldn't engage in legislation without knowing who's affected by it, and usually the people who are affected by it are the best sources of information.
>
> There are a few guys up here who vote a certain way because they're bought, but most of us don't like to deal with people who have only a short range interest in us.[19]

Most lobbying activity is directed toward reinforcing the opinions of legislators who are already in basic agreement with the group position. Instead of attempting to convert legislators, lobbyists seek to hold supporters in line or to activate those who agree with the group position but who might not vote unless convinced of the importance of that vote. This focus on legislators in agreement with the lobbyists is a result of the lobbyists' belief that most votes are already pretty well set long before an issue comes to a vote and of their desire to avoid uncertain or high conflict situations. A major study of trade policy found that:

> Lobbyists fear to enter where they may find a hostile reception. Since uncertainty is greatest precisely regarding those who are undecided, the lobbyist is apt to neglect contact with those very persons who he might be able to influence.
>
> It is so much easier to carry on activities within the circle of those who agree and encourage you than it is to break out and find potential proselytes, that the day-to-day routine and pressure of business tend to shunt those more painful activities aside. The result is that the lobbyist becomes in effect a service bureau of those congressmen already agreeing with him, rather than an agent of direct persuasion.[20]

When legislators respond to questions about lobbying, they think of instances when an organization attempted to change their vote. This happens rarely enough that most legislators consider themselves relatively free of such pressures. The main task of lobbyists (providing information and rationales to justify a legislator's already decided vote) is not considered lobbying by those on the receiving end. Although performing such functions might not change any votes, it does provide an important service for legislators.

A study of the Illinois legislature shows the importance of giving representatives reasons for having voted the way they did. In this case, a legislator brought in a law professor to testify against a tax bill; neither the legislator nor the professor felt that this testimony had really changed any votes on the bill.

> However (the legislator pointed out), do not undersell the significance of the presentation. Our arrangements (for votes) were concluded before the hearing ever started, but it was absolutely essential that members who had agreed to vote against the bill be furnished with a "cover"—with an impressive witness whose competence was unquestioned so that they could offer an explanation of their votes. The professor furnished that "cover." When we return the favor on legislation in which others are interested, we shall expect to be furnished with a cover.[21]

A second reason why most lobbying is not perceived as such by members of Congress relates to the system of cue networks. Since most voting by legislators is done in a low-information situation, members come to depend on a network of cue sources for reliable information as to how they should vote. Constituents, lobbyists, staff members, and party leaders all serve as cue sources for particular legislators on certain issues. But the most consistent source of cues for legislative voting is other senators and representatives. The information a member relies on to support his or her position will come primarily from within the Capitol Hill network rather than from external sources.[22] The most successful lobbies are thus quite often the least visible. "The key point of contact is usually between a highly specialized lobbyist and the specialized staff people of a standing committee. Intimate friendships spring up there—it's the rivet point." [23] Because of the importance of a legislator's staff, lobbyists often prefer to talk to a senator or representative's aides rather than to the legislator. This indirect approach fits in better with the internal information system of Congress. It can also be a great help to overworked staff members. Says one Senate staff member:

> My boss demands a speech and a statement for the *Congressional Record* for every bill we introduce or cosponsor—and we have a *lot* of bills. I just can't do it all myself. The better lobbyists, when they have a proposal they are pushing, bring it to me along with a couple of speeches, a *Record* insert, and a fact sheet. They know their clout is tripled that way.[24]

A professional lobbyist had this to say about the staff relationship: "The conventional wisdom today is that members are overstaffed. What so many people overlook is that members of Congress have become ombudsmen—they spend most of their time taking care of their constituents' problems with the government—so it becomes difficult to do good legislative work. So to an extent we become an extension of the staff." [25]

The importance of the internal cue network in Congress is reflected in the fact that the most effective lobbyists are senators and representatives themselves. *Inside lobbying* by legislators is generally viewed as a form of legitimate representation by members of Congress. Whether a legislator's ties to a particular group stem from his own occupational background or from that group's being an important part of his constituency, it is expected that he will try to convince colleagues to support that group's legislative goals. "Lobbying by other congressmen is the most difficult for me to resist," is the way one legislator put it.[26] Another commented:

> Congressmen tend to have a high regard for one another, and if someone has a pet bill, you tend to make efforts to accommodate him if it is at all possible. When Congressman _____ had his cranberry bill, everybody said, "let's do something for good old Nick," and so they passed the bill. It wasn't a very good bill and probably shouldn't have passed; but the "good old Nick" slogan was enough to do it. No lobby could have pushed that bill through. It was just a personal hand for a member.[27]

Inside lobbying of their colleagues by legislators became more institutionalized in the 1970s with the emergence of a vast array of caucuses formed by representatives with similar constituency, regional, background, or issue interests. In 1971, the twelve black members then serving in the House formed the Congressional Black Caucus. In 1973, representatives from New England's six states formed the first regional caucus, the New England Congressional Caucus, which was followed three years later by the 200-member Northeast-Midwest Economic Advancement Coalition. In the Ninety-fifth Congress (1977–1978), the Congresswoman's Caucus successfully lobbied enough members to pass a bill providing veteran's benefits to former Women's Air Force Service Pilots. The Textile Caucus won a similar victory in the Ninety-fifth Congress when the House passed legislation that exempted all textiles from trade talks then going on in Geneva. A list of the many House caucuses of the Ninety-sixth Congress (1979–1980) demonstrates both the informal fragmentation in the House that parallels the formal fragmentation in the subcommittee structure and the extent to which inside lobbying has become accepted in the House. In addition to the caucuses already mentioned, the House has a Steel Caucus, Mushroom Caucus, Irish Caucus, Italian-American Members of Congress, Hispanic Caucus, Ball Bearing Caucus, Shipyard Caucus, Blue Collar Caucus, Suburban Caucus, Rural Caucus, and the Vietnam-Era Veterans' Caucus.[28] The size and effectiveness of these caucuses vary a great deal, and there has not been a similar growth of caucuses in the Senate. But the range of caucuses in the House alone demonstrates the importance of inside lobbying in Congress.

A third reason why lobbying activity is often hard to find stems from the nature of the political process in Congress. Inside the legislature, members are socialized into a body emphasizing reciprocity and bargaining. These norms, coupled with a specialization that precludes a member's having a broad general overview of the cumulative effects of public policies, help to explain how special interests are able to achieve their legislative goals. Stanley Surrey points out how the nature of legislative politics brings about tax loopholes:

> The desire—sometimes the need—of a congressman to be useful often places a congressman who sits on one of the tax committees, the House Committee on Ways and Means or the Senate Committee on Finance, in a difficult position. A fellow congressman who sits on the Public Works Committee, for example, can respond to constituency pressure by approving the project involved; a member of the Appropriations Committee can respond by a favorable vote on a specific appropriation. But a congressman on a tax committee can respond only by pushing through a special tax provision.
>
> His legislative stock in trade, so to speak, is special tax treatment. This difficulty is especially acute in the case of those congressmen who come to sit on a tax committee only after they have been members of other committees and have become so accustomed to using their committee powers in helpful ways that the habit persists.[29]

Legislative bargaining among elites requires that legislators deliver tangible rewards. Although the mass public may accept symbolic rewards, legislators and lobbyists who are active in political bargaining are not so easily pacified. Instead of being satisfied with programs promising to maintain a progressive income tax, or agricultural price supports figured on parity, political elites active in legislative bargaining seek specific tax provisions and price supports for particular crops. As Surrey's description of the tax committees suggests, bargaining is the exchange of tangible benefits among political elites. Most of this process is regarded not as lobbying by interest groups, but as normal legislative politics. However, the results in terms of policy payoffs for particular groups are much the same.

In his analysis of American politics, E. E. Schattschneider has suggested that any political system develops a set of predominant values, beliefs, rituals, and rules of the game that benefit certain groups at the expense of others.[30] This *mobilization of bias* is staunchly defended by those groups who benefit from the status quo. Professors Peter Bachrach and Morton Baratz suggest that this mobilization of bias is maintained through a process of *nondecision-making* by which challenges to the values or interests of the decision-maker or other political elites are suppressed or thwarted.

> To be more nearly explicit, nondecision-making is a means by which demands for change in the existing allocation of benefits and privileges in the community can be suffocated before they are even voiced; or kept covert; or killed before they gain access to the relevant decision-making arena; or, failing all these things, maimed or destroyed in the decision-implementing stage of the policy process.[31]

One effect of this idea of power is to greatly broaden the definition of politics. Instead of focusing only on concrete decision-making by a political body, analysts must look at popular values that preclude certain issues from being seriously raised or permit their being dismissed after only superficial consideration. For instance, the power of the American Medical Association in blocking medicare for over twenty years partially reflects the importance of such values as individualism (or *volunteerism*) and belief in the free enterprise system. Because of widespread acceptance of these values, the AMA was able to successfully oppose all medicare programs by attacking them, at the symbolic level, as being socialized medicine.[32]

Similar values affect the distribution of power within the political system. Volunteerism made it difficult for organized labor to gain power in the United States and still affects the way in which labor legislation is administered.[33] *Anticommunism* benefits those groups seeking a larger defense budget and government contracts, and *economic growth* helps larger corporations in their pursuit of tax breaks for expansion and research.[34] The widespread acceptance of these values gives certain groups advantages in the political process that other groups lack. Those who profit from the existing distribution of values do not need to actively seek congressional support for beneficial programs, because the existing programs already help them. Their power is a diffuse veto power embodied in the political culture. It is exercised whenever policies that could challenge the status quo are eliminated prior to public debate or defeated by linking them with vague negative symbols. It is a kind of power that political analysts who focus on overt lobbying and concrete decision-making situations are likely to overlook or to underestimate.

A last consideration that we should include in this general discussion of interest groups and Congress is the series of descriptions and evaluations of lobbying put forward by the pluralist school of thought in American politics. In Chapter 1 we had a look at these ideas and some of the criticism leveled against them. Because so much of Madison's argument in Federalist paper #10, and later discussions of the public interest that rely on a process of special interests checking one another, have to do with the role of interest representation in Congress, it seems appropriate to end this section with some thoughts about these pluralist notions of how things work.

The competition of disparate groups seems to be a key element of pluralist thought. As long as legislators must pay heed to the demands of a wide range of groups present in heterogeneous constituencies, they will tend to support policies that satisfy the greatest number of individual demands. Pluralist explanations of lobbying emphasize the heterogeneity of constituencies and the fact that a legislator must balance the conflicting demands of many groups. This discontinuity among groups is also extended into the Congress itself and used to explain why individual legislators are relatively free from influence by any one group. The authors of one study conclude:

> If Congressman A listens when the Fruitgrowers Association speaks, Congressmen B, C, D, E, and F are indifferent to the pleas of the Association. Congressman B, in turn, might be vulnerable to a second group to which his colleagues A, C, D, E, and F are indifferent. When the patterns of individual vulnerability are overlaid on one another, so to speak, it is clear that relatively few Congressmen are vulnerable to any given group. Individual vulnerabilities cancel each other out to a considerable extent and are lost in the indifference, inertia, and invulnerability of Congress as a whole.[35]

There are two weaknesses in the pluralist description of lobbying in Congress. First, the collusion of seemingly disparate groups and trade-offs in different policy areas is downplayed or ignored. Second, there is an assumption that competing groups will prevent any one interest from dominating a particular policy subsystem, that most policy areas involve opposing groups that serve to check the demands of others. Some general studies about group interaction in American politics and specific instances of congressional lobbying illustrate how either collusion among groups or norms of mutual noninterference greatly dilute the idea of groups checking one another.

Murray Edelman's description of management-labor disputes shows how even these very different interests can evolve a pattern of settlement that gives each side expanded benefits, and indicates the scope of intergroup collusion:

> A major function of much union-management bargaining in the late fifties and sixties has been to provide a ritual which must be acted out as a prerequisite for the quiescent acceptance of higher prices and higher wages by those directly involved. Nor is it surprising that the rite is most formalized precisely in the industries in which the bargaining and the speculation about the likelihood of a strike are most widely publicized: steel, autos, meat packing, heavy machinery, electronics.[36]

When Congress was considering the Clean Air Act of 1977, under circumstances described by the House floor manager as "the heaviest lobbying I've seen in 23 years in Congress," a coalition in opposition to the bill emerged that was based on cooperation between two old enemies: the automobile companies and labor unions.[37] The industry's opposition to strict emission control standards was expressed in terms of the number of jobs that would be lost as a result of legislation. The influence of the four big automobile companies (Ford, General Motors, Chrysler, and American Motors) was greatly enhanced by their working with the experienced and respected lobbyists for the 1.5 million-member United Auto Workers. Although the industry-labor coalition did not succeed in blocking passage of the legislation, they were able to win a delay in the imposition of the new standards.[38]

Explanations of interest group activity in the legislature that emphasize the countervailing effects of different lobbies underestimate the power of these coalitions. Although an individual legislator may not be vulnerable to any given group, if many groups get together to support each other's legislative goals they may represent a political force that no elected official can ignore.

Group theorists who talk of countervailing interests also generally assume that there is some sort of representational balance that produces the public interest. But studies of interest representation in Congress do not support such a view. For instance, in congressional hearings on tax laws "there is practically no one, except perhaps the Treasury, available to represent the public." As William Cary observes:

> Perhaps the reason is that all of the pressure group proposals are of such character that no one of them would have a large adverse effect on the tax bill of any individual. Hence counterpressure groups seldom develop.
>
> A second reason why the public is not more frequently represented is the difficulty of forming pressure groups around general interests. The concentration of business organizations on appeals brought to Congress and the emphasis placed on specific and often very technical information makes it difficult even for the members of the tax committees to secure a balanced view of what is the general interest, what the public wants or, indeed, what the public would want if it were informed as to the facts.[39]

A similar point was made by the organizer of the environmental group coalition supporting the Clean Air Act of 1977: "Lobbying is a reflection of organized power, and that's the weakness of it. Those with the greatest economic resources can win. But there are 215 million people who breathe auto emissions and are concerned about air. How do these people get representation when there is no easily available means for them to be organized?"[40]

Organized economic interests are able to get tangible rewards from the legislature, not by bribing legislators, but rather by using the advantages that the political system gives them. By providing information that reinforces the position of their supporters, by relying on inside lobbyists, by invoking legislative norms and political values that strengthen their position, and by working in conjunction with other political elites for shared benefits, these groups are able to benefit from policies coming out of particular subsystems.

As this general review of lobbying in Congress has shown, there is not complete agreement as to the effects of lobbying on legislators' behavior and the content of legislative policies. Sometimes those who emphasize the great influence of pressure groups seem to be right. At other times those who downplay their importance seem more nearly correct. It is time, then, to recognize that different types of policies are handled in different ways by Congress and that these differences greatly affect the relative influence of lobbyists on legislation.[41] In the next few pages I have organized the discussion in terms of Lowi's classification of policy types and drawn on some studies of interest group activities in different policy areas. The purpose here is not to present an authoritative statement on lobbying in Congress, but rather to show the great variety of interest group behavior and influence. By employing Lowi's framework, it is hoped that some of the seeming contradictions about the importance of lobbyists in Congress will be cleared up.

Distributive Policies and Pressure Groups

A glance back at Table 6–1 will remind you that distributive policies are those that generally involve the awarding of material benefits to some narrow segment of the general population. Awarding federal funds for the development of a harbor or building a bridge, maintaining or reducing postal rates for bulk mailers, granting tax loopholes for certain industries or occupations, keeping price supports at a certain level for particular crops, or awarding defense contracts or military bases to a representative's district are all examples of distributive policies. They are generally characterized by the government's giving something away. The politics of distributive policies focus more on "Who gets what?" than on "Who pays?"

When we look at those accounts of lobbying in Congress that stress the influence of groups on policy outcomes, we find that the vast majority deal with distributive issues. The authors of *Who Runs Congress?* talk about the oil lobby, the military armaments lobby, the tobacco lobby, the automobile lobby, and the National Rifle Association among others. Their picture of lobbying is perhaps best illustrated in their characterization of the oil lobby as one that "has plenty to gun with."

> When fully mobilized, oil can send into action lawyers from the most respectable law firms, public relations consultants, numerous ex-government officials, newsmen who serve as "advisors," company executives, corporate legal departments, government officials in several of the executive departments, trade association representatives, and—though only a small fraction of the total—men who actually register as lobbyists. Whenever legislation affecting oil is on the docket, the oilers can easily afford to have a corporate vice-president or similarly impressive official assigned to persuade every member of every relevant committee. If reinforcements should be needed, the industry can call on a vast reserve of sales agents, filling station operators, and other small businessmen.[42]

The Common Cause publication, *How Money Talks in Congress*, provides a description of the lobbying campaign that was conducted in the Ninety-fifth Congress (1977–1978) for a cargo preference bill which would have required that 30 percent (rather than the 4 percent then in effect) of all oil imported to the United States be carried in U.S. flagships:

> The lobbying campaign conducted by the maritime interests for their legislation was massive. A million dollar public relations/advertising effort was undertaken. It was financed primarily by maritime companies and run by Gerald Rafshoon, the man behind President Carter's successful image in the 1976 campaign and who has since joined the White House staff. The lobbying campaign included television commercials, full page ads in major newspapers, and efforts to stimulate grass roots lobbying. In addition, the stage had been set for victory by the more than $1 million in maritime contributions made to 1976 congressional candidates.[43]

In this particular instance the intense lobbying effort was not successful: the House of Representatives defeated the cargo preference bill in the fall of 1977. The point here is not whether such lobbying is always successful but rather that these types of characterizations of intense lobbying efforts generally are associated with policies that affect particular economic interests, be they the oil industry and tax provisions, the maritime industry and unions and a cargo preference bill, the American Medical Association and a hospital cost containment bill, or trial lawyers and insurance companies and no-fault automobile insurance legislation.

More systematic studies of legislative action on tax bills lend some support to the vivid descriptions of lobbyists' influence on this policy process. Both Joseph Pechman and John Manley discuss the important role groups play in making sure that special tax provisions are maintained or inserted in tax bills before Congress. These loopholes often come in the form of amendments to the bill and are generally inserted on the Senate floor. Senators proposed 111 amendments, and accepted 70, to the 1969 Tax Reform Act in less than two weeks of debate.[44] When the Revenue Act of 1978 was passed by the House of Representatives it provided tax cuts and special provisions with a total cost of $16.3 billion. A flood of amendments in the Senate boosted the total cost of the bill to $29.1 billion. The way these special tax provisions assist specific interests can be seen by looking at some of the special provisions left in the final bill:

> Provisions exempting two large chicken farms from a law requiring farms to use accrual accounting; extending investment tax

credits to sod farms, pigpens, chicken coops and green houses; freeing restaurant owners from having to report their employees' charge account tips; phasing out the federal excise tax on slot machines; allowing an Oklahoma long term care home to escape taxation as a private foundation; enabling the Power Authority of the State of New York to use tax exempt industrial development bonds to finance power projects to serve New York City and adjacent Westchester County; liberalizing accounting rules for manufacturers who provide discount coupons and for manufacturers of magazines, books, and records; nullifying tax claims made by the IRS against Alaska Native Corporations, and preventing the IRS from taxing certain payments made to Michigan farmers to compensate them for cattle which were poisoned.[45]

It has been estimated that tax loopholes, shelters, and preferences such as those included in the 1978 Act cost the federal government about $136 billion in revenue every year.[46]

Other examples of lobbyists directly influencing legislators tend to come from similarly distributive policy fields. In 1972, a former senator from Maryland was found guilty of accepting an unlawful gratuity from a Washington lobbyist to influence his vote on postal rate legislation. The lobbyist represented a Chicago mail business that would have to pay $1 million a year for every one-penny increase in third-class postal rates. During the trial the senator's former chief assistant described his legislative office as "one where lobbyists wrote speeches, where a Federal job was purchased for cash, where money flowed into his and the Senator's pockets and where the Senator's signature was so widely copied by staff members that they even signed it to (the Senator's) final divorce decree." [47] Postal rates, like tax loopholes, are distributive policies in the sense that they have an important impact on only a narrow segment of the society (bulk mailers) and that the most intensively concerned interests are producer interests.

Farm price supports provide another example of policies that are influenced by single-issue economic interests. In addition, this policy area illustrates how the concept of representation and committee structure can make the need for overt lobbying by concerned interests unnecessary. The House Agriculture Committee is very much a constituency committee; legislators tend to sit on commodity subcommittees that permit them to have some say over price supports for crops that are important in their districts. The distribution of benefits that this system produces is similar to that of the tax-loophole system. Most of the benefits go to the biggest economic interests in the constituencies. A 1971 study showed that the wealthiest 25 percent of the farmers received 75 percent of the subsidy payments. Thus, in 1968, the 264 largest farms received $52 million in government aid, as did the 540,000 smallest farms. "This meant an average government payment of $197,000 to the wealthiest farmers, an average of $96 for the half million small farmers." [48]

We do not presently have enough studies of lobbyists and legislators covering a sufficiently wide array of different policy areas to make sound generalizations about the overall impact on legislative policies. But when we encounter statements like this: "It's like there's a bushel basket in the middle of the table. Everybody is trying to throw as many of their things into the barrel as they can," there is a good chance that the speaker is describing a distributive policy-making process.[49] Similarly, when we see descriptions that emphasize the influence of lobbyists on legislation or when we hear legislators suggest that they are not subjected to much pressure to vote one way or another, it is likely that legislative politics dealing with a distributive issue is the subject of attention. For the nature of interest group activity in distributive policy-making is such that there are close links between concerned economic interests and members of relevant committees or subcommittees and that the narrow scope of the issue provides that only a limited number of lawmakers need be directly involved.

The outline presented in Table 6–1 provides a summary of interest group activity in the distributive policy arena. There are a large number of small, intensely organized interests based on narrow economic grounds. These groups pursue their interests in a low-conflict political process that stresses the norm of mutual noninterference; when coalitions form, they consist of unlike interests brought together through a logrolling process; and the primary focus is on the subcommittee or committee that has jurisdiction over that policy area.

Regulatory Policies and Pressure Groups

Those who study Congress often bring to their research with them the distributive model of lobbying. As Lewis Anthony Dexter notes, " 'pressure' and 'pressure politics' are regarded by most 'sophisticated' people today as 'explaining' a great deal that happens." [50] There is the expectation that affected interests will marshal their forces to influence legislators directly on the matter and that the level of lobbying activity will be related to the economic stakes those interests have in the issue. The authors (Raymond Bauer, Ithiel de Sola Pool, and Lewis Anthony Dexter) of a prize-winning book on trade policy have pointed out that they "started with the notion that public officials would see themselves as under almost constant pressure from those who have a stake in the decisions they make." [51]

Sometimes these scholars find much less lobbying (in the distributive sense) than they expected. This happened with the 1963 study of trade policy and with a study of the 1970 Political Broadcast Act limiting campaign spending. In the latter, the authors observed:

> Probably the most striking aspect of pressure group activity in this case was the lack of it. Considering the importance of the measure and the potential impact of the various versions of the bill upon the broadcasting industry, it is somewhat surprising that more intense lobbying did not occur. [52]

Lowi suggests that the reason Bauer, Pool, and Dexter found little pressure group activity in their study of post-war trade policies is because trade policy, which had long been regarded as distributive policy, was becoming regulatory in the 1950s and 1960s. Instead of being conceived as domestic policy that was designed to serve the interests of a vast array of unrelated native industries, trade policy came to be regarded as an instrument of foreign policy that required cohesion and the application of a general rule to all trade decisions. A look at Table 6–1 will indicate how interest group activity in the case of regulatory policies differs from that of distributive policies.

In regulatory policy-making, interest groups are based on shared attitudes rather than just narrow economic interests. Coalitions of groups are formed through a bargaining process of conflict and compromise over goals rather than a logrolling process that produces mutual noninterference in each group's seeking its own goals. These coalitions change with different issues, but all groups in a coalition seek to build a majority on the issue by compromising with other groups in the coalition. Lastly, these groups focus their activity on the whole chamber and not just the concerned committees.

Some examples of regulatory policies are trade policies since the 1960s, federal aid to education, campaign finance regulations, and medicare. By drawing on case studies dealing with these types of policies, we can provide some general observations about the nature of pressure group activity in regulatory policy-making.

First, a characteristic of interest group activity in the regulatory arena seems to be that groups are seeking broad social goals and not just their own economic gain. Congress passed the Medicare Bill in 1965. All studies of this public health legislation point to the importance of the AFL-CIO's campaign. Says one: "It [medicare] was carried by the AFL-CIO all the way to the bill-drafting stage, and for the first few months, at least, it had only nominal sponsorship by a congressman who had doubts about it and did little to promote it." [53]

The battle over medicare produced coalitions of interest groups that were concerned with more than just the immediate delivery of benefits from the government. On one side was a coalition made up of the AFL-CIO, the National Council of Senior Citizens, and members of the Democratic political coalition and administration. The coalition of opposition included the American Medical Association (which reported spending several millions of dollars), the American Dental Association, the American Hospital Association, and the American Nursing Homes Association. The fact that medicare was passed and that the AFL-CIO won gives credence to the Nader group's evaluation of the effectiveness of the labor lobby—that "labor has been stymied on many strictly labor issues, where the unions find themselves without allies, but has had some striking successes as part of coalitions working on broader social issues." [54] The essence of these interest group coalitions that form around regulatory policies seems to be the fact that they are based on a shared attitude toward some broad policy issue and not just collections of people who agree to stay out of each other's affairs.

When we consider regulatory policies and lobbying, another characteristic comes to mind that might help to explain the fact that there is seldom a feeling among members of Congress that they are being pressured to vote a particular way. That is that coalitions of interests on regulatory policies tend to form a long time before a bill on the issue is subject to a vote. A case study of the Elementary and Secondary Education Act of 1965 reports that "the private groups that had represented the varieties of opinion on federal aid legislation began their realignment a full year before the Eighty-ninth Congress convened." [55] Similarly, labor group activity in behalf of medicare began nine years before the legislation was passed.

This early formation of coalitions on regulatory policies is related to the need to develop compromise positions among members of the coalition and to the fact that these interest groups must deal with bills when they reach the chamber floor and not just in their committee or subcommittee stage. Reaching a compromise position among different elements in a coalition obviously takes longer than mobilizing interests with the same economic base. There is bound to be some disagreement about political attitudes on broad policy, while all members of the same economic interest can readily agree on their shared interests. Effective lobbying on regulatory policies also involves the mobilization of public opinion and the building of a broader base of support than does lobbying for distributive issues.[56] Both processes take more time than those associated with distributive policies, where interest groups need only make sure that they have the standing commitment of subcommittee and committee decision-makers. In addition, effective lobbying for regulatory policies entails utilizing the internal cue network of Congress in which legislative colleagues lobby one another and public opinion campaigns reinforce the legislator's feeling that he or she is supporting constituency interests.

A classic statement of pressure groups and distributive policies was E. E. Schattschneider's 1935 study, *Politics, Pressure, and the Tariff*.[57] The author uncovered a lobbying process that sought to keep the boundaries of conflict limited to appropriate subcommittees, took the form of logrolling, and relied on a standing pattern of agreement between industries seeking tariff protection and subcommittee members. The differences between this type of pressure group activity and that which we find in regulatory areas are summed up in the case study of federal aid to education legislation. Eidenburg and Morey, authors of *An Act of Congress*, state:

> Our observation of the education issue in 1965–67 does not accord with Schattschneider's major theme of the pressure groups coercing Congress into action along lines they desire. Rather, we saw the network of forces surrounding the Congress and education pressure groups blending into a policy climate that required certain prior arrangements among the pressure groups in order for Congress to act out its role.[58]

Once again, we become aware of the gap between general statements about lobbying and Congress and case studies of specific policies. There still are not enough studies on lobbying to provide comprehensive understanding of this part of the legislative process and the impact on policies. But this comparison between distributive and regulatory policy-making and the role of interest groups in each does suggest that some of the disparities among the different pictures of pressure groups' influence on legislation that we do have stem from the fact that people are talking about different types of policies.

Redistributive Policies and Pressure Groups

The other types of policy we looked at represent the normal ones handled by the legislative system. Redistributive policies, on the other hand, occur less often and are seen as policies to meet some crisis. The nature of politics surrounding redistributive policies are quite different from the politics of distributive or regulatory policies. Stephen Bailey has characterized normal legislative politics this way:

> In the absence of a widely recognized crisis, legislative policy making tends to be fought out at the level of largely irresponsible personal and group stratagems and compromises based upon temporary power coalitions of political, administrative, and non-governmental interests.[59]

Redistributive policies are handled in a different way. They are designed to meet some crisis, whether it is widespread unemployment and economic stagnation, patterns of racial discrimination, or extensive poverty in a seemingly wealthy society.

Briefly, we can say this about legislative politics surrounding redistributive policies: the group conflict involves large coalitions made up of peak associations (such as the National Association of Manufacturers, the Chamber of Commerce, the AFL-CIO) that share a broad consensus on goals to be achieved; both sides of the conflict advance ideological, rather than self-interest, arguments; much of the discussion revolves around the possible long-term effects of the proposed policies; and the president generally plays an active role in the legislative process.

There are some fine case studies we can turn to in our attempt to sketch how pressure groups influence legislative policies of a redistributive type. Stephen Bailey's *Congress Makes a Law* looks at the Employment Act of 1946; Daniel Berman's *A Bill Becomes a Law* deals with civil rights legislation in the early 1960s; and a number of studies of the 1964 poverty program provide useful descriptions of the legislative policy process.[60]

In discussing pressure group activity surrounding the Employment Act of 1946, Bailey devotes a chapter to the "Lib-Lab Lobby," which he sees as being similar to the broad reform coalition of Liberal and Labour interests operating in late nineteenth century Britain. The 1946 "Lib-Lab Lobby" consisted primarily of the Union for Democratic Action, the CIO political action committee, the American Federation of Labor, and an ad hoc collection of interests known as the Continuations Group. A simple listing of the organizations represented in this Continuations Group shows the breadth of this coalition. Included were: the American Federation of Labor; Americans United for World Organization; the Brotherhood of Maintenance of Way Employees; the Brotherhood of Railway Trainmen; Business of America, Inc.; the Congress of Industrial Organizations; the Council for Social Action of the Congregational Christian Churches; the Independent Citizens Committee of the Arts, Sciences, and Professions; the National Association for the Advancement of Colored People; the Young Women's Christian Association; the National Catholic Welfare Conference; the National Conference of Jewish Women; the National Farmers Union; the National Women's Trade Union League of America; the Railway Labor Executive Association; the Union for Democratic Action; and the National League of Women Shoppers.[61] In addition, support for the bill came from a variety of other groups such as university professors; religious, racial, and educational groups; veterans; welfare workers; the National Lawyers Guild; and independent businessmen. Opposition to the bill also drew on a broad coalition of interests including the National Association of Manufacturers, Chambers of Commerce, the Committee for Constitutional Government, and the American Farm Bureau Federation.

Pressure group activity for the Civil Rights Act of 1964 and the poverty program show a pattern similar to that of the Employment Act of 1946. The most active lobby for civil rights legislation was the Leadership Conference on Civil Rights, which was a broad coalition of labor, liberal, race, and church groups. By 1963, a total of seventy-nine organizations were represented in the Leadership

Conference. The endless parade of witnesses for the bill provided by the Leadership Conference led one southern congressman to scold those "cardinals, bishops, elders, stated clerks, common preachers, priests, and rabbis" coming to Washington to support the bill.[62] When a House subcommittee began hearings on the Economic Opportunity Act of 1964, the lead-off witnesses supporting the measure included the Secretaries of Defense, Labor, Commerce, Agriculture, HEW, and the Attorney General.

> Later, spokesmen for an impressive range of civic, welfare, and religious groups appeared to endorse the bill. AFL-CIO President George Meany and the National Urban League's executive director, Whitney Young, Jr., led off, followed by representatives of such groups as the National Council of Churches, the National Catholic Welfare Council, the National Education Association, the American Public Welfare Association, the National Farmers Union, the National Grange, the American Friends Service Committee, and the General Federation of Women's Clubs.[63]

We have seen that pressure group activity for regulatory policies differed from that of distributive policies. When a distributive issue is involved, the outside interests seeking to influence Congress generally represent a single economic interest or industry that is seeking only to maximize the benefits it receives from government. There is a little concern for what others are doing, and any group coalitions that do form are based on an agreement not to interfere with each other's interests. Regulatory policies, however, saw some broadening of group goals and a tendency for groups sharing some common social policy to compromise their differences and jointly seek legislative action. The nature of group activity in relation to redistributive policies is a continuation of this expansion of the scope of the conflict and the breadth of the coalitions involved. This is clearly seen in the above descriptions of the composition of pressure group alliances formed over the Employment Act, Civil Rights Act, and the Economic Opportunity Act. Differences in the structure of the group conflict are also accompanied by differences in the form of the debate.

Arguments advanced on both sides in considering redistributive policies are much broader and more ideological than those put forward in debates over distributive policies ("this is in the interest of cotton growers, the construction industry, etc.") or regulatory policies ("this is in the interest of certain broad segments of the population such as school children or the elderly"). The participants in redistributive policy-making invoke broad ideological symbols such as free enterprise, the right to work, or political freedom versus totalitarianism. A sampling of the arguments put forth in the Employment Act and Civil Rights Act debates clearly shows the ideological nature of the debate and a concern for the possible long-term effects of these policies.

The hearings of the House committee on the Employment Act contained the following statement issued by the Ohio Chamber of Commerce:

> The Communist-sparked C.I.O.-P.A.C., aided by its political fellow-travelers, is now making the drive which has been in preparation for years. Everything that has happened up to now has been but a preliminary.
>
> This is the hour, almost the moment, of historic decision. The basic goal of C.I.O.-P.A.C. is to overturn our system of competitive, private enterprise and substitute for it complete government control over capital and labor alike. . . .
>
> Keystone of the new group of "crisis" legislative enactments, devised by the same cunning brains that have guided this boasted bloodless revolution, is the full employment bill, now being seriously considered in Washington.
>
> Labeled in fraud and deception as a bill designed to preserve private enterprise, if enacted, it would be the scaffold on which private enterprise could be dropped to its death. . . .[64]

The Committee for Constitutional Government, in opposing the bill, said that it "may turn America permanently from constitutional private enterprise toward a system of collective statism." The National Association of Manufacturers talked about "state socialism" in their literature against the bill. And other opponents emphasized the potential long-term effects of the bill in suggesting that "there is an implicit threat that if 'free private enterprise' cannot supply jobs, then the task will be taken over by the government. The final step would be for the government to provide all the employment there is." [65]

The conflict over civil rights legislation reveals the same sort of emphasis on ideological concerns. Proponents of the legislation spoke in terms of constitutional guarantees, equality, and the moral responsibilities of the government. Those who opposed the various bills invoked the same values of freedom from federal government coercion seen in the Employment Act debate.

> We can keep our country free if we keep our elections free. We cannot keep our elections free if the electorate is to be determined by registration officials who owe their allegiance to a President who owes his allegiance to a political party which elected him. To those who think otherwise, I would point out the stark fact of history that Adolf Hitler's dictatorship became absolute when he was given power to appoint members of the German Reichstag.[66]

Assorted quotes are not, of course, sufficient evidence to prove or disprove any proposition. At best, they can only suggest a pattern. But it does seem clear that redistributive policy-making is not the same as distributive or regulatory policy-making. And part of the difference is reflected in pressure group activities and their influence on legislative policy.

We have had a look at some of the different evaluations of pressure groups' impact on legislative policy. They range from no impact to a great deal, from pictures of benign lobbyists helping the members of Congress do a better job, to conspiratorial rumblings about boodlers, bagmen, and sellouts to the highest bidder. By recognizing that different types of policies are handled in different ways, we have perhaps made a small step toward understanding the contradictory reports about lobbyists and legislators. Pressure groups do have some influence, but the nature and effectiveness of that influence will vary with the type of policy being considered. Senator Borah was not lying when he said that he "hadn't seen any lobbyists around here this year," nor was Senator Richard Russell when he talked about the "most intensive, extensive, and effective lobby assembled in Washington in many years." [67] They were talking about different types of legislative policy-making.

Policies and Pressure Groups in the 1980s

Earlier in this chapter it was mentioned that the nature of interest group and congressional activity will depend, to a large extent, on how a particular policy is perceived. A policy that allocates benefits to a narrow segment of the economy will be perceived as distributive and handled through the normal channel of subcommittee decision-making. Issues that are perceived as having a greater potential impact on society as a whole, the less frequent regulatory or redistributive policies, are more likely to involve the president, broad interest group coalitions, congressional party leaders, and the full membership of the House and Senate. During the 1970s there have been two developments that suggest a fundamental change has taken place in how policies are being perceived and in the political reaction to them. The first development is a general perception that American politics has entered what has been called an age of scarcity, a recognition that resources are limited and a concomitant shift in politics from demand management to resource management, from allocative decisions to production decisions. The second development is the growing force of single-issue politics and single-issue groups in the American system.

The *New York Times* officially ushered in this new political era in a 1974 editorial entitled "An Age of Scarcity." One of the best descriptions of this phenomenon was provided a year later by Elizabeth Drew:

> The country is confronting a third generation of issues involving government intervention. These issues have several common characteristics: they are technological and highly complicated; they are not subject to resolution by spending; they cut across the interests of a wide variety of interest groups; and they concern economic resources that are seen to be shrinking rather than expanding.
>
> They cannot be settled by the traditional method of buying off (doing a little something for) the various competing interests. The new issues—food, raw materials, energy—have brought us to a new kind of politics: a politics of what might be called resource constraints.[68]

What such a new political era means for the politics of Congress is that fewer issues will be perceived as distributive ones in which the decision to be made is how best to allocate seemingly unlimited resources. In structural terms, this means that fewer congressional decisions will be made *seriatim* by autonomous subcommittees and more will be made collectively by the whole membership. Some of the trends discussed earlier in this book—the growth of congressional staff, an increase in the coordinating powers given to party leaders, the success of the new centralized budget process, and the resort to creating extraordinary ad hoc committees on issues such as energy—are probable manifestations of this general shift in the perceptions of issues.[69] The caution with which the Ninety-sixth Congress (1979–1980) approached all spending issues, the normal politics of allocation, is another indication that Congress was moving from an era of distributive politics to one of resource constraints. "This is the most boring session I've seen in my years on the Hill," is the way one staff member characterized the Ninety-sixth Congress. "Nobody wants to move on anything. Everybody is gun shy. It's hard to get co-sponsors on any bill that costs anything, and, of course, most of them do." [70] A continuation of this trend in the 1980s would lead to a reduction in the overall volume of legislation produced by Congress and by a continuation of the centralizing and coordinating role of strengthened party leaders and the budget process. The politics of Congress, in other words, is likely to exhibit more characteristics of regulation and redistribution than it has in the past.

At first glance, the second development mentioned, the emergence of single-issue politics and groups, would seem to be moving congressional politics in the other direction, toward fragmentation rather than centralization. Single-issue politics is similar to distributive politics in the sense that groups are independently seeking political goals rather than engaging in coalition politics in pursuit of comprehensive and compromise goals. But there is a key difference. In distributive politics, groups are seeking government benefits for a narrow segment of the economy and are not in direct opposition to other groups with similar claims. Single-issue politics, on the other hand, often revolve around government decisions that would impose regulations on the behavior of everyone in society or directly take something of value from one group or segment of the economy and give it to another. Examples of single-issue politics in recent years include those whose foci have been gun control, abortion, and busing.

One observer of the Washington scene had this to say about the dominance of single-issue politics: "I can't remember a time when interest-group issues and politics so dominated events. And every day the units of protest and concern seem to be subdividing into even smaller and more specialized groupings." [71] During a political period in which one Senator's defeat had been attributed to the anti-abortion lobby, in which single-issue groups were calling for constitutional amendments requiring a balanced budget and prohibiting busing to integrate schools, and in which farmers from the American Agriculture Movement brought their protest campaign to the streets of Washington, Senator John Culver of Iowa talked about both the causes and the effects of single-issue politics:

> The problems are of such enormous complexity that the public is frustrated and senses it can't influence these situations by traditional forms of political action, and so it turns in other directions. People are increasingly turning to issues that they feel they can understand and do feel strongly about, and are devoting all their energy and resources to one particular issue.
>
> For a lot of reasons, the parties have lost their strength, their traditional power as the reconcilers of competing interests. So you've had balkanization into these splinter groups. When you have these rifle-shot constituencies, with their money and discipline, their influence on the outcome of elections is obviously disproportionate to their numbers. You can form a necklace of all these single-issue constituencies devoid of common purpose or values, and an unprincipled politician can cynically exploit them.[72]

While the increasing importance of single-issue groups obviously represents a decentralizing or fragmenting force in American politics, it is quite possible that the willingness of many members of Congress to support centralizing trends within Congress, which give greater control to the leadership, stems from a desire to protect themselves from the demands being made by single-issue groups. By delaying or not scheduling floor votes on volatile issues such as anti-abortion, anti-busing, and balanced budget amendments, the congressional leadership can serve as a useful buffer between individual members and single-issue groups.

A concrete measure of the growing importance of single-issue groups is the spectacular increase in the number of political action committees (PACs) in American politics. The Federal Election Commission defines political action committee money as "separate, segregated funds to be utilized for political purposes."[73] The Federal Election Campaign Amendments of 1974 and 1976 greatly enhanced the development of PACs and shifted the focus of political money from presidential to congressional campaigns.[74] Between 1974 and 1978, the number of PACs tripled: there were 1,938 in existence during the 1978 campaign. The amount of campaign money provided by political action committees also tripled during this period. PACs spent $12.5 million in the 1974 election, $22.6 million in the 1976 election, and $35.1 million in the 1978 election.[75] Three types of PACs—labor; corporate; and trade, membership, and health—contributed about equal amounts of money to congressional candidates in 1978, with about 57 percent of the total going to incumbents. Political action committees contribute to the fragmentation of American politics because they can impose heavy campaign funding sanctions on legislators who oppose them on the single issue or limited number of issues about which the political action committee is concerned. The limited range of issues to which a political action committee gives its attention is demonstrated by the remark of the director of a restaurant chain political action committee. How a legislator votes on minimum-wage legislation and the "three martini lunch" tax deduction is really all that this particular PAC cares about. "We don't get too concerned about their positions on the neutron bomb, you know," the PAC director noted.[76]

The two trends discussed in this section are mentioned here not because they suggest that Congress has been captured by special interests, but rather because a continuation of these trends in the 1980s will certainly test whether a representative institution is also capable of the integrative decision-making that is the essence of lawmaking. The president and the executive branch also represent a potential source of comprehensive policy integration in the American political system, and it is to this topic of executive influence in Congress that we now turn.

EXECUTIVE IMPACT ON LEGISLATIVE POLICIES

In his justification of checks and balances and separation of powers in the U.S. Constitution, James Madison indicated that such a system was needed to prevent Congress from dominating the other branches of government. "In republican government, the legislative authority necessarily predominates," Madison warned.[77] About two hundred years later, however, the authors of the Ralph Nader Congress Project book on the national legislature suggest that Madison's fear of dominance had been directed at the wrong branch of government. "No matter how hard the Congress may struggle on one issue," say the authors of this study, "it is overwhelmed by the vastly greater forces of the presidency. Whether Congress wins or loses, the President ends up on top." [78] Yet a scholarly study of Congress and social policy, published shortly after the Nader book, comes to a different conclusion. Professor Gary

Orfield discusses pervasive and unchallenged myths about power in American society, which "include a view of Congress as a declining and hopelessly fragmented body trying with little success to cope with the expansive and even dangerous power of a stronger institution, the Presidency." His review of congressional action and social change led to an assessment of congressional and presidential power that is in marked contrast to that of the Nader group study. "It should be evident," says Orfield, "that the President is often neither the dominant nor the progressive partner in the shaping of domestic policy." [79] Another study of the relative congressional and presidential influence over defense policies, published the same year as the Nader group study, supports Orfield's conclusions. "Congress did not docilely accept and ratify the defense policy positions of the executive," reports this political scientist. "On the contrary, it played a relatively lively role in particular policies, an activism whose level seemed to be associated with a perceived inadequacy of presidential decisions and actions." [80]

A glance at other discussions of the president and Congress reveals that such contradictory evaluations of presidential influence on legislation are quite common. Following are some examples:

> It is a simple fact that for the past thirty-six years, Congress has become almost exclusively dependent on the Executive Branch for any forward motion.[81]

> If Congress legislates, it subordinates itself to the President; if it refuses to legislate, it alienates itself from public opinion.[82]

> Within American political institutions, the center of initiative and decision has shifted from the Congress to the executive.[83]

On the other hand, we have these assessments made by a political scientist, a former White House staffer, and a former President:

> While the legislators do not obstruct, neither do they surrender. At times it has been they who led and the President who followed. The substantial contributions of members of Congress to legislation on air and water pollution, civil rights, education, medicare, and other measures come nearer to genuine partnership than to subordination.[84]

> The President does not "control" Congress at any time, not even at periods of great popularity when it is politic for most legislators

to go along with him. His true relationship to Congress is basically that of a highly important factor which the legislators must take into account.[85]

The fact is, I think, the Congress looks more powerful sitting here than it did when I was there in Congress. But that is because when you are in the Congress you are one of a hundred in the Senate or one of 435 in the House. So that the power is so divided. But from here I look at a Congress, and I look at the collective power of the Congress, particularly the bloc action, and it is a substantial power.[86]

Assessments of executive influence on legislation show a similarity to assessments of pressure groups' influence on legislation. Some observers, looking at particular instances, find that the president and the executive bureaucracy wield great power. Others, focusing on different issues or different periods of time, find that the impact of these outside actors on legislation is not very great. We hear warnings about the president becoming an absolute monarch who can completely ignore Congress and make policies by executive fiat, about an emerging dictatorship of the bureaucrats that would relegate both the president and Congress to minor roles in the policy-making process, and about a powerful but unresponsive Congress that fails to tailor policies to meet pressing social needs and prevents the president from doing so.

Discussions of presidential power relative to Congress are more valuable when a distinction is made among different types of policies. We find, for instance, that people who stress the president's growing dominance of the policy process often point to foreign policy or strategic defense issues to support their assertions. The use of executive agreements rather than treaties and the minor congressional role in making decisions about the war in Vietnam are excellent cases to support the suggestion that Congress has little say in the policy process. "The United States has one President, but it has two presidencies," says Aaron Wildavsky. "One presidency is for domestic affairs, and the other is concerned with defense and foreign policy. Since World War II, Presidents have had much greater success in controlling the nation's defense and foreign policies than in dominating its domestic policies." [87] In discussing the relative influence of the executive and the legislature over policies, it is useful to distinguish between foreign and domestic policies.

The president seems to have the upper hand in the first, while Congress is generally agreed to have some say over the second.

Another distinction among types of policies is that of Samuel Huntington in *The Common Defense*. He suggests that there are two different types of defense policies. One is strategic and deals with questions about the strength of military forces, their makeup, and their ability to be deployed; choices about the development of certain weapons; and matters having to do with the development of military forces. The other is structural and concerns the amount of money to be spent to maintain overall levels of men and material and how these force levels should be organized. Congress plays a major role in deciding structural issues, but the focus of decision on strategic matters lies within the executive branch. As Huntington notes, "structural issues of military policy are usually handled through what might be termed the domestic legislative process," while strategic issues fit more correctly into the foreign policy category.[88]

Distinguishing between foreign and domestic policies and between strategic and structural defense policies makes sense when talking about the relative influence of the executive and legislative branches on policy. We can go beyond this and consider different types of domestic policies as well. Lowi's essay consciously omits foreign policy in classifying different policy types. If we think of the continuum moving from distributive to redistributive policies as reflecting a broadening of the scope of issues and the number of people directly affected by them, we could put foreign policy and strategic defense issues in with redistributive policies and use the Lowi framework as a way to organize the discussion of executive influence on congressional policies.[89] Again, I should warn that these policy classifications are not mutually exclusive, that there is some overlap among the different categories. What the scheme helps us to do is to move away from overly general statements that Congress has lost all influence over policies to the executive or that the legislative branch maintains a decisive role in all policy-making.

Three major actors need to be considered in any discussion of executive-legislative influence on policy: the president and his or her administration officials, who represent the president's political source of power; the executive bureaucracy, whose source of power is its expertise based on long-term association with a government agency working in some specialized field; and the legislature, which consists of members who represent expertise in some areas based on extended familiarity with a policy area and a political base that might be quite different from that of the president. In short, we have a political world that is much more complicated than that represented by the evening news portrayals of an ideologically committed president versus a recalcitrant Congress or an arrogant president being held in line by the wisdom of a thoughtful Congress. The battles about who should determine policies are likely to involve many people in both the executive and legislative branches, not just the president and Congress.

Using the Lowi classification as a starting point, we can offer the following generalizations. Distributive policies are determined chiefly by subgovernments made up of congressional subcommittees and representatives of executive bureaus, with little direct intervention by the president. Regulatory policies are more likely to involve political actors in the president's administration, with the president often playing a direct role in the legislative process, and they are decided by the whole Congress rather than by committees or subcommittees. Redistributive domestic policies and foreign policies are settled in a process that comes closest to being one of executive dominance. The executive's near monopoly on information in this last policy category often leaves Congress with a minor role of legitimizing decisions made elsewhere. Let us now turn to some examples of presidential, bureaucratic, and congressional interaction in these different areas. We shall find again that not all cases fit so neatly into the overall framework, nor do they always support my generalizations about the different types of policy-making. Organizing the discussion in this way does help us to realize, though, that the influence of the executive on legislative policies varies with the types of policies under consideration.

Distributive Policies and Subgovernments

President Kennedy sometimes responded to policy suggestions put forward by friends or advisors with this comment: "Well, I agree with you, but I'm not sure the government will." [90] The government to which the president was referring has been variously called subsystems, subgovernments, and whirlpools by political analysts. To understand why some policies come out the way they do we have to look at the president and the Congress, and at the collection of actors who make up these subgovernments. This includes "(1) a federal administrative agency within the executive branch; (2) a heavily committed group of congressmen, usually members of a particular committee or subcommittee; (3) a private (or quasi-private) association representing the agency clientele; (4) a quite homogeneous constituency usually composed of local elites." [91]

The types of policies that are dealt with in such subgovernments are generally distributive ones: use of public lands, rivers and harbors legislation, agricultural subsidies, and specific tax benefits. Douglass Cater gives us a graphic description of the "tight little subgovernment which rules the nation's sugar economy."

> Political power within the sugar subgovernment is largely vested in the chairman of the House Agricultural Committee who works out the schedule of quotas. It is shared by a veteran civil servant, the Director of the Sugar Division in the U.S. Department of Agriculture, who provides the necessary "expert' advice for such a complex marketing arrangement. Further advice is provided by Washington representatives of the . . . producers.[92]

All farm subsidies reflect the same sort of policy-making by subgovernments. The president generally plays no direct role in the policy process, nor does Congress as a whole. Decisions about how to allocate the bulk of government expenditures through the Department of Agriculture are made by a subgovernment consisting of bureaucrats in the central agency, legislators on appropriate committees and subcommittees, and local farm committees.

> These self-governing agriculture systems have such institutional legitimacy that they have become practically insulated from the three central sources of democratic political responsibility: (1) Within the Executive, they are autonomous. Secretaries of Agriculture have tried and failed to consolidate or even to coordinate related programs. (2) Within Congress, they are sufficiently powerful within their own domain to be able to exercise an effective veto or to create a stalemate. (3) Agriculture activities and agencies are almost totally removed from the view of the general public.[93]

All of the characteristics we associate with distributive policies are included in such discussions of policy-making by subgovernments. The nature of the overall policy is such that it can be separated into component parts and dealt with in piecemeal fashion. Only special segments of the general population are concerned with the policy outcome. The policy is a low-visibility one that carries no great political implications for the president or for most legislators.

The normal legislative process for dealing with such policies is that of logrolling, of gaining support from unconcerned interests in return for support on other issues important to them. Because the outcome is of no great importance for the president or for most legislators, influence over distributive policies goes, by default, to bureaucrats, some legislators, and interest groups who do have a stake in the policy outcome.

Distributive policy-making, then, is not one that reflects a growing dominance of the president in legislative decision-making. For the most part, he stays out. If we want to find out who does determine the eventual policy outcome in these areas, we should look to the executive and the legislative bureaucracy. The currency of power in distributive policy decisions seems to be one of technical information and expertise. A top senatorial assistant captures the essence of this reliance on bureaucrats and their expertise in his observation:

> It's not bad enough that the Senators rely so totally on us. We rely on the executive branch's bureaucracy downtown. I can't tell you if we need a bill for V.A. benefits until I check with the Veterans Administration. We make hundreds of calls a day to the agencies. All these bills are so complex that we can't understand them without help from the bureaucrats.[94]

The executive impact on distributive policies is not manifested by a strong president's wielding power over members of Congress. Rather, it is a process in which experts from executive agencies, congressional committees and subcommittees, and concerned interest groups come together to determine who gets what from the government. Descriptions emphasizing an overall diminution of legislative influence relative to that of the president's are not accurate portrayals of distributive policy-making. Those who talk about the increasing power of the executive bureaucracy are probably closest to home in describing the distributive policy process. However, this is not always the case, and we will see that the president's influence on legislative policy follows a somewhat different pattern in relation to regulatory and redistributive issues.

Regulatory Policies: Passing Laws and Implementing Them

When we look at the president's role in the policy process dealing with regulatory policies such as medicare or federal aid to education, we find that the president is more actively involved than with distributive policies. Initiative on such programs generally rests with the president, and when a policy finally emerges it is the product of what James Sundquist calls the "dual legislative process." Policy consideration within the executive branch is similar to that within Congress. "In both branches, information is gathered and appraised, experts are consulted, formal or informal committees are created to draft bills, political prospects and consequences are weighed, and finally decisions are made." [95]

You will recall that a major difference between distributive policies and regulatory policies is that the former consists of many small decisions affecting only special groups while the latter represents a coordinated, overall policy affecting most or all of the public. The president's role in regulatory policy-making seems to be that of coordinating different demands made by various interests and shaping some compromise legislative program through a bargaining process. Studies of the 1965 Elementary and Secondary Education Act illustrate the president's important coordinating role in the early stages of the legislative process. A central conflict in this case was whether the bill should apply only to public schools or to parochial schools as well. One study sums up the president's mediating role in observing: "The most significant contribution the President made to the passage of the 1965 act was his initial effort to work out a bill which would appeal to federal aid advocates and avoid the church-state controversy." [96] The bill that came from the White House was said to have "just enough aid to parochial schools to push away the veto of the Roman Catholic Church but not enough to drive away the support of the National Education Association." [97]

Sometimes we find that the president's role in regulatory policy-making goes beyond that of serving to mediate and compromise conflicting demands. President Johnson's activities on behalf of medicare are a case in point. Richard Harris describes the highly visible efforts put forward by Johnson in this case:

> Leaving nothing to chance, President Johnson went on television at eleven o'clock in the morning of March 26th to describe the new bill. After giving a brief account of its provisions, he introduced nine other Democrats—from the House there were Mills, Speaker McCormack, Majority Whip Boggs, and Majority Leader Albert, and from the Senate there were Anderson, Smathers, Majority Leader

Mike Mansfield, and Byrd. All but Byrd spoke glowingly of the new measure—even Smathers said, "I'm delighted with the bill." Then the President turned to Byrd, who had opposed all the earlier, and far more modest, versions of the bill, and who, it was feared, as chairman of the Senate Committee on Finance, might hold up the present version by postponing hearings on it.

In a dialogue that Representative Albert described later as not only an outstanding example of the famous "Johnson treatment" but the first instance of it ever to be shown on a national television hookup, the President smiled at Byrd and said, "I know that you will take an interest in the orderly scheduling of this matter and give it a thorough hearing." Byrd looked at him blankly, whereupon Mr. Johnson asked, "Would you care to make an observation?"

Byrd, who had engaged in many conversations with Presidents but never before with millions of people watching, shook his head. "There is no observation I can make now, because the bill hasn't come before the Senate," he replied gruffly. "Naturally, I'm not familiar with it."

President Johnson pressed on. "And you have nothing that you know of that would prevent (hearings) coming about in reasonable time, not anything ahead of it in the committee?" he asked.

"Nothing in the committee now," Byrd answered, shifting uneasily.

"So when the House acts and it is referred to the Senate Finance Committee, you will arrange for prompt hearings and thorough hearings?" the President asked, leaning forward intently.

Senator Byrd, in a voice that was barely audible, said, "Yes." [98]

In 1979, the Carter Administration undertook a similar, but untelevised, lobbying campaign in behalf of its hospital cost containment bill. After being defeated on this measure in the Ninety-fifth Congress (1977–1978), the Carter Administration moved its lobbying campaign from the Department of Health, Education, and Welfare to the White House itself and began what was described as the "most intensive lobbying effort this year on a piece of domestic legislation." [99] The presidential role of coordinating the efforts of different interest groups was seen when the White House put together a coalition of over twenty-five different organizations to lobby for the Administration's bill. Included were groups representing the elderly, labor, state and local government, and the insurance industry. The description of this lobbying effort provided by the *Congressional Quarterly Weekly Report* demonstrates both the scope of the effort and the involvement of high officials in the executive branch: "Some 1,200 county officials meeting in Washington, D.C., the week of March 5 (1979) were dispatched to Capitol Hill to discuss the bill with their representatives and senators. And a meeting of about 250 coalition members held at the White House March 15 with Vice President Mondale was followed by a lobbying foray to the Hill." [100]

Those who talk about the increasing power of the president to influence legislation, no doubt have such instances as this in mind. Even here the president does not control the eventual policy outcome. Rather, he or she is able to coordinate different elements in the policy initiation stage so as to present Congress with an overall legislative package and to overcome the fragmentation inherent in congressional structure. At times the president visibly invokes the symbol of his or her representing a truly national constituency and being the spokesperson for the general public interest, as in the medicare example. At other times the president's role is the less visible one of compromising the many group demands made during the policy initiation stage, as in the case of federal aid to education.

A major area of regulatory policy important to this consideration of executive influence is that of expenditures for programs approved by Congress. The president is the chief political officer held responsible for maintaining a healthy economy. Because of this, he or she may sometimes decide not to spend funds allocated for certain programs. The justification for such impounding of funds is that they would exceed the limits of the federal budget and be inflationary.

This practice of the executive determining the real impact of policies by withholding funds and transferring money from one agency to another has been a common practice since World War II and represents another facet of the president's power to affect policies. Although executive impounding of funds is found in both distributive and redistributive areas, it seems that the general practice is one that reflects characteristics of regulatory policies. For while the effects of impounding funds might be felt in specific and narrow programs that give funds to specialized segments of the population, the guiding principle behind such withholdings is the regulatory one of maintaining fiscal integrity and controlling overall government spending.

During the Nixon Administration, presidential impoundment of funds appropriated by Congress rose to new heights. The president was using impoundment as a way not only to control government spending but also to circumvent the goals of Congress in providing funding for programs. The president withheld funds that Congress had appropriated for programs in such areas as public housing, water and sewer grants, highways, rural electrification, water pollution control, and education. The total amount of money that had been voted for specific programs by Congress and witheld by impoundment in the Nixon Administration was $18 billion.[101] Congress responded to this excessive use of the impoundment power by passing the Congressional Budget and Impoundment Control Act of 1974, which requires the president to report all impoundments and provides a means for Congress to limit the amount of funds impounded by the president. Passage of this act led to a much more limited use of the impoundment power by both the Ford and the Carter Administrations.[102]

One of the criticisms made of the presidential impoundment of funds was that it gave the president, in effect, an item veto, i.e., the power to accept parts of a law passed by Congress and to reject other parts. This power was specifically denied the president in the Philadelphia Convention of 1787. In recent years Congress has been exercising its own form of an item veto in an attempt to control what it sees as lawmaking by the federal bureaucracy. The legislative veto consists of a requirement that Congress review and/or approve any executive action. Legislative review provisions range from the major requirements of congressional approval written into the War Powers Act of 1973 and the Federal Election Campaign Act to relatively minor requirements that certain executive agencies inform Congress of new regulations. The practice of including legislative veto provisions in laws dates back to 1932, but most of the more than 200 provisions for congressional review that exist in current law were enacted during the 1970s.[103] The legislative veto is seen by many legislators as a way for Congress to control the federal bureaucracy, which, according to Representative Elliott Levitas of Georgia, "has evolved into a fourth-nonconstitutional-branch of government with a thick tangle of regulations that carry the force of law without the benefit of legislative considerations." In one year, the congressman pointed out, sixty-seven federal agencies issued 7,496 rules and regulations having the same effect as laws, while Congress itself enacted only 404 public laws.[104] Both Presidents Ford and Carter have contended that the legislative veto represents a violation of the constitutional principle of separation of powers and have lobbied strongly against legislation that would give Congress a broad legislative veto over all executive regulations. Members of Congress who support a broad legislative veto power, on the other hand, see it as an instrument for bringing regulatory policy-making under popular control.

Before moving to a consideration of executive influence in the area of redistributive and foreign policy-making, let us first summarize the general characteristics of executive influence over regulatory policies that we have looked at. First, the president plays a more direct and active role in regulatory policy-making than in distributive policies. Sometimes this is chiefly a coordinating role of bringing in various interests' demands in the bill-drafting stage and working out a compromise through a bargaining process. At other times, the president plays a more public role and uses that office to build support for a measure pending in Congress. The executive also influences these policies through their implementation. Impoundment, impoundment control, and the legislative veto represent an on-going contest between the highest levels of the executive branch and the entire Congress to control regulatory policy-making. As we move from distributive to redistributive policies, we find that the president's influence increases. The expanded power of the executive that we have seen in the regulatory area becomes even more pronounced when we look at redistributive and foreign policy-making.

Presidential Influence over Redistributive and Foreign Policies

Domestic redistributive policies and foreign policies are somehow different from distributive and regulatory policies. Many of the distributive and regulatory issues discussed so far are relatively unimportant, the sort of thing that presidents might ignore without serious repercussions. Most domestic policies in the United States, if they represent change at all, are incremental in nature. They are what one political scientist has called "experimental adjustments to an existing situation." [105] But redistributive policies and foreign policies carry with them the sense of being irrevocable. They call for basic decisions that will in turn affect other policies for a long time. They are seen as commitments to follow through with basic value decisions involved in that one particular choice. I have mentioned the fact that the tone of policy debate over redistributive policies is determined more by what the policy might lead to than by what the immediate policy decision could involve in the more distant future. There is, then, a sense of importance about redistributive issues that greatly surpasses that of distributive or regulatory policies. The same sort of aura hangs about foreign policy decisions. As President Kennedy observed: "Domestic policy . . . can only defeat us; foreign policy can kill us." [106]

Because of the great importance attached to such decisions, we find that redistributive and foreign policies are not generally determined in a political process demonstrating logrolling or bargaining. These types of policies require that both Congress and the president make some *overall* commitment to the general direction of policy in that area. There is no room to say "Yes, but . . ." or to accept parts of a policy while delaying decision on others to a future time, in order to reach an immediate compromise. This overall coherence of redistributive and foreign policies is further reflected in the ideological slant to the debate surrounding them. We have seen the ideological nature of the arguments presented by interest groups for and against the Employment Act of 1946 and the Civil Rights Act of 1964. Such a characteristic means that political leaders may do one of two things. Either they disagree with the basic value premises embodied in a policy proposal and fight it on ideological grounds or they accept the basic ideological framework and concern themselves with the best means for achieving the accepted end. In either case, legislators are in an inferior position relative to the president. If they choose to fight on ideological grounds they face an elected official who can claim to represent the general electorate's basic ideological sense of direction, no matter how crudely expressed. If they accept the executive's delineation of goals, they are subjected to the fact that the executive branch has overwhelmingly superior sources of information on which to base his specification of means for best achieving those agreed-upon ends.

Those who talk about the growing presidential domination of Congress in the policy process are probably closest to the mark in defining the existing redistributive policy process. For it is here that we find legislators playing a relatively passive role of ratifying decisions made in the executive branch. Case studies of the Economic Opportunity Act of 1964 and the Civil Rights Bill of 1964 suggest the extent of presidential influence on the eventual outcomes. In discussing the 1964 poverty program, James Donovan notes that "the Congressional role in developing the Economic Opportunity Act was essentially a minor one . . . it was written in the executive branch and subsequently endorsed by Congress." [107] "The most significant feature of the Economic Opportunity Act," report the authors of another study, "was that it was legislated almost entirely within the executive branch and, indeed, virtually without prodding from Congressional or other outside clienteles. . . . Thus, Congress was asked not to draft the war on poverty, but rather, to ratify a fully prepared Administration program, and invited, though hardly encouraged, to propose marginal changes." [108] James Sundquist observes in his review of policies during the sixties: "The war on poverty represents the most extreme case of legislative initiative by the President almost to the exclusion of Congress." [109]

President Johnson's role in securing passage of the Civil Rights Act of 1964 demonstrates the great influence of the executive in redistributive policies and the characteristic of such policies that they be decided *in toto,* with no side bargains to eliminate certain aspects of the issue. One of the best descriptions of the president's role here is provided by Washington journalists, Rowland Evans and Robert Novak:

> Johnson's contribution—and it was a highly significant one—was to pass the Civil Rights bill *without* much horse-trading. "Part III" (giving the federal government power to intervene in Civil Rights cases) had been added to the bill in the House Judiciary Committee and FEPC was adopted on the House floor, bringing the bill up to the highest hopes of the Civil Rights leaders. . . .
>
> Even before the bill passed the House on February 10 by a vote of 290 to 130, Johnson had laid down the no-compromise edict. In a private session in his office with Clarence Mitchell of the NAACP and Joseph Rauh of ADA, Johnson pledged there would be no changes in the bill even if that required suspending all other activity in the Senate for months.
>
> . . . Johnson reiterated he wanted the Senate to pass the bill intact.[110]

The relatively minor role that Congress has played in the foreign policy process has been noted by both legislators and political scientists. Representative Donald Riegle of Michigan talks about his experiences on the Foreign Operations Subcommittee.

> The House has long since abandoned its responsibility to dig into policies of the executive branch. While he can be a scrooge on specific items in the budget, Otto Passman (the subcommittee chair-

man) makes it clear he has little interest in pursuing policy questions, and today he used the reform rules to effectively squelch any penetrating cross-examination of the Secretary.

Riegle goes on to describe his frustrated attempts to gain information from Secretary of State William Rogers during the latter's testimony before the subcommittee:

> When my turn came to cross-examine, I thanked the Secretary for his initiatives in the Middle East, then asked immediately about his testimony before the subcommittee last year, which had been stricken verbatim from the public record. Rogers had appeared before us six days prior to the U.S. move into Cambodia. At that time he had indicated, rather forcefully, that the U.S. was not contemplating sending troops into Cambodia. He said emphatically that such a move would "destroy our Vietnamization program." If circumstances changed, he added, and the Administration decided to enter Cambodia, either he or someone else would surely inform Congress in advance—and seek Congressional authorization.
>
> Six days later the U.S. did precisely what Rogers had said the U.S. wouldn't do. The Congress had been misled. So this morning I read portions of last year's classified transcript aloud and asked Rogers why his testimony had been so unreliable. Then I asked, "Has sufficient time passed for this material to be declassified and printed in the record?"
>
> Passman fidgeted and came to the Secretary's defense. That testimony should remain classified, he said. It was necessary to protect "national security."
>
> I continued to press Rogers, asking for explanations. He smiled and hemmed and hawed and offered only vague and indirect responses.
>
> "The gentleman from Michigan," Passman interrupted, "has now consumed *seven* minutes."
>
> Rogers knew my time was up and that I'd have no further chance to cross-examine him this year. He smiled at Passman appreciatively.[111]

James Robinson's study, *Congress and Foreign Policy-Making,* comes to similar conclusions about the minor role played by Congress in this process.

> The role of Congress in the U.S. system of government has been shifting gradually away from the initiation of public policies toward the legitimization and emendation of policies originally devised in

the executive branch. This alteration of the major role in the legislative process has been especially notable in foreign affairs.[112]

During the 1970s, Congress took a number of steps to improve its position relative to the president in foreign policy-making. In 1972, Congress passed a law requiring that all executive agreements be transmitted to both the House and the Senate within sixty days of their signing. The Arms Control Export Act of 1976 gives Congress a legislative veto power over all arms sales above $25 million. In the same year, Congress required the executive to issue "human rights reports" on all countries receiving U.S. military assistance and provided a way for Congress to cut off aid to nations violating human rights. The Nuclear Nonproliferation Act of 1978 gives Congress a veto power over executive decisions about exporting nuclear fuel and technology. And perhaps most important, the War Powers Act of 1973 requires congressional approval before troops sent to another country by the president may stay there for more than sixty days and insists that the president inform and consult Congress in making decisions during an international crisis. While these many reforms in the foreign policy-making process do involve Congress in the policy process at an earlier stage and do provide it with more information than it had prior to the 1970s, many would still question whether the reforms have altered the pattern of presidential dominance in the area of foreign policy. Assessments of the War Powers Resolution test case in the *Mayaguez* incident of 1975, for example, indicate that the president was able to exclude Congress from the crisis decision-making process.[113] The key to presidential influence in the area of foreign policy seems to be the executive's monopoly on the information that is needed to make rational decisions. In the realm of foreign affairs, legislators must generally make decisions based only on the information given to them by the executive branch. "Unless the administration volunteers the information, Congress is pretty helpless. We lack the expert staff to do the effective cross-examination needed to get the facts," is the way one representative put it. Other legislators express similar complaints:

> The terrifying thing is that what we are talking about is the ability of Congress to make decisions on the basis of information furnished by the executive, and the indications are, on relatively superficial study, that in the field of defense we don't have an effective decision making apparatus in the executive. The basic decision is never made by Congress. We may choose between "A" or "B" missile systems,

but we never get all the facts to determine whether the choice should
then be made between "A" or "B." Perhaps the choice should be "C"
or "D." [114]

There's no real hot line to let you know what is really going on.
What do you do when they say the Dominican Republic is being
taken over by Communists? I looked at the fifty-eight names, too, but
they meant nothing to me.[115]

The executive branch's control over information required for
any effective decision-making gives it a great edge over Congress in
these areas. And it is not the sort of imbalance that can be righted
by simply expanding congressional staffs and information systems.
As long as the primary source of foreign policy and defense intelligence is located in the executive branch, the legislature can never
hope to play a major role in the determination of such policies.

The extent of executive influence goes from the relatively
minor influence of the president and control by subgovernments
that we found in distributive policy areas to virtual domination by
the president and the executive branch that we find in redistributive and foreign policies. We come back, then, to the basic premise
stated at the beginning of this chapter: that different policies are
handled in different ways by the American political system and that
broad statements about Congress being the tool of pressure groups
or the president in formulating policies are misleading. Sometimes,
these outside groups are found to have a great deal of influence over
policy, while at other times their impact is minor.

CONCLUDING NOTE

We began this book with a discussion of various normative frameworks for evaluating Congress. Most judgments of Congress rest on
procedural grounds, on the nature of the congressional process. The
intent of Chapter 6 was to show that the congressional process is
many different patterns of behavior, all of which depend on the
nature of the policy under consideration. Blanket statements that
Congress reacts to pressures from voters, interest groups, and the
executive branch generally ignore the variety of possible congressional responses. Congressional response to, and congressional initiative in, policy decisions as they relate to outside pressure will depend on the type of policy under consideration. Lowi's framework
of distributive, regulatory, and redistributive policies provides one

way to see the great variation in the nature of the congressional role in policy-making. The framework is valuable (even if the specific categories were to have little correspondence to the actual perceptions of legislators) because it highlights the fact that there are many different policy processes in American politics.

Beneath this variety of congressional responses to different policy demands is an institution with a life of its own, with a general response pattern for dealing with all policy demands in the political system. This pattern may best be summarized in Lowi's terms: Congress is most effective as a policy-maker and most powerful *vis-à-vis* the executive branch when it is dealing with distributive issues. A corollary to this statement is that, whenever possible, Congress will attempt to transform regulatory or redistributive policies into distributive policies. This can be done by breaking down general legislation into component parts that can be handled within the normal legislative process. This distributive side to congressional policy-making serves also as one of the chief distinctions between congressional and presidential approaches to policy. David Mayhew captures the essence of this distinction when he observes that in times of recession legislators reach for accelerated public works bills listing projects for their districts, while presidents prefer more general fiscal effects. In the education field a congressional favorite is the *impacted areas* program with its ostentatious grants to targeted school districts. Here again, presidents prefer ventures of more diffuse impact. Presidents are capable of closing a dozen veterans' hospitals in the interest of efficiency; legislators work to keep them open.[116]

Within Congress, the tendency to transform redistributive or regulatory policies into distributive ones (to break up omnibus legislation into separate pieces of legislation or to focus on the distributive characteristics of more general legislation) cuts across all types of substantive policy areas. Mayhew cites programs involving the use of categorical grants and water pollution control legislation as examples of the typical congressional favoritism toward limited, controllable, dispersal of material benefits for which individual legislators can take credit.[117] Even when Congress is faced with a general defense policy or foreign policy decision, there is a strong urge to draw out distributive aspects or the distributive potential of the policy. In the spring of 1976, when the House International Relations Committee was considering the general strategic issue of selling airplanes with advanced radar warning systems to NATO, many members began focusing on the distributive aspects of the decision. Legislators questioned where the planes and the components of the warning system would be built and assembled. Their main concern was which district would be affected by this sale to NATO. Legislators' interest in these distributive aspects of the decision far overshadowed their interest in the strategic military implications of the proposed sale.

The same pattern of behavior was seen in House consideration of a military aid bill for fiscal years 1976 and 1977. As reported by the International Relations Committee, the bill contained a provision limiting military aid to Korea to $290 million for 1976 and 1977 and limiting agricultural assistance (under P.L. 480 provisions under Title I) to $175 million for the same period. These limits were established, in committee, as a signal that the United States would not condone the repressive practices of the Park regime in South Korea. However, when the House first began considering the military aid bill on the floor, it became clear that the limit to agricultural assistance to Korea was being considered in a distributive sense rather than in terms of broad foreign policy concerns. The primary opposition came from representatives from farming districts. Their opposition was not phrased in terms of foreign aid to repressive governments; rather, it focused on the loss of material benefits to their own constituents that would come about as a result of such policies. "It means $104 million in lost sales to the American farmer at a time when we are searching for new markets for our agricultural products," is the way a congressman from Ohio expressed it.[118] Those members of the committee who had sponsored the aid restriction on South Korea as sensible foreign policy were quick to bow to the distributive benefit loss such a policy would have for farm-state legislators. The chief sponsor of the Korea limitations in the military aid bill dropped the limitation on agricultural assistance from the bill before it came up for final consideration on the floor. In order to gain support for military aid limits to Korea, he realized that he would have to cater to the overriding distributive policy interests of representatives from farm districts.

If you think back on some of the points discussed earlier, such as the increasingly district-oriented representational role played by legislators and the decentralizing structure of subcommittees, it becomes clear that the emphasis on distributive policies that provide limited material benefits for constituents (for which legislators can take credit) represents a rational response by politicians who face periodic reelection. These structural factors greatly influence how members of Congress perceive policies and make policy. Together, they account for a large part of the human behavior that represents the politics of Congress.

NOTES

1. Thomas E. Cavanagh, "The Two Arenas of Congress: Electoral and Institutional Incentives for Performance," a paper prepared for delivery at the 1978 annual meeting of the American Political Science Association, New York, N.Y., August 31 to September 3, 1978, appendix, Table 5, "Volunteered Public Reasons for Performance Rating of Congress."

2. For a recent survey of the political science literature on Congress, see David W. Rohde and Kenneth A. Shepsle, "Taking Stock of Congressional Research: The New Institutionalism," a paper prepared for delivery at the 1978 annual meeting of the Midwest Political Science Association, Chicago, Illinois, April 20–22, 1978.

3. Theodore Lowi, "American Business, Public Policy, Case Studies, and Political Theory," *World Politics*, vol. 16, no. 4 (July, 1964), pp. 689–690. For a refinement and expansion of Lowi's framework, see Randall B. Ripley and Grace A. Franklin, *Congress, The Bureaucracy, and Public Policy* (Dorsey, 1976).

4. See, for instance, the essays in Austin Ranney, ed., *Political Science and Public Policy* (Markham, 1968), especially pp. 41–52 and 151–175, and Jerrold E. Schneider, *Ideological Coalitions in Congress* (Greenwood Press, 1979), pp. 30ff.

5. Schneider provides a good example of how a bill to reimburse farmers for destroying contaminated chickens, normally considered a distributive issue, was perceived by one senator as a redistributive one and defeated on the basis of this perception, in *Ideological Coalitions in Congress*, pp. 32–33.

6. See Grant McConnell, *Private Power and American Democracy* (Vintage, 1966), pp. 11ff for a discussion of the *New York World* articles and their effect. The Report of the Association of the Bar of the City of New York's Special Committee on Congressional Ethics, *Congress and the Public Trust* (Atheneum, 1971), pp. 80ff discusses Phillips' earlier work.

7. Mark J. Green, James M. Fallows, and David R. Zwick, *Who Runs Congress?* (Bantam, 1972), p. 32.

8. *How Money Talks in Congress: A Common Cause Study of the Impact of Money on Congressional Decision-making* (Common Cause, 1979), p. 7.

9. Quoted in Carl P. Chelf, *Congress in the American System* (Nelson-Hall, 1977), p. 166.

10. Quoted in McConnell, *Private Power and American Democracy*, p. 14.

11. Donald R. Matthews, *U.S. Senators and Their World* (Vintage, 1960), p. 177.

12. John J. Fialka, "Capitol Lobbying," *Washington Star*, December 15, 1975, p. A14. This is part of a five-part series on congressional lobbying by Fialka that appeared in the *Star* from December 15–December 19, 1975. Spending figures cited here were also taken from Congressional Quarterly Service, *Legislators and Lobbyists* (1968), p. 28. A good general discussion of lobbying on the Hill can be found in Congressional Quarterly Service, *The Washington Lobby*, 2nd edition, 1974.

13. The 1967 figure comes from *Legislators and Lobbyists*, p. 28, cited above. The 1975 figure comes from "Lobby Registration," *Congressional Quarterly Weekly Report Index*, supplement to vol. 34, no. 4 (January 24, 1976), pp. 58–65. The Nader Congress project estimated an even higher figure of 5,000 or more full-time lobbyists in Washington, or ten for each member of Congress. See Green et al., *Who Runs Congress*, p. 30.

14. *How Money Talks in Congress*, p. 31.

15. Ibid., p. 33.

16. Alan Berlow, "House Passes Lobbying Disclosure Bill," *Congressional Quarterly Weekly Report*, April 29, 1978, p. 1028.

17. Matthews, *U.S. Senators and Their World*, p. 178.

18. Lester Milbraith, *The Washington Lobbyists* (Rand McNally, 1963) and Lewis Anthony Dexter, *How Organizations Are Represented in Washington* (Bobbs-Merrill, 1969).

19. Quoted in Elizabeth Drew, "A Reporter at Large (Lobbyist)," *The New Yorker*, January 9, 1978, p. 41.

20. Raymond Bauer, Ithiel de Sola Pool, and Lewis Anthony Dexter, *American Business and Public Policy* (Atherton, 1963), pp. 352–353. Matthews' discussion of the effects of lobbying uses the framework of reinforcement, activation, and conversion. The idea that most votes are decided by elections rather than lobbying is expressed by one lobbyist in *U.S. Senators and Their World*, p. 193:

> Ninety percent of what goes on here during a session is decided on the previous election day. The main drift of legislation is decided then: it is out of our control. There is simply no substitute for electing the right folks and defeating the wrong folks.
>
> Our job is a little like that of a football coach. Our material is given. By carefully coaching we can sometimes improve the effectiveness of the material.

21. Gilbert Steiner and Samuel K. Gove, *Legislative Politics in Illinois*

(University of Illinois Press, 1960), p. 77. Quoted in Murray Edelman, *The Symbolic Uses of Politics* (University of Illinois Press, 1964), p. 136.

22. Donald Matthews and James Stimson, "The Decision Making Approach to the Study of Legislative Behavior," paper delivered at the annual meeting of the American Political Science Association, New York, 1969; David Kovenock, "Influence in the U.S. House of Representatives: Some Preliminary Statistical Snapshots," paper delivered at the annual meeting of the American Political Science Association, Chicago, 1967, p. 22.

23. Edwin M. Yoder, "Washington Report," *Harpers*, June 1970, p. 34.

24. Quoted in Norman J. Ornstein and Shirley Elder, *Interest Groups, Lobbying and Policymaking* (Congressional Quarterly Press, 1978), p. 85.

25. Quoted in Drew, "A Reporter At Large (Lobbyist)," p. 41.

26. Charles Clapp, *The Congressman: His Work as He Sees It* (The Brookings Institution, 1963), p. 203.

27. Ibid., p. 204.

28. Rachelle Patterson, "Strength in Numbers? That's a Capitol Idea," *Boston Globe*, December 10, 1978, p. A3. For more on caucuses see Michael J. Malbin, "Where There's a Cause There's a Caucus on Capitol Hill," *National Journal*, January 8, 1977, pp. 56–58, and Burdett A. Loomis, "Informal House Groups and the Policy Process: The Case of the New Members Caucus," a paper prepared for delivery at the 1978 annual meeting of the Midwest Political Science Association, Chicago, Illinois, April 20–22, 1978.

29. Stanley Surrey, "The Congress and the Tax Lobbyist—How Special Tax Provisions Get Enacted," *Harvard Law Review*, May 1957, pp. 1155–1156.

30. E. E. Schattschneider, *The Semi-Sovereign People* (Holt, Rinehart & Winston, 1961).

31. Peter Bachrach and Morton Baratz, *Power and Poverty* (Oxford University Press, 1970), p. 44. Grant McConnell discusses attitudes toward government shared by business, labor, and agriculture in *Private Power and American Democracy*, pp. 89ff.

32. For an excellent history of the AMA fight against medicare see Richard Harris, *A Sacred Trust* (Pelican, 1969). Representative Aimé Forand tried to get behind the symbolic smokescreen of socialized medicine by asking for a definition of the term:

DR. LARSON: Mr. Forand, I think it is very difficult to define "socialized medicine." I know of nothing in the record of our Association that would spell out what the Association thinks is socialized medicine.

MR. FORAND: Dr. Allman (President of the AMA) labelled my bill "socialized medicine." I would like to know just what you mean by "socialized medicine."

DR. LARSON: He was speaking as the president of the American Medical Association and as an individual sir. [*A Sacred Trust,* p. 81.]

During these hearings the AMA seemed to make the mistake of using, in congressional hearings, political rhetoric designed for mass consumption. Edelman discusses how this backfired in *The Symbolic Uses of Politics,* pp. 123 ff. After the hearings a committee member said:

They were invited to appear as expert witnesses, but they displayed no expertise at all. I know that I didn't care for their presentation, and a number of my colleagues didn't either. We know there was something in the air—those millions of old people stirring out in our districts—and some of us were sure that sooner or later a bill like this was inevitable. And the members of the committee who didn't like the bill—by far the majority at the time—were looking to the AMA for some help, some way to defend their position back home. I'm afraid they didn't get anything except the usual hokum. [*A Sacred Trust,* pp. 81–82.]

33. The Taft-Hartley Act says that the National Labor Relations Board cannot use staff members for economic analysis, that the hearing examiner cannot make recommendations in representation cases, and that the trial examiner in unfair labor practices cannot be present when the board considers the case at which he presided. The pro-management implications of these procedures is noted by Edelman:

Such provisions quite explicitly bar the board from paying overt attention to certain types of data or points of view, particularly facts and values growing out of observation of what occurred, or allegedly occurred, in the plant. The board is thus encouraged to behave less like an investigating administrative agency and more like a court, confining its attention chiefly to past interpretations of the law. Such ignoring of actual behavior in the plant is practically certain to mean overlooking much of the evidence that an employer charged with an unfair labor practice did things which indicate he has an anti-union bias. [*The Symbolic Uses of Politics,* p. 67.]

34. For an interesting discussion of the corporate bias in policies designed to stimulate economic growth see Kenneth Dolbeare and

Murray Edelman, *American Politics: Power and Change* (D. C. Heath, 1971), pp. 147ff.

35. Andrew Scott and Margaret Hunt, *Congress and Lobbies: Image and Reality* (University of North Carolina Press, 1966), pp. 95–96.

36. Edelman, *The Symbolic Uses of Politics*, p. 60. Grant McConnell also discusses how the countervailing power notion does not apply to union-management interaction in the steel industry:

> The most serious and illuminating example of this is the history of events in the steel industry since the end of World War II. This is a record of repeated contests between the industry, led by the United States Steel Corporation and the United Steel Workers. The outcome of these contests, with slight exceptions, has been a pattern of settlement in which the union has obtained higher wages and the industry has obtained prices sufficiently higher to cover not only the added costs of the wage increases but something additional. Perhaps the most startling feature of this history is that the effects of collaboration between labor and industry have been achieved in the face of genuinely sharp and even bitter hostility between the two sides. [*Private Power and American Democracy*, p. 251.]

37. Representative Paul Rogers (D-Fla.), quoted in Ornstein and Elder, *Interest Groups, Lobbying and Policymaking*, p. 182.

38. For a good case study of the Clean Air Act, see Ornstein and Elder, *Interest Groups, Lobbying and Policymaking*, Chapter six.

39. William Cary, "Pressure Groups and the Revenue Code: A Requiem in Honor of the Departing Uniformity of the Tax Laws," *Harvard Law Review*, March 1955, p. 778. A study of testimony before the House Committee on Banking and Currency on federal housing policy showed the same sort of bias in favor of representation of organized economic interests; see Jay S. Goodman, "Federal Policy and Urban Impact" (mimeograph, Wheaton College, 1971).

40. Ornstein and Elder, *Interest Groups, Lobbying and Policymaking*, pp. 167–168.

41. James Sundquist gives a good discussion of relative interest group activity influence on different policies in the 1950s and 1960s in his *Politics and Policy* (The Brookings Institution, 1968), pp. 392ff.

42. Green et al., *Who Runs Congress?* p. 33.

43. *How Money Talks in Congress*, p. 11.

44. Joseph Pechman, *Federal Tax Policy* (W. W. Norton, 1971), p. 43. John Manley's *The Politics of Finance* (Little, Brown, 1970) provides an excellent description of the role of lobbyists in formulating tax legislation.

45. *Congressional Quarterly Weekly Report,* October 21, 1978, pp. 3031–3032.

46. Robert Sherrill, *Why They Call It Politics* (Harcourt Brace Jovanovich, 1979), p. 327.

47. *New York Times,* November 18, 1972, p. 20.

48. Nick Kotz, *Let Them Eat Promises* (Anchor, 1971), pp. 43 and 60. Also see Theodore Schultz, *Economic Crisis in World Agriculture* (University of Michigan Press, 1965) and Charles L. Schultze, *The Distribution of Farm Subsidies* (The Brookings Institution, 1971).

49. The statement is by a former committee staff member. Quoted in Green et al., *Who Runs Congress?* p. 40.

50. Lewis Anthony Dexter, "The Representative and His District," in Nelson Polsby and Robert Peabody, eds., *New Perspectives on the House of Representatives* (Rand McNally, 1969), p. 24.

51. Bauer, Pool, and Dexter, *American Business and Public Policy,* pp. 434–435.

52. Robert Peabody, Jeffrey Berry, William Frasure, and Jerry Goldman, *To Enact a Law* (Praeger, 1972), p. 60.

53. Sundquist, *Politics and Policy,* p. 392.

54. Green et al., *Who Runs Congress?* p. 36.

55. Eidenburg and Morey, *An Act of Congress,* p. 60.

56. David Truman discusses these differences between forming an alliance and engaging in logrolling in *The Government Process* (Alfred A. Knopf, 1962), pp. 362ff. For an example of this broader base of lobbying on regulatory policies, see Lawrence E. Gladieux and Thomas R. Wolanin, *Congress and Colleges* (D.C. Heath, 1976), p. 119.

57. E. E. Schattschneider, *Politics, Pressure, and the Tariff* (Prentice-Hall, 1935).

58. Eidenburg and Morey, *An Act of Congress,* p. 222.

59. Bailey, *Congress Makes a Law,* p. 236.

60. Sundquist, *Politics and Policy;* John C. Donovan, *The Politics of Poverty* (Pegasus, 1967); and John Bibby and Roger Davidson, *On Capitol Hill* (Holt, Rinehart & Winston, 1967), pp. 219–251 are the major sources used for the poverty program discussion.

61. Bailey, *Congress Makes a Law,* pp. 75–76.

62. Berman, *A Bill Becomes a Law,* p. 114 and Sundquist, *Politics and Policy,* p. 268.

63. Bibby and Davidson, *On Capitol Hill,* pp. 239–240.

64. Quoted in Bailey, *Congress Makes a Law,* p. 141.

65. See Bailey, *Congress Makes a Law,* pp. 145, 134, and 130 for the respective citations.

66. Quoted in Berman, *A Bill Becomes a Law*, p. 53.

67. Sundquist, *Politics and Policy*, p. 266.

68. Elizabeth Drew, "A Reporter At Large (The Energy Bazaar)," *The New Yorker*, July 21, 1975, p. 35, cited in Schneider, *Ideological Coalitions in Congress*, p. 163.

69. For more on this, see Phillip Brenner, "Marxism and the Study of Congress," in Lawrence C. Dodd and Bruce I. Oppenheimer, eds., *Congress Reconsidered* (Praeger, 1980, second edition).

70. Quoted in Warren Weaver, Jr., "96th Congress Is Off To A Sluggish Start," *New York Times*, May 15, 1979, p. 17.

71. Meg Greenfield, "Thinking Small," *Washington Post*, April 19, 1978, p. A13.

72. Elizabeth Drew, *Senator* (Simon & Schuster, 1979), pp. 112–113. Copyright © 1978, 1979 by Elizabeth Drew. Reprinted by permission of Simon & Schuster, a Division of Gulf & Western Corporation.

73. Randall Rothenberg, "The PACs Go To Market On the Hill," *The Nation*, November 18, 1978, p. 536.

74. Herbert A. Alexander, *Financing Politics* (Congressional Quarterly Press, 1976).

75. Rhodes Cook, "Political Action Committee Spending Soared in 1978," *Congressional Quarterly Weekly Report*, June 2, 1979, p. 1043.

76. Quoted in Aaron Epstein, "Political Action: The Cash Flows In," *Boston Globe*, November 9, 1978, p. 64.

77. James Madison, "Federalist Number 51," in Alexander Hamilton, John Jay, and James Madison, *The Federalist Papers* (Washington Square Press, 1964), p. 123.

78. Green et al., *Who Runs Congress?* p. 94.

79. Gary Orfield, *Congressional Power: Congress and Social Change* (Harcourt Brace Jovanovich, 1975), pp. 3 and 20.

80. Arnold Kanter, "Congress and the Defense Budget: 1960–1970," *American Political Science Review*, vol. 66, no. 1 (March 1972), p. 142.

81. From Arthur Blaustein, "536 Characters in Search of a Legislative Program," *Harper's*, March 1969, p. 31.

82. Samuel P. Huntington, "Congressional Responses to the Twentieth Century," in David Truman, ed., *The Congress and America's Future* (Prentice-Hall, 1965), p. 6.

83. C. Wright Mills, *The Power Elite* (Oxford University Press, 1956), p. 229.

84. Sundquist, *Politics and Policy*, p. 535.

85. George E. Reedy, *The Twilight of the Presidency* (World, 1970), p. 130.

86. John F. Kennedy, quoted in Louis W. Koenig, *The Chief Executive* (Harcourt, Brace and World, 1964), p. 126.

87. Aaron Wildavsky, "The Two Presidencies," reprinted in his reader, *The Presidency* (Little, Brown, 1969), p. 230. Presidential dominance in this area is also supported by James Robinson's findings in *Congress and Foreign Policy-Making* (Dorsey, 1967).

88. Samuel P. Huntington, *The Common Defense* (Columbia University Press, 1961), p. 124.

89. For a good discussion of the crisis/noncrisis distinction in policies and the relative congressional/executive influence over foreign and defense policies, see Ripley and Franklin, *Congress, The Bureaucracy, and Public Policy* (Dorsey, 1976).

90. Quoted in Roger Hilsman, *The Politics of Policy Making in Defense and Foreign Affairs* (Harper & Row, 1971), p. 1.

91. Grant McConnell, *Private Power and American Democracy* (Vintage, 1966), p. 244. Other descriptions of these subgovernments may be found in Ernest S. Griffith, *The Impasse of Democracy* (Harrison-Hilton Books, 1939), p. 182; Douglass Cater, *Power in Washington* (Random House, 1964), and J. Leiper Freeman, *The Political Process* (Random House, 1965).

92. Cater, *Power in Washington,* pp. 17–18.

93. Theodore Lowi, *The End of Liberalism* (W. W. Norton, 1969), p. 112.

94. Quoted in Robert Sherrill, "Who Runs Congress?" *New York Times Magazine,* November 22, 1970, p. 85.

95. Sundquist, *Politics and Policy,* p. 490.

96. Eidenburg and Morey, *An Act of Congress,* p. 230.

97. Sundquist, *Politics and Policy,* p. 212.

98. Harris, *A Sacred Trust,* pp. 190–191. Copyright © 1966 by Richard Harris.

99. Alan Berlow, "Carter Administration Pits Its Lobbying Efforts Against Hospital Industry's On Cost Control Issue," *Congressional Quarterly Weekly Report,* March 17, 1979, p. 474.

100. Ibid.

101. Joel Haveman, *Congress and the Budget* (Indiana University Press, 1978), p. 177.

102. William G. Munselle, "Presidential Impoundment and Congressional Reform," in Leroy N. Rieselbach, ed., *Legislative Reform: The Policy Impact* (D.C. Heath, 1978), pp. 173–181.

103. Martin Donsky, "New Legislative Veto Battle Brews Over HUD Bill Provision," *Congressional Quarterly Weekly Report*, March 31, 1979, p. 585.

104. Mary Russell, "Hill Increasingly Taking Veto Weapon Into Its Own Hands," *Washington Post*, September 5, 1976, p. A10.

105. Wildavsky, "The Two Presidencies," p. 232.

106. Ibid., p. 242.

107. Donovan, *The Politics of Poverty*, p. 87.

108. Bibby and Davidson, *On Capitol Hill*, pp. 220 and 238.

109. Sundquist, *Politics and Policy*, p. 493.

110. Rowland Evans and Robert Novak, *Lyndon B. Johnson: The Exercise of Power* (New American Library, 1966), pp. 378–379.

111. Donald W. Riegle, Jr. and Trevor Armbrister, *O Congress* (Doubleday, 1972), pp. 81–83. Copyright © 1972 by Donald W. Riegle, Jr. and Trevor Armbrister. Reprinted by permission of Doubleday and Co.

112. Robinson, *Congress and Foreign Policy-Making*, pp. 173–174.

113. See, for instance, Richard M. Pious, *The American Presidency* (Basic Books, 1979), pp. 410ff.

114. Quoted in Clapp, *The Congressman: His Work as He Sees It*, pp. 310 and 311. Copyright © 1963 by The Brookings Institution.

115. Quoted in Richard Fenno, *Congressmen in Committees* (Little, Brown, 1973), p. 30.

116. David R. Mayhew, *Congress: The Electoral Connection* (Yale University Press, 1974), p. 128.

117. Ibid., pp. 129, 134. A similar pattern of emphasis on distributive policies is reflected in increasing use of congressional vetoes to give Congress specific and particularistic control over more general executive-initiated policies. For discussions of this phenomenon, see Mary Russell, "Hill Eyes Its Own Veto Power," *Washington Post*, December 27, 1975, p. A2; Arlen J. Large, "New Veto Powers for Congress," *Wall Street Journal*, February 6, 1975, p. 10; Donsky, "New Legislative Veto Battle Brews Over HUD Bill Provision"; and Russell, "Hill Increasingly Taking Veto Weapon Into Its Own Hands."

118. *Congressional Record*, May 19, 1976, p. H4606.

INDEX